Archaeological Research

Archaeological Research

A Brief Introduction

PETER N. PEREGRINE

Lawrence University

Prentice
Hall

Upper Saddle River, New Jersey 07458

Library of Congress Cataloging-in-Publication Data

PEREGRINE, PETER N. (PETER NEAL) (date)
    Archaeological research : a brief introduction / Peter N. Peregrine.
        p.   cm.
    Includes bibliographical references and index.
    ISBN   0–13–081127–0 (pbk.)
    1. Archaeology—Methodology.   I. Title.

CC75.P375 2001
930.1'028—dc21
                                                99–462089

VP, Editorial Director: Laura Pearson
Publisher: Nancy Roberts
Project Manager: Joan Stone
Prepress and Manufacturing Buyer: Ben Smith
Electronic Art Manager: Guy Ruggiero
Artist: Maria Piper
Cover Director: Jayne Conte
Cover Photo: Neil Beer/PhotoDisc Inc.
Director of Marketing: Gina Sluss

This book was set in 10/12 Palatino by Stratford Publishing Services
and was printed and bound by Courier Companies, Inc.
The cover was printed by Phoenix Color Corp.

© 2001 by Prentice-Hall, Inc.
A Division of Pearson Education
Upper Saddle River, New Jersey 07458

Printed in the United States of America

10 9 8 7 6 5 4 3 2 1

ISBN 0-13-081127-0

PRENTICE-HALL INTERNATIONAL (UK) LIMITED, *London*
PRENTICE-HALL OF AUSTRALIA PTY. LIMITED, *Sydney*
PRENTICE-HALL CANADA INC., *Toronto*
PRENTICE-HALL HISPANOAMERICANA, S.A., *Mexico*
PRENTICE-HALL OF INDIA PRIVATE LIMITED, *New Delhi*
PRENTICE-HALL OF JAPAN, INC., *Tokyo*
PEARSON EDUCATION ASIA PTE. LTD., *Singapore*
EDITORA PRENTICE-HALL DO BRASIL, LTDA., *Rio de Janeiro*

Contents

PREFACE   **xiii**

ABOUT THE AUTHOR   **xxiii**

CHAPTER 1:   The Archaeological Research Process   **1**

1.1   Phase I: Asking Questions   *2*

1.2   Phase II: Building Models   *5*

1.3   Phase III: Collecting Data   *9*

1.4   Phase IV: Analyzing Data   *12*

1.5   Phase V: Evaluating Results   *15*

1.6   Summary   *17*

Suggested Readings   *18*

Notes   *18*

CHAPTER 2:   The Archaeological Record   20

2.1   What Do Archaeologists Find?   *22*

2.2   What Is Context?   *23*

2.3   What Theories Do Archaeologists Use to Interpret
the Archaeological Record?   *24*

2.4   Summary   *30*

Suggested Readings   *31*

Notes   *31*

CHAPTER 3:   Measurement and Sampling   33

3.1   How Do Archaeologists Make Measurements
Through the Archaeological Record?   *34*

    3.1.1   Types of Data   35

    3.1.2   Validity and Reliability   36

    3.1.3   Units of Analysis   37

3.2   How Do Archaeologists Sample
from the Archaeological Record?   *38*

    3.2.1   Random Sampling   38

    3.2.2   Stratified Sampling   39

    3.2.3   Cluster Sampling   39

    3.2.4   Nonrandom Sampling   40

3.3   Summary   *41*

Suggested Readings   *41*

Notes   *42*

CHAPTER 4:   Survey Methods and Strategies   43

4.1   How Do Archaeologists Find Sites?   *44*

    4.1.1   Literature Search   44

    4.1.2   Landowner and Collector Interviews   47

4.2   What Is Archaeological Survey?   *48*

    4.2.1   Pedestrian Survey   48

    4.2.2   Probing and Testing   50

    4.2.3   Remote Sensing   51

    4.2.4   Aerial Photography and Imagery   57

4.3   How Do Archaeologists Conduct Surveys?   *58*

    4.3.1   "Top-Down" Surveys   58

    4.3.2   "Bottom-Up" Surveys   58

    4.3.3   "Shotgun" and Predictive Surveys   62

4.4   Summary   *63*

Suggested Readings   *64*

Notes   *64*

CHAPTER 5:   Excavation Methods and Strategies   **66**

5.1   What Techniques Do Archaeologists Use to Excavate Sites?   *68*

    5.1.1   Horizontal Controls   68

    5.1.2   Vertical Controls   70

5.2   What Strategies Do Archaeologists Use to Excavate Sites?   *73*

    5.2.1   Standard Excavation Strategies   74

    5.2.2   Special-Case Excavation Strategies   79

5.3   What About the Digging Itself?   *81*

5.4   Summary   *83*

Suggested Readings   *84*

Notes   *84*

CHAPTER 6:   Recordkeeping   **86**

6.1   How Do Archaeologists Record Context?   *87*

6.2   What Types of Records Do Archaeologists Keep?   *89*

    6.2.1   Excavation Records   92

    6.2.2   Accession Records   95

    6.2.3   An Example: Kaminaljuyu   97

6.3   Summary   *103*

Suggested Readings   *103*

Notes   *104*

CHAPTER 7:   The Analysis of Spatial Patterns   **105**

7.1   What Is Point-Pattern Analysis?   *106*

    7.1.1   Quadrat Methods   107

    7.1.2   Distance Methods   108

    7.1.3   Dispersal Methods   110

7.2   What Is Regional Analysis?   *112*

    7.2.1   Central Place Theory   112

    7.2.2   Network Methods   114

    7.2.3   Relational Methods   116

7.3   What About Context?   *121*

7.4   Summary   *122*

Suggested Readings   *122*

Notes   *123*

CHAPTER 8:   Ceramic Analysis   **124**

8.1   What Are Ceramics Made From?   *125*

8.2   How Are Ceramics Made?   *127*

8.3   How Do Archaeologists Analyze Ceramics?   *132*

8.4   What Can Archaeologists Learn from Ceramic Analysis?   *138*

8.5   Summary   *144*

Suggested Readings   *144*

Notes   *145*

CHAPTER 9:   Lithic Analysis   **146**

9.1   What Are Lithics Made From?   *147*
9.2   How Are Chipped Stone Tools Made?   *148*
9.3   What Types of Chipped Stone Tools Are There?   *150*
9.4   What Types of Ground Stone Tools Are There?   *152*
9.5   How Do Archaeologists Analyze Lithics?   *154*
9.6   What Can Archaeologists Learn from Lithic Analyses?   *160*
9.7   Summary   *164*
Suggested Readings   *164*
Notes   *164*

CHAPTER 10:   Floral and Faunal Analysis   **166**

10.1   How Do Archaeologists Find Remains of Ancient Plants
        and Animals?   *167*
10.2   What Kinds of Plant Remains Are Found in the Archaeological
        Record?   *170*
        10.2.1   *Microbotanical Remains*   *170*
        10.2.2   *Macrobotanical Remains*   *171*
10.3   What Kinds of Animal Remains Are Found in the Archaeological
        Record?   *174*
        10.3.1   *Microfaunal Remains*   *174*
        10.3.2   *Macrofaunal Remains*   *175*
10.4   What Information Do Archaeologists Obtain from Plant and Animal
        Remains?   *176*
10.5   Summary   *178*
Suggested Readings   *180*
Notes   *180*

CHAPTER 11:   Dating Archaeological Materials   182

11.1   Relative Dating   *183*

    11.1.1   Association   183

    11.1.2   Seriation   185

11.2   Absolute Dating   *187*

    11.2.1   Radiocarbon   187

    11.2.2   Thermoremnant Magnetism   190

    11.2.3   Thermoluminescence   192

    11.2.4   Dendrochronology   192

    11.2.5   Some Less Common Dating Techniques   192

11.3   Summary   *194*

Suggested Readings   *195*

Notes   *195*

CHAPTER 12:   Presenting Results   197

12.1   Why Publish?   *198*

12.2   What Types of Publication Are There?   *201*

12.3   What Are the Standard Forms of Publication?   *202*

12.4   Are There Nonprint Forms of Publication?   *205*

12.5   Summary   *207*

Suggested Readings   *207*

Notes   *208*

CHAPTER 13:   Legal and Ethical Issues   209

13.1   What Laws Regulate Archaeology in the United States?   *210*

13.2   What Principles Regulate the Behavior of Professional
    Archaeologists?   *214*

Principle 1: Stewardship *214*

Principle 2: Accountability *214*

Principle 3: Commercialization *215*

Principle 4: Public Education and Outreach *216*

Principle 5: Intellectual Property *216*

Principle 6: Public Reporting and Publication *217*

Principle 7: Records and Preservation *217*

Principle 8: Training and Resources *218*

13.3 Summary *218*

Suggested Readings *219*

Notes *219*

CHAPTER 14:   Research Opportunities   **221**

14.1 How Can I Gain Field Experience in Archaeology? *222*

14.2 Summary *224*

Suggested Readings *225*

Note *225*

GLOSSARY   **226**

PHOTO CREDITS   **239**

INDEX   **241**

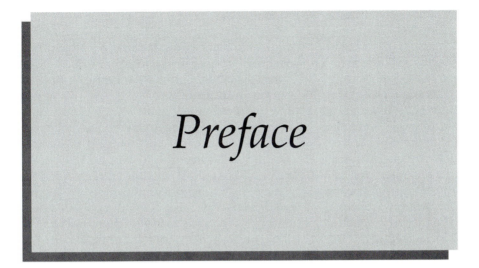

Preface

WHY DO ARCHAEOLOGY?

I was recently at a reception with one of my Wisconsin state legislators. I told him how troubled I was with the deep cuts that were being proposed to the state's archaeology budget. His response was: "Tell me how to sell archaeology to my colleagues and I'll try to put the money back." Sell archaeology. The comment threw me for a loop. The value of archaeology has always been obvious to me, and I thought it was obvious to others, too. Certainly some artifacts recovered through archaeological research are in demand: I was in an art gallery in Santa Fe a few months back where I saw prehistoric Puebloan ceramic vessels selling for more than my annual salary! Someone must think they are valuable. So why do I have to sell archaeology to my state legislators? I think it's because the archaeology sponsored by the state of Wisconsin, the archaeology I will try to introduce you to in this book, is not really all that concerned with artifacts, not even fancy or valuable ones. Archaeology, as I and more than 10,000 other scholars around the world practice it, focuses on the careful recovery, description, and analysis of *the relationships between and among artifacts*—what we call **context**. Most artifacts, by themselves, tell the archaeologist very little. Artifacts in context, on the other hand, speak volumes to those trained to listen.

Indiana Jones is a lousy archaeologist

Most archaeologists like the Indiana Jones movies. We find his adventures exciting and dream (often while grading papers) of flying off to some remote part of the world to discover lost treasures. But in all honesty, no serious archaeologist would survive past the first scene in *Raiders of the Lost Ark,* where Indy navigates an underground temple complex, replete with booby traps and large spiders, to procure a golden idol. The booby traps would have gotten me, and I think every other trained archaeologist in the world. We would never stomp through ancient buildings, breaking though collapsed walls to get into and out of the central chamber. We would start at the entrance, meticulously mapping the location of even the smallest piece of material we found. That's how the booby traps would get us—we'd be shot with a poisoned dart while trying to photograph the trip mechanism, or we'd fall through a trap door setting up our transit, or we'd unleash that giant rolling boulder and get squished measuring the width of the corridor. But that's what archaeology is all about—recording context, not grabbing artifacts—and that's why Indiana Jones is a lousy archaeologist.

 Why is context so important? What does it tell us? Let me illustrate with the following example: A E I G M N N. Huh? You don't understand because the letters (think of them as artifacts) are not in context. They are all very pretty letters, and we have them nicely organized on the page (in alphabetical order, perhaps like they might be displayed in a museum or private collection), but we can't read them because they are out of context. If we put them in context, we get: MEANING. Clever, eh? Context provides meaning, it allows us to read the archaeological record. In fact, you could think of this book as a simple outline of methods to record and read artifacts in context.

 But back to our question: Why do archaeology? One important answer, at least in the United States, Canada, Mexico, and most of the rest of the industrial world, is that the government mandates it. In the United States a series of laws dating back to the Antiquities Act of 1906 establish the basic principle that the archaeological record is essentially a part of the public record just like deeds, birth certificates, and marriage licenses. Like such public documents, the archaeological record cannot be wantonly destroyed. If the archaeological record is threatened, then either the threat must be removed or careful choices must be made about what can be destroyed and what must be preserved. This is why the state of Wisconsin and other state governments, as well as the federal government, fund some archaeological research: to collect and preserve parts of the archaeological record that are threatened with destruction. But that only covers one part of archaeology—data collection. What about reading context, reading the story the archaeological record has to tell us about the past? Why is that important?

I think the first, and perhaps most obvious, answer to the question of why do archaeology is that archaeology is interesting and entertaining. That's (in part) why the Indiana Jones movies are so popular. We share a genuine fascination about the past. Who lived here before us? What were they like? What happened to them? Those questions intrigue us, and it's a valid activity to try to answer them, if only to satisfy our own interest. In the United States today there are over 100 archaeological societies, many with several thousand members.[1] *Archaeology* magazine is circulated to some 200,000 people. We regularly see television documentaries on archaeology, and there are even several television series devoted to archaeology. Archaeology provides engaging entertainment and is a serious pastime for many thousands of people. But there are, I think, some more important reasons than either amusement or legal statutes for doing archaeology.

"Man . . . hangs on the past: However far or fast he runs, that chain runs with him"[2]

One important reason we do archaeology is to recognize the contributions and achievements of our predecessors. We have all inherited the legacy of Western civilization—both the good and the bad—and it is important for us to understand the contributions of those who came before us, for several reasons. The first is simply humanitarian—to honor our predecessors. We exist because they did, and it is right to acknowledge that. For those of us who live in North America, we must also reckon with the fact that our homes and schools are built on lands once occupied by Native Americans whom our predecessors either conquered or displaced. It is important that archaeology help us understand their contributions and achievements, too, even though their legacy is one of loss.

A related reason for us to understand the past is that the past provides precedents for the way we do things today. I think Karl Marx put this idea best when he wrote: "Men make their own history, but they do not make it just as they please; they do not make it under circumstances chosen by themselves, but under circumstances directly found, given and transmitted from the past. The tradition of all the dead generations weighs like a nightmare on the brain of the living."[3] What we do today is in part based on what we did yesterday. There is very little that is really "new" in any society, just things transformed. It is valuable for us to understand where the things we do today started, if only to return to that starting place and try again if our transformations have failed or have created unanticipated problems.

The link we have to the past is also used for political purposes, and it is important for us to understand how the past is used in political maneuvering. When we reelect representatives we are using the past, sending persons to office based on what they did previously. We often use the past conservatively, to argue against change, since "that's the way we've always done it." We can use the past to promote change, arguing for a transformation of past practices or for the prevention of previous mistakes. But the past can be used for more far-reaching political purposes. A clear example was given in the recent Gulf War, where part of Saddam Hussein's claim to Kuwait was that Iraq was the direct inheritor of the Assyrian Empire, an empire that had the area now known as Kuwait within its borders. Many less extreme, yet still politically powerful, claims are made on the basis of archaeological evidence. In the United States, for example, Native American groups have made extensive use of archaeological evidence in pursuing federal recognition and treaty rights. So archaeology is also important because it is used as a political tool.

"Those who cannot remember the past are condemned to repeat it"[4]

A second reason we do archaeology is that it offers us vital information about experiments in technology, economics, society, and political organization—experiments that more often than not were failures and thus only survive in the archaeological record. If we think about the great civilizations of the past—Pharaonic Egypt, Sumeria, the Inca Empire, to name a few—we'll notice one important commonality: They are all gone. Indeed, most civilizations that have ever existed ultimately collapsed or were conquered. Why? That's a very important question because it seems likely that our civilization will ultimately collapse, too, if the established pattern continues. One way to hedge against our civilization's downfall is to understand how and why previous civilizations fell. That answer has to include conquest as well, because it is always a question why a conqueror succeeds in overthrowing an established civilization. The conqueror's success points to either overwhelming strength or, more likely, some preexisting weakness in the conquered civilization.

In addition, conquerors or those remaining in a given area following a civilization's collapse often alter or neglect established patterns of life that may offer unique adaptations to that area. For example, the potato was exported to Europe following the Spanish conquest of the Andes; unfortunately, the rich diversity of potatoes, each variety adapted to specific environmental conditions, was not exported. Three centuries later Irish civilization nearly collapsed through a potato famine, a famine caused by a blight that spread rapidly because of the uniformity of potato varieties being grown in Ireland. Understanding the past adaptation—the diversity of potatoes that helped prevent such a catastrophic crop failure—has now taught us how valuable it is to preserve plant varieties, just as the Inca had done 500 years ago. It would have been helpful if we had learned that a bit earlier, don't you think? And it's those kinds of lessons that archaeology can teach us.

We are starting to take lessons from the past. In the Bolivian Andes, for example, archaeologists found that in pre-Incan and Incan times farmers used "raised" fields for their crops. They dug ditches for irrigation and piled the soil from those ditches into linear mounds on top of which they planted their crops. Wetland plants grew wild in the irrigation ditches and these were collected annually and spread on top of the raised fields, too, acting as fertilizer. The whole system worked beautifully—the irrigation system provided both water and fertilizer, and the raised fields surrounded by water helped to prevent animals and other pests from gaining access to the crops and also provided a hedge against frost damage. When the Spanish took over the region they transformed indigenous agriculture into a Spanish open-field model, and the ancient raised-field systems stopped being used. With the help of archaeologists, raised-field systems are being established once again in highland Bolivia and are proving themselves superior to modern farming techniques, both in the cost to produce crops and in their yield.[5]

"The past is never dead. It's not even past"[6]

A third and perhaps more important reason for doing archaeology is that archaeology helps us better understand ourselves. How? Well, it has to do with the rather strange nature of the past. We can never go back to the past (at least until someone creates a time machine), so the past only exists in the present, in our own minds. This does not mean, as some overzealous theorists have suggested, that a real past doesn't exist, nor does it mean that we can never accurately reconstruct the past. What it does mean is that our reconstructions are always subject to question and revision. For example, suppose I were to type %*(&). What? What is that? Did my fingers slip? Did I mean %*(&) to represent some vulgar word? Or did I type %*(&) purposely to prove a point? How can you know? The act is already done; the symbols are on the page. You cannot go back and examine the event of my typing as it occurred, you can only view the results and try to understand them. That's the nature of the past. Here, if we examine the symbols in context (and I will be harping on context throughout this book), we can see that it is unlikely that %*(&) was the result of my fingers slipping. It would have required one finger to slip onto the shift key and fingers from both hands to slip onto the erroneous symbols. So we can conclude that this was purposeful. We can also anticipate that there should be a noun in the spot where %*(&) occurs. We know this because we know something about the rules of English (just as we might know something about the rules governing behavior in a past society). There are several vulgar nouns, so perhaps that's what I meant, but in context (again) that doesn't seem to make sense. What would I be trying to convey? The most likely reconstruction is that I was trying to make a point. Can we ever know that for sure? No. Does that mean that a "real" past doesn't exist? Of course not. All it means is that our reconstruction is based on a set of assumptions and hypotheses that may change (for example, if you were to find out that I frequently use vulgar words . . . which I don't!).

There is an important lesson here. Since our reconstructions of the past are based on our thoughts, assumptions, insights, and hypotheses in the present, examining the past can tell us as much about ourselves in the present as it can tell us about the past. As Immanuel Wallerstein explains elegantly: "Recounting the past is a social act of the present done by men of the present and affecting the social system of the present."[7] This is something we cannot ignore. We can never know the past as it truly was but only the way it exists today in our imagination, and given the information we have about it. As Marc Bloch explains, "The past is, by definition, a datum which nothing in the future will change. But the knowledge of the past is something progressive which is constantly transforming and perfecting itself."[8] Our understanding of the past, then, is a product of both our knowledge of the past and how we interpret it. Both change constantly, and while we do gain a better understanding of the past the more we study it, we simultaneously gain a better understanding of ourselves, our biases, and our social world as we examine how our interpretations of the past have changed. Just consider how our view of Christopher Columbus's "discovery" of the New World has changed from 1892 to 1992. In 1892 a massive exhibition in Chicago celebrated the conquest of the Americas; in 1992 even Columbus, Ohio, had difficulty offering a celebration, and the United States as a whole held a "commemoration" that itself was not without controversy. I think this change tells us a lot about our society.

So, why do archaeology? Because the archaeological record is an irreplaceable part of our heritage that we must record and preserve. It is a powerful, and sometimes misused, political tool. It provides us with important insights about our society and ourselves. It offers us ideas about how to, and how not to, organize our society, technology, and economy. And it's fun! That is probably not a good enough answer to convince my Wisconsin legislators to spend more money on archaeology, but I hope it's good enough to get you interested in learning more about how archaeology is actually done, because that's what this book is all about.

OVERVIEW OF THE BOOK

As the title suggests, this is designed to be a *brief* introduction to archaeological research, and certainly not all aspects of archaeology are covered. What I have attempted to do is to focus on the one element common to archaeology wherever it is done: the research process itself. Archaeologists have developed a standard process for archaeological research, and this book attempts to clearly and concisely describe and illustrate it. You might notice that I keep referring to three research projects to help illustrate this process: my research in northeastern Wisconsin, a project I am part of in northern Syria, and a project in Oaxaca, Mexico, that my mentors were completing while I was in graduate school. These are not the only, or even the best, projects I could have chosen to use as examples, but they are projects I've been involved in and that I hope I can describe more completely than others I don't know as well. I also hope they tie the book together somewhat and give you a sense of how many dimensions there are to even the most basic archaeological projects. I also give examples from other projects, and I've tried to select them from all over the world. Obviously, in a book of this kind, not all the good ones can be noted, but let me assure you that there are many more out there than I refer to here.

My focus on the research process also means that I have either glossed over or left out many aspects of archaeological data collection and analysis, as well as issues of the history of archaeology and the battles that have been fought over archaeological research. I have, for example, not included discussions of how metals, glass, and textiles are analyzed, largely because they are not found in the archaeological record in many parts of the world. Instead, I have spent a bit more time than I might have discussing ceramics and lithics, as these are found everywhere archaeology is done. I don't intend this to be an apologia for what I have left out of the book; rather, I hope that it establishes at the start one of the book's central themes—that archaeologists do things for a reason. We don't dig holes, collect artifacts, or perform analyses just for the fun of it (although it can be fun!); we do those things to answer questions and we do them as part of an established and effective research process.

In Chapter 1 we'll look at the archaeological research process itself; that is, how archaeologists go about doing research from asking questions through evaluating results. In Chapter 2 we'll gain an understanding of the archaeological record and the three primary categories of archaeological material recovered: artifacts, ecofacts, and features. Chapters 3 through 6 describe how archaeologists collect data and record context. In them we'll look at archaeological survey and excavation strategies, we'll consider how particular strategies are chosen, and we'll examine the various methods of recordkeeping that archaeologists employ to record context. Chapters 7 through 11 focus on analyzing the data collected through archaeological survey and excavation. We'll look both at how the context and spatial patterns of artifacts are analyzed and at how information can be gleaned from artifacts themselves. We'll also learn how archaeological materials are dated. Finally, in Chapters 12 through 14 we'll consider how archaeology is actually done today. We'll look at publication and other ways archaeologists present the results of their research, we'll discuss legal and ethical issues that they face, and we'll find out about opportunities for doing archaeology.

ACKNOWLEDGMENTS

There are many people who have helped to take this book from an idea to a reality, and many, many more who have influenced the ideas I have presented here. I want to thank them all. In particular I want to thank my mentors in archaeology, Richard Blanton, Duane Esarey, Robert Fry, Ronald Mason, Neal Trubowitz, and Richard Zettler, who were kind enough to allow me to learn archaeology by working on their projects. I also want to thank all of the students who have studied archaeology under my instruction—I learned a lot from all of you—perhaps more than you did! I offer my most heartfelt thanks to Carol and Mel Ember, whose support and encouragement over the past decade have helped me grow from a naïve new Ph.D. into the scholar and teacher I am today. I offer thanks to the reviewers whose many suggestions have tremendously improved this book: Michael Fuller, St. Louis Community College; Perry L. Gnivecki, Appalachian State University; Jian Leng, University of Missouri–St. Louis; Michael J. O'Brien, University of Missouri; Susan Riches, Fort Lewis College; Lorraine P. Saunders, State University of New York College at Brockport; Gary M. Shaffer, Scottsdale Community College; Michael Stewart, Temple University; and Michael R. Waters, Texas A&M University.

I must also thank the wonderful people at Prentice Hall, particularly Nancy Roberts and Maureen Diana, who have been exceptionally supportive and helpful thoughout the sometimes difficult process of getting this work into print. Finally, I thank my family for putting up with my late nights and resulting irritation in the morning. Thanks to all.

SUGGESTED READINGS

Bahn, Paul. 1996. *Archaeology: A Very Short Introduction*. New York: Oxford University Press. Just what the name says—a short, well-written introduction to archaeology.

Bloch, Marc. 1953. *The Historian's Craft*. New York: Vintage. An essay on the nature of the past and how we learn about it in the present, written by one of the great historians of the twentieth century.

Gibbon, Guy. 1984. *Anthropological Archaeology*. New York: Columbia University Press. In my opinion, the single best introduction to archaeology ever written. Mandatory reading for anyone interested in understanding what archaeology is all about.

Taylor, Walter. 1983 (1948). *A Study of Archaeology*. Carbondale: Southern Illinois University Press. An influential critique on American archaeology as it was practiced in the 1940s. Taylor's discussion of why archaeology is important and what its aims should be, particularly his focus on the recovery of context in the archaeological record as a means of inferring past behavior, has influenced generations of archaeologists and should be required reading for anyone wishing to pursue the discipline.

Trigger, Bruce. 1978. *Time and Traditions*. New York: Columbia University Press. A collection of essays on the purposes and methods of archaeology written by an archaeologist whose work transcends archaeology, history, and anthropology.

NOTES

1. A list of the archaeological societies in the United States is published annually in the fourth issue of the journal *North American Archaeologist*.

2. Friedrich Nietzsche, *The Use and Abuse of History* (New York: Macmillan, 1985/1874).

3. Karl Marx, *The Eighteenth Brumaire of Louis Bonaparte* (Chicago: C. H. Kerr, 1913/1852). In *The Eighteenth Brumaire of Louis Bonaparte* Marx attempts to understand why the French elected Louis Bonaparte, nephew of Napoleon Bonaparte, as president of France. He had been deposed only thirty years before following his second attempt to overthrow the government. Eighteenth Brumaire is the date in 1799 that Napoleon Bonaparte staged a coup d'etat and overthrew the French revolutionary government, establishing himself as emperor, a reign that lasted until 1814. Louis Bonaparte spent only two years as president before he staged his own coup d'état and ultimately established himself as dictator, an occurrence that Marx, at least, felt should have been easily foreseen.

4. George Santayana, *Life of Reason* (New York: Scribner's, 1905–1906), Ch. 12. William L. Shirer used this quote as an epigraph in his *Rise and Fall of the Third Reich* (1959).

5. For information on raised-field agriculture, see Clark L. Erickson, "Prehistoric Landscape Management in the Andean Highlands: Raised Field Agriculture and Its Environmental Impact," *Population and Environment* 13 (1992):285–300. For information on how modern Bolivian farmers are using ancient agricultural methods, see Baird Straughan, "The Secrets of Ancient Tiwanaku Are Benefiting Today's Bolivia," *Smithsonian* 21(February 1991):38–49.

6. William Faulkner, *Requiem for a Nun* (New York: Random House, 1951).

7. Immanuel Wallerstein, *The Modern World System* (New York: Academic Press, 1974), p. 9.

8. Marc Bloch, *The Historian's Craft* (New York: Vintage, 1953), p. 58.

About the Author

Peter N. Peregrine is Associate Professor and Chair of the Department of Anthropology at Lawrence University in Appleton, Wisconsin. Dr. Peregrine received his Ph.D. in 1990 from Purdue University, where he did research on the late prehistoric Mississippian culture of the midwestern United States. Dr. Peregrine has dedicated his career to teaching undergraduates and regularly teaches courses on archaeology, research methods, and human evolution. He has also conducted archaeological fieldwork in the United States and Syria trying to understand how and why complex societies evolve and collapse. He is the author of more than 30 articles and book chapters and has authored or edited six books, including *Mississippian Evolution: A World-System Perspective* (1992) and *Archaeology of the Mississippian Culture* (1996).

The Archaeological Research Process

OVERVIEW

1.1   Phase I: Asking Questions

1.2   Phase II: Building Models

1.3   Phase III: Collecting Data

1.4   Phase IV: Analyzing Data

1.5   Phase V: Evaluating Results

1.6   Summary

Archaeologists do research all over the world, but regardless of where they work they follow a standard process for conducting research. This process consists of five separate phases: asking questions, building models, collecting data, analyzing data, and evaluating results. Each takes different amounts of effort and money (asking questions, for example, may only take a moment of free thought, while analyzing data may take years and cost thousands of dollars), but all are vital to reading the archaeological record. In this chapter I'll try to introduce you to each phase of the archaeological research process using examples from my own research and training.

1.1 PHASE I: ASKING QUESTIONS

All archaeological research begins with questions. One morning during the summer I started working for Lawrence University I was sitting on my front porch when the phone rang. It was Lawrence's president. Now, when you are a junior faculty member in a new job and your president calls you at home it's usually not a good thing. So, after the pain from the scalding hot coffee I spilled all over myself subsided and I started actually listening, I was pleased to hear that the president was not calling to tell me that they had made a mistake and I wasn't actually hired, but because he had an archaeological question for me. Lawrence had just broken ground for a new conference facility on property the university owns in Door County, Wisconsin. Some artifacts had been found there and the president wanted to know if I would take a look at the site. I agreed, and a new archaeological research project was born—the Bjorklunden Archaeological Survey. (Bjorklunden, pronounced "be-york-lun-den," is the name of the property and supposedly means *birch forest* in Norwegian.)

This might seem a bit different from how I said archaeological projects begin—asking questions. Here I didn't ask a question but was asked to look at a site. However, *my* work, as an archaeologist, began not when the president asked me to visit Bjorklunden, but after I visited the site and saw that it was indeed a likely location for prehistoric habitation. At that point I asked a fundamental archaeological question: "Is there a preserved and recoverable record of human behavior at this location?" I also asked a number of secondary questions, such as "What types of material might be preserved here?"

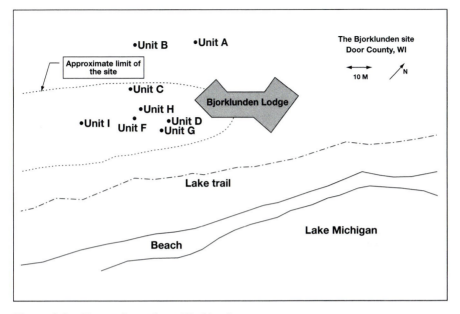

Figure 1.1   Excavation units at Bjorklunden.

and "What peoples likely lived here, and what kind of archaeological record would they have left?" These are the kinds of simple questions that start many archaeological projects.

Of course, other projects start with much more sophisticated or specific questions in mind. As a graduate student I was lucky enough to come in on the tail end of one of the most significant archaeological projects ever undertaken: the Valley of Oaxaca (pronounced "wa-ha-ka") Settlement Pattern Project. My mentor, Richard Blanton, was the project's principal investigator, and my dissertation research (and indeed much of what I have done since graduate school) focused on questions stemming from the project and its findings.[1] A powerful state evolved in the Valley of Oaxaca, centered at a site called Monte Albán, and the Valley of Oaxaca Settlement Pattern Project was designed to answer the question: "Why did the Monte Albán state evolve?" That question really had three parts, all of which required answers: "Why did the state evolve?" "Why did it evolve at Monte Albán and not elsewhere?" and "Why did it evolve when it did, not earlier or later?"[2]

These questions are much more specific than the ones I had starting research at Bjorklunden, but recognize that they are preceded by a substantial understanding of the existing archaeological record. Indeed, the Valley of Oaxaca was chosen specifically as a research locale because it (1) was a place where a state evolved that (2) had a reasonably well-understood archaeological record that (3) was easily accessible through archaeological survey. Thus, the

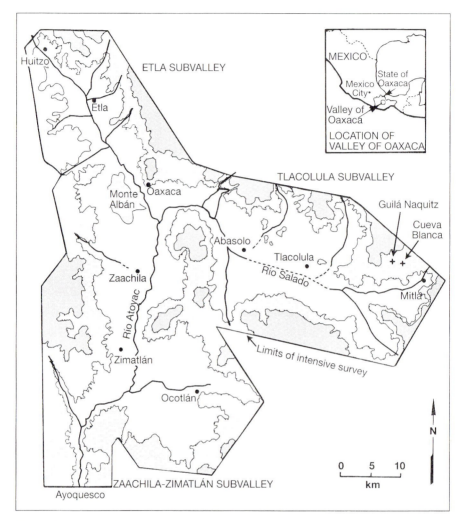

Figure 1.2   The Valley of Oaxaca, Mexico, showing survey boundaries.

Source: Figure from *Guilá Naquitz: Archaic Foraging and Early Agriculture in Oaxaca, Mexico* by Kent Flannery, copyright © 1986 by Academic Press, reproduced by permission of the publisher.

question of state origins started the whole project. Once the question was framed, a location where answers could be found was sought, and that location turned out to be the Valley of Oaxaca.

These two examples illustrate the two major types of questions asked by archaeologists: descriptive and processual. **Descriptive questions** ask about the nature of the archaeological record and can be thought of as questions that start with who, what, when, or where. They ask what material is present, what the state of preservation is, when the material was deposited, and, ultimately, who made the material. Answers to descriptive questions often lead to a **culture-history**, which is a history of the cultures that inhabited a particular location or region. **Processual questions** assume that a location's culture-history is known and move beyond it to ask how and why the culture-history takes the form it does. In other words, processual questions ask about the processes of cultural stability and change over time. Most archaeologists find processual questions the most interesting to pursue, but I hope it's clear that descriptive questions have to be asked—and answered—before processual ones can be addressed.

1.2 PHASE II: BUILDING MODELS

Once a question has been posed, archaeologists begin to devise model answers to the question, or more simply, models. Model answers for descriptive questions are based on two fundamental assumptions: (1) The archaeological record accurately preserves the material remains of human behavior and (2) human behavior can be accurately reconstructed from its material remains. There has been considerable discussion and criticism of these two assumptions, and we will spend part of the next chapter examining them more closely. Suffice it to say that almost all archaeologists accept them, and most archaeological work directed at answering descriptive questions proceeds under a fairly generic model.

Model answers for processual questions are based on some theory of human behavior. In archaeology two schools of theory predominate: materialist and eco-functional. **Materialist theories** posit that the way humans organize labor and technology to get resources out of the material world is the primary force shaping culture. Major forces promoting change are innovations in technology, environmental changes or catastrophes, and internal conflicts over labor organization and access to resources. **Eco-functional theories** posit that human culture is an adaptation to the environment, and thus culture functions to maintain humans and the environment in a sustainable balance. The major force promoting change, then, is the environment itself—as the environment changes, so do human cultures. However, a basic assumption in many eco-functional theories is that human population has an overall tendency to grow, and this often puts pressure on resources and the environment as a whole—pressure that leads to change. I hope it is obvious that these two schools of theory are closely related and that both share a common focus on the environment and how humans use it. This should not be all that surprising, given that the best information we can get from the archaeological record is about human interaction with the natural world.

While some model answers for processual questions aim at broad processes like those just mentioned—human use of or interaction with the environment—most are aimed at evaluating very specific theories within those larger schools. The Valley of Oaxaca project was directed toward evaluating an eco-functional theory proposed by the agricultural economist Esther Boserup. Boserup suggested that as population grows in societies that practice agriculture, the society will find ways to intensify agricultural production to support the growth.[3] Thus, cultural change is seen as stemming from population growth. As population increases, the society will have to innovate to continue to support itself. Archaeologist William Sanders applied this idea to the rise of the Teotihuacan state in the Valley of Mexico, arguing that the state evolved as a way to centrally control the agricultural economy and intensify production to support a growing population.[4] The Valley of Oaxaca project was designed to test this idea in a different location; in other words, to **replicate** the findings from the Valley of Mexico.

The basic model used in the Valley of Oaxaca project was a population growth one, based on Boserup's theory. The model answer to the question "Why did the state evolve?" was that population grew to the point where a state was required to control the agricultural economy. The model answer to "Why did it evolve at Monte Albán and not elsewhere?" was that Monte Albán

Figure 1.3   The main plaza at Monte Albán, Oaxaca, Mexico.

was located on prime agricultural land where production could easily be centralized and intensified. The model answer to "Why did it evolve when it did, not earlier or later?" was that it evolved when population reached a point where it could no longer be intensified without centralized control. Based on these model answers, the project team developed a series of **hypotheses** or predictions for how the archaeological record should look. Most fundamentally, they suggested, was that there should be evidence of population growth through time, particularly right before the founding of the Monte Albán state. Once that primary hypothesis was established, a clear set of variables that needed data became obvious, the most obvious being data on changes in population density through time in the Valley. Thus, the question led to a model answer that told the archaeologists precisely what data needed to be collected. This is how the archaeological research process is supposed to work.

Of course, many projects are not so clear-cut in being directed at answering a particular descriptive or processual question or in having such a specific model answer. For example, I have been working since 1990 on a project with colleagues at the University of Pennsylvania Museum and the Semitic Museum at Harvard University trying to understand settlement in part of a large Early Bronze Age city in northern Mesopotamia called Tell es-Sweyhat (pronounced "sway-hot").[5] The city is divided, as are virtually all northern Mesopotamian cities, into an inner town or acropolis containing a palace and temple complex and elite residences and an outer town containing workshops and common residences. Unfortunately, little work has been done in the outer towns of northern Mesopotamian cities. We know, in general, what to expect in the outer town of Tell es-Sweyhat, but many descriptive questions remain. Our primary question, however, is a processual one concerning the political and economic relationship between residents in the inner and outer towns. Clearly the residents of the inner town were supported by the craftspeople and agricultural workers who lived in the outer town, but what was the nature of their relationship? How did the residents of the inner town "earn" support? Why did residents of the outer town support elites in the inner town?

Our model answers for both the descriptive and processual questions are based on prior research and theory. We know something about the archaeological record in outer towns from other excavations, and we also know something about it from Bronze Age documents. We have several bodies of theory on the relationship between elites and commoners in early cities like Tell es-Sweyhat, and the basic model we've taken from them is that elites provided military and religious services to the commoners who were basically coerced to support them, but who also willingly gave support for the military defense provided by the city and for the supernatural services provided through the temple complex. Our main hypothesis, then, is that clear distinctions will be present in the activities taking place in the inner versus the outer town, with the inner town focused on military and religious activities and the outer town on craft and agricultural production. We need to gather a variety of data, then,

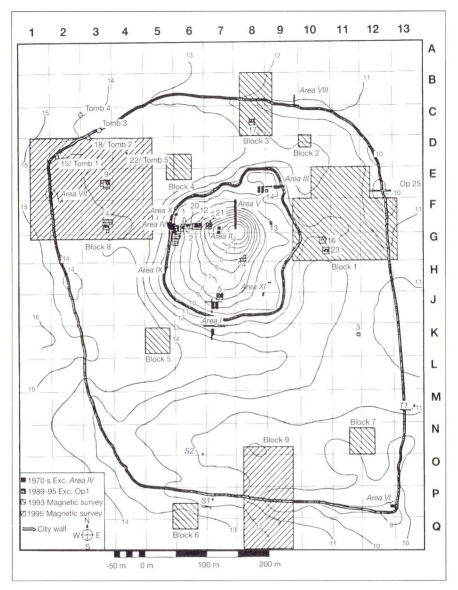

Figure 1.4 Excavation units and survey areas at Tell es-Sweyhat.

Source: From *Subsistence and Settlement in a Marginal Environment* by Richard Zettler, ed., Museum Applied Science Center for Archaeology, Vol. 14, copyright © 1997, University Museum, University of Pennsylvania, p. 6. Reprinted by permission of University Museum, University of Pennsylvania.

on settlement patterns and residential activities in order to answer both our descriptive and processual questions.

1.3   PHASE III: COLLECTING DATA

The outer town of Tell es-Sweyhat covers roughly 40 hectares. How do we go about collecting a variety of data on settlement patterns and residential activities over such a large area? We can't possibly excavate that whole area, and indeed, since all of the information is buried, we can't even tell where the most informative data are buried—we don't know where to dig. The Valley of Oaxaca researchers faced an even larger problem: how to gather information on changes in population density over an area of more than 2,000 square kilometers! But archaeologists are always faced with these problems. Even my fairly simple project at Bjorklunden has archaeological deposits that cover an area at least several football fields in size. So how do archaeologists know where to start? How do they collect data over such large areas? There are three basic methods used, and which one is employed on a given project depends on the data required to answer a particular question. The three methods are pedestrian survey, test excavation, and remote sensing.

Pedestrian survey is the primary way archaeologists find archaeological deposits. All archaeologists know that pedestrian survey is problematic, since much of the archaeological record is deeply buried or may not otherwise be visible on the surface, so in most cases pedestrian survey is used only to find general site locations, not as a primary means of data collection. There are rare situations where pedestrian survey can, however, be used to collect the data needed to answer questions. The Valley of Oaxaca project, for example, was based almost entirely on pedestrian survey. As I mentioned earlier, the location had been chosen specifically because most of the Valley was under cultivation

Figure 1.5   Tell es-Sweyhat.

and thus subsurface deposits were regularly brought to the surface. Also, ancient houses had been built on raised platforms that were still visible throughout the Valley.[6] If you'll recall, the main data the researchers needed concerned population change through time. Because population can be estimated by both community size and house size, pedestrian survey provided all the information needed. This is an unusual case, however. Most archaeological projects use pedestrian survey only to locate sites, not to collect primary data.

Often archaeologists combine pedestrian survey with small **test excavations** to determine how much of the archaeological record is actually visible on the surface. Test excavation is more difficult and time consuming than pedestrian survey, but it offers a much better knowledge of the actual archaeological deposits and is the only technique available when the ground surface is not visible or when deposits are thought to be deeply buried. At Bjorklunden, for example, no artifacts are visible on the surface; indeed, most of the ground surface is covered with a thick blanket of pine needles. The artifacts that were found the summer the president called me were located where the ground had been scraped clean in order to build the new conference center. In order to find where the site was located I conducted a series of **shovel tests**, taking a shovel full of dirt out of the ground and sifting it through a one-quarter-inch mesh screen to separate the dirt from artifacts. By doing shovel tests over a large area, I was able to roughly delineate the boundaries of the archaeological deposits. I followed that with a series of small excavation units, designed to define the artifact-bearing strata—but we'll get into that in the chapter on excavation.

Figure 1.6   Shovel testing at Bjorklunden.

The term **remote sensing** covers a variety of techniques that share the ability to locate archaeological deposits below the ground without having to dig. In other words, these techniques allow archaeologists to sense buried archaeological deposits remotely, from the surface. I have been using one remote sensing technique—geomagnetics—to map the outer town at Tell es-Sweyhat. If you'll remember, the outer town is roughly 40 hectares in size, and most of the archaeological deposits are buried under about a meter of soil, so pedestrian survey is only of marginal utility. And pedestrian survey can't really give us the information we need to plan excavations, as we are interested in locating and excavating a representative variety of residences, workshops, and the like. What the geomagnetic maps provide, in combination with pedestrian survey and test excavations, is a detailed map of the outer town, one that offers us a good idea of both how the outer town is laid out and where the best places to excavate should be.

Excavation, the careful recovery of buried archaeological data in context, is the primary data collection method used by archaeologists, and probably the one that comes to mind when we think of archaeologists doing their work. But excavation, like site location, is not a uniform or simple process. Rather, it is designed to recover the specific information needed to answer the

Figure 1.7   Excavations at Tell es-Sweyhat.

question the archaeologists are pursuing. In the outer town at Tell es-Sweyhat, for example, we have a carefully planned schedule of excavation that will likely take the careers of several scholars to complete. So far we have excavated a segment of the external fortifications, a residence built against the fortification wall, several additional residences, and two workshops. This has taken about five years, and we only have the first glimpse of how the outer town was structured, but this is really not that long for an archaeological project. The Valley of Oaxaca project took about fifteen years from beginning to end, and that was without excavation. I anticipate my project at Bjorklunden will continue for at least five years. Why do archaeological projects take so long to complete? Largely because excavation must be meticulous. Once a site is excavated it can never be reexcavated—it has to be done right the first time. We'll talk more about that when we discuss excavation later in the book.

1.4   PHASE IV: ANALYZING DATA

Excavation, while itself a long and sometimes tedious process, only collects data. **Data analysis** is an even longer and more tedious process. In fact, it has been estimated that archaeologists spend a week doing data analysis for every hour spent collecting data! That may seem extreme, but a lot goes into data analysis. All materials collected have to first be cleaned, stabilized (if they are decaying or breaking), and preserved. They then need to be catalogued— numbered, photographed, and described. That alone can take hours for any given piece of material, and that's before analysis can even begin!

As we'll discuss in the next chapter, archaeologists consider everything used or affected by humans to be part of the archaeological record, but many of our analyses are focused on only two types of materials: lithics and ceramics. **Lithics** are stone tools, and there is a vast array of types, styles, and means of manufacture. We'll look in some detail at stone tools in a later chapter. **Ceramics** are utensils, often containers for storing food and water, made of baked clay. As with lithics, a vast array of types, styles, and means of manufacture exist. We'll be looking at ceramics in a later chapter, too. A third and also important type of data that we'll look at is floral and faunal materials. These are used to reconstruct the environment and how humans used it. The importance of this information should be obvious from our brief discussion of materialist and eco-functional theory.

Why are lithics and ceramics primary forms of archaeological data? Largely because lithics and ceramics preserve well and are readily recoverable in the archaeological record, and so they are two items we can pretty generally count on finding. They are found all over the world—literally everywhere humans have lived—and so archaeologists in all world areas learn how to analyze them. Also, lithic and ceramic styles of manufacture and decoration change regularly through time, and that makes them good temporal markers and excellent tools for developing culture histories. Finally, since both lithics and ceramics are important in the economies of the peoples who use them (particularly lithics), their analysis can tell us a lot about how a group of people used their environment, and that (like floral and faunal data) is important in both materialist and eco-functional theory.

A good example of how ceramics can be used as temporal markers comes from the Valley of Oaxaca project. Recall that the researchers wanted to determine population size through time. They used settlement size to estimate population, but how did they know when a particular settlement had been occupied? You guessed it—by the ceramics! Oaxacan ceramic styles of decoration and manufacture changed regularly, and these changes gave the researchers clear temporal markers for when particular locations were occupied. They were occupied when the type of ceramic found there was made. But ceramics also told the researchers a lot about social and political changes. When the Monte Albán state emerged, ceramics changed dramatically; they became standardized and quite plain. The researchers have argued that the Monte Albán state took control of ceramic production and mass-produced them for the population as part of an overall strategy for controlling the economy in the valley.[7]

Figure 1.8   Diagnostic ceramics of the Rosario phase (ca. 700 B.C. to 500 B.C.) in the Valley of Oaxaca: (a, b, c) fine gray bowls; (d) tripod bowl.

Source: Figure from *The Cloud People* by Kent Flannery and Joyce Marcus, copyright © by Academic Press, reproduced by permission of the publisher.

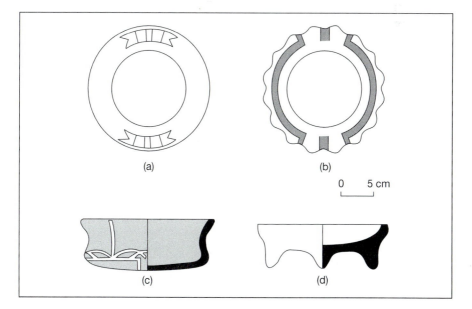

Figure 1.9   Projectile points from Bjorklunden.

I am using lithic data exclusively right now in my project at Bjorklunden because I haven't found any ceramics. Why not? Well, perhaps because I simply haven't looked in the right place. Ceramics were first introduced to the Door County region about 500 B.C., and several projectile points we've found date to a time period after that. Just like ceramics, forms and manufacture of stone tools change regularly through time, and so lithics are often good temporal markers, too. The projectile points we've found at Bjorklunden date from before 2500 B.C. to after A.D. 500, well into the ceramic period. Another reason why we haven't found ceramics yet might be that people weren't using ceramics at the site. The site may have been used as a hunting camp or flint-knapping area. It is located between two very large village sites and may have been a place hunters simply stopped, rested, and made projectile points.

Not everything excavated can be removed from the site; for example, you can't take the pyramids away from Giza. Archaeologists call such non-removable artifacts **features.** At Tell es-Sweyhat, one of the things we are most interested in is variation in architecture. Houses at the site were constructed of mud-brick walls built atop stone footings. Preserved today are about a half-meter of the mud-brick walls and the stone foundations. We could remove these from the site, but we really wouldn't learn much from the pile of stones and crumbling bricks we'd have. Together, in context, the foundation and walls tell us much more—they tell us about the form, construction, and function of the houses. Within the houses we have found hearths, another type of feature often found on archaeological sites. Finally, we have found a number of pits: holes dug into the ground for storage or to bury garbage (in fact, we found seven whole pots in one pit!). Pit features are perhaps the most common on archaeological

sites and are sought after by archaeologists because even if their original function was to store material, they are often filled in with garbage, and garbage
provides an excellent record of the materials people were using.

1.5   PHASE V: EVALUATING RESULTS

Once data have been collected and analyzed, the process of evaluating them
in terms of the original question and model answers can begin. This might
seem to be a fairly straightforward phase of the research process, but it isn't.
Usually the data answer only part of the original question, or the data are
contradictory. Sometimes they even contradict the originally proposed model.
In the Valley of Oaxaca, for example, the researchers found not only that population was never high enough to put pressure on resources, but also that it
actually fell dramatically in some areas over time.[8] In fact, the researchers found
that the population was extremely dynamic, and this dynamism may have
had more impact on cultural change in the Valley of Oaxaca than population
growth! These kinds of problems are found all the time in archaeological
research. They are really part of the whole evaluation process, and they are one
reason why evaluation is an ongoing part of any archaeological project.

While formal evaluation of the original question happens only at the
end of the research process, more informal evaluation goes on all the time. As
data are recovered and analyzed it often becomes clear that they won't be suf-
ficient to answer the question posed. Sometimes, as in the case of Oaxaca,
they confuse or even contradict original models or assumptions, and the entire
research process itself has to be called into question. Indeed, surprises are part
of the game in archaeology, a part of the research process that keeps it from
being too highly formalized or procedural. We can never know what the
ground is going to hold until we dig it up, and what we dig up is often a surprise. So while I've outlined here a rather formal process, recognize that it is
a process built to be flexible and to allow for change mid-stream. Most important, it is a process that allows new questions to arise.

A few years ago my colleagues at the University of Pennsylvania visited Tell es-Sweyhat to check on things between seasons. The farmer who
owns the southern part of the outer town complained to them that our excavation holes were draining all his irrigation water. This sounded a bit strange,
since our excavations in that part of the site were rather shallow, so my colleagues went out to look at the holes the farmer was complaining about. It
turned out that the irrigation water had percolated through the soil and had
eaten through limestone caps that covered Early Bronze Age shaft tombs. Several tombs were now open and filling with water. This is the kind of surprise that
often occurs in archaeology. We now think there may be as many as 120 tombs

on the western side of the site, and we have spent two seasons with part of the crew excavating the disturbed ones. So, while formal, the archaeological research process has to be flexible enough to allow us to pursue surprises like these. And indeed, this surprise should lead to very interesting questions about the relationship between the inner and outer towns, since these tombs precede architecture in the outer town and indeed are covered up by it. The people building houses some two centuries after these tombs were capped apparently didn't know the tombs were there!

New questions not only arise from surprises but also are an important aspect of the evaluation phase for any project. Indeed, most archaeological projects end in new questions, not in answers to old ones. As I said earlier, my dissertation research and much of what I have done since has focused on questions arising from the Valley of Oaxaca project. Imagine the researchers' surprise when they found that their population pressure model could not alone explain the rise of the state. What could? Clearly the Monte Albán state had attempted to take control of the economy, as evidenced by mass-produced ceramics. How would emergent leaders gain economic control? Under what conditions could this happen? Warfare seems to have been endemic in the Valley of Oaxaca before the rise of Monte Albán. Could conquest and pacification by a single group have led to this state? Could it have led to economic control, too? These were the sorts of questions the researchers in Oaxaca were left with and are the sorts of questions I was directed toward by my mentors and colleagues who were part of the Oaxaca project. The archaeological

Figure 1.10   The entrance to a tomb at Tell es-Sweyhat.

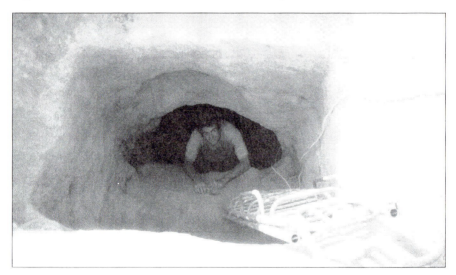

research process, then, never really ends. It leads to new questions that are, in turn, addressed—sometimes by a new generation of archaeologists.

In order for the archaeological research process to be a continuing one, however, archaeologists have to disseminate their findings. An essential aspect of any archaeological project, therefore, is publishing the results. In fact, conscientious archaeologists will produce a report during each phase of the research process, and often several for the data collection and analysis phases. Unfortunately, not all do. The bulk of contemporary archaeological literature consists of data analysis reports. Altogether too few archaeologists produce final reports for the evaluation phase, which is a continuing problem in archaeology today.[9] It is an understandable problem, however, since projects always end in new questions and it can be difficult to stop the research process to take the time to answer the questions already asked. Also, as projects evolve, sometimes those old questions turn out to be either unanswerable or at least the wrong ones to ask, and writing a report about them is almost impossible. Still, archaeologists are required to disseminate the results of their research. If they don't, they are no better than looters who take artifacts from sites for personal collections or monetary gain. Indeed, the thing that most clearly separates archaeologists from artifact collectors (like Indiana Jones, for example) is the research process we've just examined and the responsibility of reporting the results of research to the larger community of archaeologists and to the public as a whole. Publication is the only thing that can give life to the archaeological research process—that can give it the ability to continue through new questions and new archaeologists pursuing answers.

1.6 SUMMARY

All archaeological research begins with questions. We go about answering those questions through the research process, which begins with questions and ends with answers (and usually more questions). The first step in answering questions is to propose a possible answer or a set of answers. These possible answers are called models and are based on particular bodies of theory that provide a set of assumptions for how humans behave. Models propose specific hypotheses or predictions about what the archaeological record will contain. Once hypotheses are selected for testing, the variables necessary to evaluate them are **operationalized** (that is, made measurable through the archaeological record).

Field research—survey and excavation—is initiated only after questions have been asked and models built. Why? Because we can't possibly collect everything, so we have to determine beforehand what specific data we need to gather in order to evaluate our hypotheses. **Sampling** also helps us determine precisely what data to collect. Once collected, data must be interpreted to determine what they mean. Archaeologists have developed a powerful set of analytical tools to recover meaning from the archaeological record, and, as I will try to impress upon you, most are based on patterns and **context** rather than the intrinsic properties of artifacts themselves. Once data have been analyzed and interpreted, they can be evaluated in relation to the theoretical model and associated hypotheses under which they were collected. The outcome of most evaluations is a new set of questions, and that, in essence, starts the process of archaeological research all over again.

SUGGESTED READINGS

Ashmore, Wendy, and Robert Sharer. 1996. *Discovering Our Past: A Brief Introduction to Archaeology*. Mountain View, CA: Mayfield. As the title says, a brief introduction to archaeology. Readable, nicely illustrated, and concise. This is a good book to read to start going deeper into the nature of archaeological research.

Binford, Lewis. 1983. *In Pursuit of the Past: Decoding the Archaeological Record*. New York: Thames and Hudson. One of the most influential archaeologists of our time uses his own research to explain how archaeological research is carried out.

Fagan, Brian. 1991. *In the Beginning: An Introduction to Archaeology*. New York: Harper-Collins. A classic introduction to archaeological research.

Patterson, Thomas. 1994. *The Theory and Practice of Archaeology: A Workbook*. Englewood Cliffs, NJ: Prentice Hall. This workbook takes the reader through practical exercises in how archaeological research is performed.

Renfrew, Colin, and Paul Bahn. 1996. *Archaeology: Theories, Methods, and Practice*. New York: Thames and Hudson. Perhaps the best single introduction to archaeological research. This is a comprehensive and detailed overview of archaeology written by two of the world's finest archaeologists.

Thomas, David Hurst. 1989. *Archaeology*. Fort Worth, TX: Holt, Rinehart & Winston. Perhaps the most readable of the several good introductions to archaeology.

NOTES

1. You can read about Richard Blanton's career and work in his article "Archaeologist at Work," in *Research Frontiers in Anthropology*, ed. Carol R. Ember, Melvin Ember, and Peter N. Peregrine (Upper Saddle River, NJ: Prentice Hall, 1998).
2. The Valley of Oaxaca project findings are summarized in Stephen Kowalewski et al., *Monte Albán's Hinterland, Part II* (Ann Arbor: University of Michigan, Museum of Anthropology, Memoir 23, 1989).

3. Esther Boserup, *The Conditions of Agricultural Growth* (Chicago: Aldine, 1965).

4. William Sanders, Jeffrey Parsons, and Robert Santley, *The Basin of Mexico* (New York: Academic Press, 1979).

5. Our initial findings are summarized in *Subsistence and Settlement in a Marginal Environment,* ed. Richard Zettler (Philadelphia: Museum Applied Science Center for Archaeology, University of Pennsylvania, 1998).

6. See the chapter on field methods in Richard Blanton et al., *Monte Albán 's Hinterland, Part I* (Ann Arbor: University of Michigan, Museum of Anthropology, Memoir 7, 1982).

7. Richard Blanton, Stephen Kowalewski, Gary Feinman, and Jill Appel, *Ancient Mesoamerica* (New York: Cambridge University Press, 1981), pp. 92–97.

8. Gary Feinman and Linda Nicholas, "Settlement and Land Use in the Valley of Oaxaca," in *Debating Oaxaca Archaeology,* ed. Joyce Marcus (Ann Arbor: University of Michigan, Museum of Anthropology, Anthropological Papers 84), pp. 71–113.

9. Brian Fagan, "Archaeology's Dirty Secret," *Archaeology* 48 (1995):14.

The Archaeological Record

OVERVIEW

2.1 What Do Archaeologists Find?

2.2 What Is Context?

2.3 What Theories Do Archaeologists Use to Interpret the Archaeological Record?

2.4 Summary

"**D**r. Pergriani?" the voice on the other end of the phone asks.

"Dr. Peregrine, yes," I answer.

"Boy, have I found an important artifact!" the voice says with enthusiasm.

"Really?" I reply, trying not to sound facetious. One thing I've learned dealing with folks who find artifacts is that when they think something is important, it's usually not.

"What is it?" I ask.

"A rock with Indian writing on it!" the voice responds with a twinge of awe.

"Is the writing scratched on the rock or painted?" I ask.

"Scratched."

"You found this in a field?"

"Yeah," the voice says. "How did you know?"

"Plow marks," I reply. "It was hit by the plow a couple of times."

"Can't be," the voice replies. "The marks are too regular." Denial. I've heard it all before.

"Well," I say, "the native peoples who lived around here didn't have written languages."

"Huh?" the voice responds. I can sense anger rising in the voice, so I try to end the conversation quickly.

"Bring it by here if you want, and I'll take a look at it, OK?"

"Uh, yeah, OK." The voice sounds confused.

"I can tell you this, though, it's definitely an artifact." That cheers the voice up, and he hangs up with a thank you. I feel good, too, because I didn't actually lie to him. What he had was an artifact. As I mentioned in the last chapter, archaeologists define an **artifact** as anything that has been used or modified by humans. A rock scratched by a plow is an artifact—it has been modified by humans. In fact, the field the rock was found in is an artifact, as the landscape has been modified by humans. The plow that struck the rock is of course an artifact, as is the tractor that pulled it, but so are the footprints of the farmer who walked through the field where he found the rock. Even the hole in the ground left by the rock is an artifact. It would not be there if the farmer had not picked the rock up.

2.1   WHAT DO ARCHAEOLOGISTS FIND?

By convention, archaeologists divide the vast realm of artifacts into three major types: artifacts, ecofacts, and features. The formal, archaeological use of the term *artifact* is not as general as the one just given. To an archaeologist, *artifact* refers specifically to objects of human manufacture or modification that can be collected or otherwise removed from a site. The rock the farmer found is an artifact. Ceramics and lithics are artifacts. Clothing, decorations, weapons, utensils, and almost any other material objects you can think of are artifacts. Well, then, what are ecofacts?

Ecofacts are natural materials that have been used by humans. Typical ecofacts include the remains of plants and animals that were eaten by a group of people. They can include seeds, pollen, or even chemicals that help archaeologists reconstruct the environment people lived in and used (recall how important human use of the environment is in both major schools of archaeological theory). Among the most important ecofacts are the remains of humans themselves—their bones, their tissues, and the chemical residues of their bodies.

As we discussed briefly in Chapter 1, **features** are artifacts or ecofacts that cannot be removed from their context. They are things like the remains of houses, buildings, or monuments; storage and garbage pits; hearths and ovens; and the like. Several less obvious but no less important types of features are activity areas, living floors, and middens. **Activity areas** are locations on a site where a group of artifacts associated with a particular activity (for example, stoneworking, pottery making, food processing) are found together. Often the artifacts found are the refuse from the activity. **Living floors** are locations on a site where artifacts associated with a household are found. Living floors are basically the floors of houses, encampments, and the like. Frequently living floors will be compacted and will be quite noticeable while excavating and in archaeological strata. Materials found on living floors tend to be small refuse from daily life. **Middens** are substantial and well-defined accumulations of artifacts and ecofacts. Middens can be the product of natural processes; for example, rainwater can collect materials in low spots. However, middens are often created by humans dumping refuse in one location over a long period of time. Middens are one of the most informative deposits archaeologists can find. Almost everything a group of people uses will be thrown away eventually, and most of what is discarded ends up in a midden. Middens typically contain everything from broken tools to kitchen refuse to human remains.

Artifacts, ecofacts, and features are the basic building blocks of archaeological data, but they are not themselves archaeological data. Archaeological data consist of the relationships between and among artifacts, ecofacts, and features; that is, archaeological data are archaeological materials in **context**.

2.2 WHAT IS CONTEXT?

Why do I keep harping on this context thing? Well, perhaps an example would make the notion of context clear.

What if we found a set of artifacts like those shown to the right? What are we to make of them? How do we make sense of them? What picture do they give us? We can't tell. There are literally thousands of ways they could be combined. But if we know something about the context they were found in, we might be able to understand them.	
What if we knew that the circles were found next to one another, and the straight line was below them? What would this tell us? Not much, but we begin to see some pattern.	
What if we knew that the arc was found below the line and was actually rotated 90 degrees from the position we see it here? Ah, now we're getting somewhere.	
Finally, what if we knew that all of the smaller shapes were found inside the large oval? Now we have a picture we can understand. That's what context does for archaeologists. It allows us to take artifacts, ecofacts, and features and make of them a picture we can understand.	

When we find a location where archaeological material (artifacts, ecofacts, and features) exist in context, we call that location an *archaeological site*. Archaeological sites exist everywhere, and we are creating them all the time. However, sites containing the data archaeologists need to answer specific questions are quite rare. Why? Because most archaeological materials decay over time and literally disappear. Those that do survive often lose context. Natural processes like erosion or freezing and thawing move archaeological materials out of their original locations. Humans are pretty good at disturbing archaeological materials, too. We dig new storage pits where old ones were located, we cover old house foundations with new ones, we drag plows across ancient fields and farmsteads. Because of poor preservation and destruction of context, it is the rare exception when ancient human behavior is preserved in an archaeological site. And ancient human behavior is what we are really talking about when we speak of archaeological data, for that is what archaeologists assume is preserved in the context of artifacts, ecofacts, and features.

2.3 WHAT THEORIES DO ARCHAEOLOGISTS USE TO INTERPRET THE ARCHAEOLOGICAL RECORD?

In the first chapter I said that most archaeological research takes place under two assumptions: (1) The archaeological record accurately preserves the material remains of human behavior and (2) human behavior can be accurately reconstructed from its material remains. The truth is actually much more complex, and there are a variety of schools of thought on the nature of the archaeological record. All of them, at some level, come back to one idea: We can know the past from the material record of human behavior, if only quite imperfectly. If archaeologists didn't believe that, they couldn't possibly be archaeologists—there would be no point at all to it. So, while some of these schools of thought may seem to suggest that a knowable past is unattainable, no one can actually believe that and still be an archaeologist.

The most basic school of thought in archaeology consists of what I call **culture-historical theory**. Culture-historical theory suggests that we can reconstruct the cultural history of a location from the superpositioning of archaeological materials. Materials near the surface are more recent than materials underlying them, and if those materials show differences, that allows us to create a simple chronology of cultures, or a culture-history. Culture-historical theory was essentially the only school of thought in archaeology until the 1940s, and other schools of thought (particularly the behaviorist, which I discuss next) didn't become widespread until the 1970s. That's not to downplay its importance. Culture-historical theory still underlies virtually all archaeological research. We use it to define change through time, and so any processual theory (which, as we discussed in Chapter 1, attempts to explain change) must rely on culture-history to define the changes to be explained.

Perhaps the classic work of culture-historical theory is Philip Phillips and Gordon Willey's 1953 article, "Method and Theory in American Archaeology."[1] In this work, Phillips and Willey attempt to create an overarching scheme for classifying archaeologically known groups into large, culture-historical frameworks. They define two formal taxonomic units, the phase and the component.

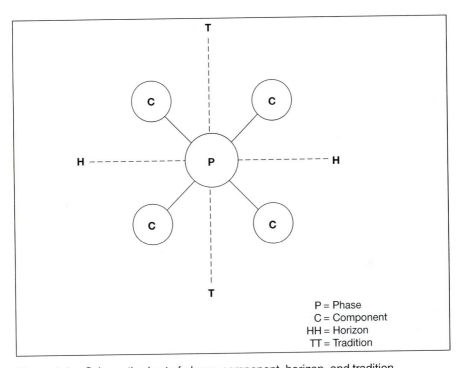

P = Phase
C = Component
HH = Horizon
TT = Tradition

Figure 2.1   Schematic chart of phase, component, horizon, and tradition.

Source: From *Method and Theory in American Archaeology* by Gordon R. Willey and Philip Phillips, copyright © 1958, University of Chicago Press, p. 41. Reprinted by permission of The University of Chicago Press.

The phase is the basic taxonomic spacio-temporal unit for culture-history, and Phillips and Willey define it as simply a space-time-culture unit that possesses characteristics that distinguish it from all other similar units. In practice, phases are composed of distinct components, manifestations of the phase at specific sites. Phillips and Willey also define two "integrative" taxonomic units, the horizon and the tradition. Horizons are spatially extensive but temporally short manifestations of shared cultural traits. Traditions are temporally long term (but not necessarily spatially widespread) manifestations of shared cultural traits. These four taxonomic units, Phillips and Willey suggest, can together create comprehensive culture-histories for regions, continents, and even the entire world. The fact that these terms are still commonly used by many archaeologists suggests that their utility is genuine.

Behaviorist theories, as I call them, suggest that the archaeological record is really a snapshot of ancient behavior. The archaeologists' job, in behaviorist theory, is twofold. First, they must determine how human behavior affects or is transmitted to the archaeological record. Second, they must determine how to apply that knowledge to reconstruct the behavior that is manifested in the archaeological record.

One of the most influential behaviorist theorists is Lewis Binford. In *Nunamuit Ethnoarchaeology,* for example, Binford examined how contemporary Inuit hunters created a material record of their behavior as they waited for game at a small hunting camp.[2] Binford compared the patterns of material remains he saw the hunters create to those he excavated at an ancient hunting camp nearby. Through this comparison, Binford was able to reconstruct the behavior of those ancient hunters—hunters who, not surprisingly, behaved quite similarly to the way contemporary ones did.

Figure 2.2   Lewis Binford's depiction of Nunamuit activities at a small hunting camp.

Source: Figure from *Working at Archaeology* by Lewis Binford, copyright © 1983 by Academic Press, reproduced by permission of the publisher.

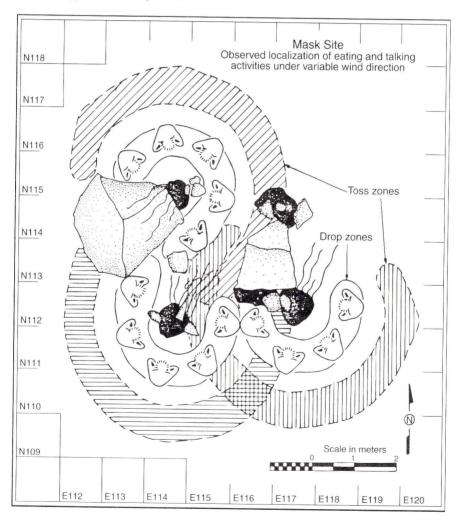

What I call **interpretive theories** are in many ways parallel to behaviorist theories in suggesting that the archaeological record is a record of human behavior, but go beyond that to suggest that from the archaeological record we can sometimes recover ancient thoughts, beliefs, motivations, and even feelings. I call these *interpretive theories* because the thoughts of ancient peoples are not as clearly manifest in the material record as most think human behaviors are, but must be teased out of the archaeological data through an interpretive (often called a hermeneutic) process. In fact, one of the most influential proponents of interpretive theories, Ian Hodder, suggests that the archaeological record can be understood as a text that, like a book, can be read to understand the characters and action or can be interpreted to get at the underlying meanings, motivations, and feelings of those characters.[3]

Hodder's work has been diverse, but perhaps his most influential has focused on the Neolithic period in Europe. The Neolithic was a time of transition from a mobile hunting and gathering lifestyle to a sedentary agricultural one. In works like *The Domestication of Europe*,[4] Hodder attempts to move beyond behavioral understandings of how this transition took place to more interpretive understandings of what the transition meant to the people who took part in it. For example, Hodder interprets an increase in contrasting patterns on ceramics in southern Scandinavia as reflecting the increasing differentiation in society and argues that the transition to farming must have led to an undercurrent of social conflict and unease that is represented, perhaps unconsciously, by individuals decorating their pottery. Similarly, ceramic decorations in northern Europe during the same period show a different pattern—one of sharply segregated but repeating patterns. Hodder interprets this as reflecting a marked territorialization of once fluid social groups as agricultural land comes to be a valued resource. Again, Hodder suggests these underlying social conditions are transferred to pottery decorations, and such decorations can be "read" and interpreted to disclose their underlying meaning.

While interpretive theories might be seen as a step forward in teasing more information from the archaeological record, what I call **taphonomic theories** represent a step back, questioning how much information is actually there. The basic position taken by taphonomic theories is that, while the archaeological record may manifest a record of human behavior and even thought when it is deposited, the natural world steps in after deposition and, through a variety of processes from frost heave to burrowing rodents, mixes those materials to the point where we often can't be certain what they tell us. Most taphonomic theorists are not completely nihilistic in their view; that is, they don't go so far as to suggest that the past can never be re-created through the archaeological record. They do, however, caution that even the most apparently well-preserved archaeological site might in reality be significantly disturbed.

The primary work of taphonomic theorists has been to identify the processes that can disturb the archaeological record. For example, Michael Schiffer's *Formation Processes of the Archaeological Record*[5] describes dozens of

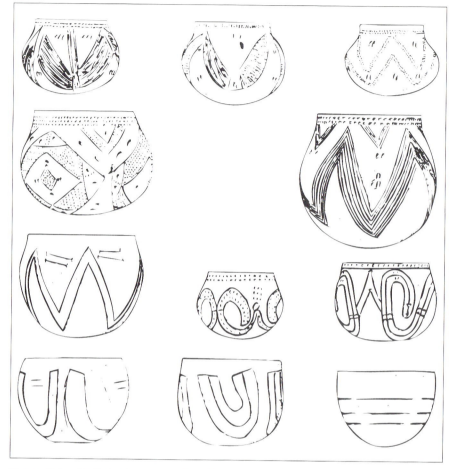

Figure 2.3   Stylistic changes on Neolithic ceramics from southern Scandinavia and northern Europe. Bottom row shows the earliest vessels, top row the latest.

Source: Figure "Stylistic changes on Neolithic ceramics from southern Scandinavia and northern Europe" by Louwe Kooijmans, 1976, in *Symbolic and Structural Archaeology* by Ian Hodder, ed., copyright © 1982, Cambridge University Press, p. 173.

natural and cultural processes that affect the context, patterning, and characteristics of artifacts and sites. Through several case studies he demonstrates that "evidence of the cultural past is created by a variety of cultural and noncultural processes that have varied and ubiquitous effects, introduce variability into the historical and archaeological records, and must be taken into account in [archaeological] inference."[6] Indeed, Schiffer ends his book on a rather incendiary note: "A large task looms ahead, that of reevaluating all previous [archaeological] inferences with respect to how well formation processes have been understood and taken into account."[7] The implication is that if for-mation processes have not been understood, the inferences may well be wrong. While this is a valid and important point, if we take this view to its log-ical extreme we have to toss out almost everything we think we know about the past—an extreme that I am certain even Schiffer doesn't really think is necessary.

In the 1980s, as part of a larger reaction against empirical and scientific forms of knowledge that has come to be known as poststructuralism, post-modernism, or postprocessualism, a group of archaeologists began to develop a set of what I call **reactionary theories** against the established schools of archaeological thought. These theories tend to promote two interconnected positions: (1) We can never describe or understand a real past because (2) our knowledge of the past is filtered through our own uniquely individual inter-pretations of the archaeological record and of the reports, books, and articles written by archaeologists about the archaeological record. In a sense, reac-tionary theories suggest that sites and artifacts are nothing more than mirrors of ourselves. We look at them and see only our own thoughts, beliefs, moti-vations, and biases, not those of ancient peoples.

The work of Michael Shanks and Christopher Tilley perhaps best cap-tures the thinking of reactionary theorists. In their controversial book *Re-Constructing Archaeology*,[8] Shanks and Tilley argue that "there can be no *objective* link between patterning perceived in material culture and processes which produced that patterning."[9] By this they mean that archaeological knowledge is the product of archaeologists' minds and, in turn, of their edu-cation, life history, and social world. As Shanks and Tilley put it: "While real, objects of archaeological knowledge are nevertheless meaningless in them-selves. They are raw matter which require completion to turn them into dis-cursive objects. It is at this point they become meaningful, can be discussed, be known."[10] From what we've already discussed, I hope you can understand that most archaeologists respond to this point with a resounding "Duh." But for Shanks and Tilley, this conclusion leads to a stifling subjectivity: "There is no *independently definable* reality or past as far as we are all concerned," and they yield archaeological knowledge to the vagaries of the powers that be: "Archaeology . . . [is] a passive function of the present, producing pasts rele-vant to and/or in support of particular interest groups."[11]

There is much truth in reactionary theories such as those put forward by Shanks and Tilley. Archaeological knowledge is created in the minds of archae-ologists and in the act of collecting, analyzing, and evaluating data. Yet is it really subjective of me to say that people lived, worked, and died at Tell es-Sweyhat some 4,200 years ago? Are the houses I've excavated only mean-ingful in my own subjective presentation of them? I don't think so, and, when pushed, I don't think Shanks and Tilley would think so either. There is a past. Things really happened before us and they left real, observable material traces. Our job as archaeologists is to figure out what those traces can tell us. Surely how we do that will be affected by our education, our opinions, our theories, and our social world. But, just as surely, there were people living in the houses at Tell es-Sweyhat four millennia ago.

I want to end this discussion of the archaeological record by considering two quotes from Marc Bloch which capture some of the difficult issues we face in dealing with the past. The first is this: "Misunderstanding of the present is the inevitable consequence of ignorance of the past. But a man may wear himself out just as fruitlessly in seeking to understand the past, if he is totally ignorant of the present."[12] I live in a small frame house. If this was the only experience I had before I excavated mud-brick houses at Tell es-Sweyhat, I would be completely incapable of recognizing the cobble foundations and mud-brick debris there as houses at all. I cannot be ignorant of the way people live in north Syria today, or of the way ancient texts and the work of other excavators describe the houses of third-millennium B.C. northern Mesopotamia. If I had no knowledge of mud-brick houses and their construction, I would be incapable of recognizing them when I found them in the archaeological record. We always bring information from the present to the past, simply because that is the only means we have for understanding what we find.

Clearly our dependence on the present for understanding the past raises some concern. And as Shanks and Tilley make all too clear, our application of present-day objects and behaviors to the past is not without ambiguity or bias. But this brings me to the second quote from Bloch: "Even those texts or archaeological [materials] . . . which seem clearest and most accommodating will speak only when they are properly questioned."[13] The process of archaeological research is not an uncritical one. We don't simply look at the archaeological record and say "this is a house and that is a workshop" solely because that's what they appear to be. We examine the archaeological record. We tear it apart and piece it back together. We examine it from all angles. We ask a myriad of questions. For example, if I were to find a line of cobbles I would not immediately leap to the assumption that I had found an ancient house foundation. I would first ask, "Are these associated with one another?" "Is there a living floor within them?" "Is this a likely location for a house?" "Does this fit the style of house found at other sites of the same period?" And many similar questions. Knowledge of the past doesn't come passively, but from an active, critical process of questioning and analysis.[14]

2.4 SUMMARY

The archaeological record consists of artifacts, ecofacts, and features. Artifacts are movable objects of human use or manufacture. Ecofacts are natural objects that have been used or altered by humans. Features are objects of human manufacture that cannot be moved from a site—they are a part of or embedded in the context of the site. While the archaeological record consists of these material objects, it is the context between and among artifacts, ecofacts, and features that makes up archaeological data. Archaeological sites are locations where artifacts, ecofacts, and features are preserved in context and can be recovered by a trained archaeologist.

Archaeologists use a variety of theories to interpret and bring meaning to the archaeological record. Culture-historical theories suggest that we can use the archaeological record to reconstruct the history of human habitation in a given locale. Behaviorist theories go beyond to suggest that the archaeological record can be used to reconstruct ancient behaviors. Interpretive theories suggest we can use the archaeological record to understand the thoughts, motivations, and beliefs of ancient peoples. Taphonomic theories caution that the archaeological record is more a record of natural processes affecting artifacts, ecofacts, and features than it is a record of human history, behavior, or thought. Finally reactionary theories suggest that the archaeological record is a mirror that reflects only ourselves, not a real past.

SUGGESTED READINGS

Binford, Lewis. 1964. "A Consideration of Archaeological Research Design," *American Antiquity* 29:425–441. This article is the basic defining statement on artifacts, ecofacts, and features.

Deetz, James. 1967. *Invitation to Archaeology.* Garden City, NY: Natural History Press. A wonderful introduction to archaeology with good discussion of the archaeological record.

Schiffer, Michael. 1978. *Formation Processes of the Archaeological Record.* Albuquerque: University of New Mexico Press. A key text for understanding how material becomes a part of the archaeological record and how artifacts, ecofacts, and features are transformed through time.

NOTES

1. Philip Phillips and Gordon R. Willey, "Method and Theory in American Archaeology," *American Anthropologist* 55 (1953): 615–633.
2. Lewis Binford, *Nunamuit Ethnoarchaeology* (New York: Academic Press, 1978).
3. Ian Hodder, *Reading the Past: Current Approaches to Interpretation in Archaeology,* 2nd ed. (Cambridge, UK: Cambridge University Press, 1991).
4. Ian Hodder, *The Domestication of Europe* (Oxford, UK: Basil Blackwell, 1990).

5. Michael Schiffer, *Formation Processes of the Archaeological Record* (Albuquerque: University of New Mexico Press, 1978).

6. Ibid., p. 23.

7. Ibid., p. 363.

8. Michael Shanks and Christopher Tilley, *Re-Constructing Archaeology: Theory and Practice,* 2nd ed. (London: Routledge, 1992).

9. Ibid., p. 14.

10. Ibid., p. 250.

11. Ibid., pp. 250, 245.

12. Marc Bloch, *The Historian's Craft* (New York: Vintage, 1953), p. 45.

13. Ibid., p. 64.

14. Ibid., pp. 143–144.

3

Measurement and Sampling

OVERVIEW

3.1   How Do Archaeologists Make Measurements Through the
       Archaeological Record?

    3.1.1   Types of Data

    3.1.2   Validity and Reliability

    3.1.3   Units of Analysis

3.2   How Do Archaeologists Sample from the Archaeological Record?

    3.2.1   Random Sampling

    3.2.2   Stratified Sampling

    3.2.3   Cluster Sampling

    3.2.4   Nonrandom Sampling

3.3   Summary

In a faculty meeting at a college where I once taught there was a heated discussion of the curriculum. The college's motto was "Truth Sets Free," and the discussion had turned to the nature of truth. A colleague in the chemistry department bluntly announced, "I know science is truth because bridges don't fall down," to which a colleague in the history department retorted, "But Tom, they do fall down." I had to ask myself the question: Do the forces of gravity hold bridges up, or do angels? How can I know? My answer was that I really can't. I had faith in the reality of gravity, but both science and religion are built on faith, faith in clearly different things, but faith nonetheless. Gravity, it seemed to me, is nothing more than a vectored angel, a computational seraphim we use to explain how the world works. Yet the more I thought about it, the more I came to see that gravity is really quite different from an angel, because we have devised ways to measure its presence. No one has ever seen gravity itself, but we can see—and measure—its effects. In the same way, archaeologists can never go back to see past events, but they can measure the effects of those events in the archaeological record and, from those measurements, see the past.

3.1 HOW DO ARCHAEOLOGISTS MAKE MEASUREMENTS THROUGH THE ARCHAEOLOGICAL RECORD?

Archaeology begins with questions that lead to models that define the variables for which data are needed (remember?). When archaeologists sit down to figure out how to actually go and get those data, what they are really doing is trying to figure out how to measure a variable of interest through the archaeological record. As we discussed in Chapter 1, the Valley of Oaxaca researchers wanted data on population density in the region over time. Population density was their key variable. They determined to measure it by measuring the total area of inhabited sites for a given time period, because total area of habitation has been shown ethnographically to represent population density fairly well.[1] However, for any variable (population density included) there are always a number of different ways it could be measured. The only real limitation is archaeologists' imagination, and time, and money. How do archaeologists decide what measurement to use? Usually the answer is based on the type of data the measurement provides. There are three basic types of data that archaeologists, and indeed all social scientists, can create through their measurements: nominal, ordinal, and interval.

3.1.1   Types of Data

Nominal data are also called *categorical data,* since the data are segregated into distinct categories. The ceramic typology used to determine the age of habitations in the Valley of Oaxaca, for example, is nominal data. A piece of pottery can be polychrome, red-on-black, grey ware, or some other type. It cannot be more than one; it is placed in one and only one category. In addition, these ceramic categories cannot be ordered in any meaningful way; that is, grey ware is not greater than or lesser than red-on-black on any meaningful dimension, nor are two grey ware pottery pieces equivalent to one polychrome piece—that's silly! So, nominal data is information that is organized into distinct categories that cannot be meaningfully ordered in any way.

   Ordinal data, as the name suggests, provide information in categories that are ordered in a meaningful way. My office building is located on the 500 block of East College Avenue. The University's bookstore is on the 300 block. From that you can tell that the two are separated by about two blocks. How? Because street addresses in Appleton (and most other places) are ordinal; that is, they have an origin and increase or decrease in a meaningful way. Street addresses are not, however, interval, because there is no meaningful interval between numbers. A house at 1002 East College might be located next to a house numbered 1004, but it might also be next to one numbered 1040. We know those other numbers mean the neighbors are to the east of the first house, but we can't tell how far because the numbers don't have a standard interval between them. The difference between 1002 and 1040 isn't always the same distance or the same number of houses. So while the categories of ordinal variables are ordered in a meaningful way, there is no standard or constant interval between those categories.

   Not only are the categories that segregate **interval data** (sometimes called *ratio data* if there is an absolute zero point) ordered in a meaningful way, but there is also a constant interval between each category. Money is a good example. The standard category of U.S. currency is the penny. If we start a pile of pennies with one and add a second, the value of the pile is now worth twice as much as with one penny. If we add eight more pennies to the pile (bringing the total to ten), the value is now ten times as much. The interval remains constant, and we always know that as each penny is added the value of the pile increases by the same amount. That is the defining nature of interval data—there is a constant interval between categories.

Why do archaeologists choose one kind of data over the others? In some cases the choice is clear. You can't develop an interval ceramic typology, for example, but you can use the weight of ceramic pieces of a given type per house to create an interval measure of ceramic use. So why aren't interval measures always developed when they can be? The basic answer is that interval data are always preferred, but often measures that are both valid and reliable cannot be developed to obtain interval data from the archaeological record. In such cases, information may be validly and reliably measured only on an ordinal scale, or perhaps only in nominal categories. Data are almost always more valid and reliable if they are in fewer categories, yet analyses are almost always less powerful the fewer categories there are. So archaeologists (and any other researchers in fact) have to strike a balance between the desire for more specific data and the need for validity and reliability.

3.1.2   Validity and Reliability

Validity basically means that archaeologists are actually measuring what they think they are. This would seem pretty obvious, but it isn't always. In the Valley of Oaxaca project, as I've already mentioned, one of the key variables of interest was population. To measure population the researchers determined the total area of habitation for a given site, then used a standard measure of habitation area per resident developed from cross-cultural data to estimate the total population of that site.[2] This would seem reasonable, that each person needs a given area of space to live in, and hence that total habitation area would be a valid proxy measure for population. However, this relationship is only true for nonindustrial societies. If we were to use this measure for Chicago, for example, we'd find we grossly underestimated population. Similarly, if we applied the same value to both Chicago and River Forest, Illinois (a town called by resident Frank Lloyd Wright "the land of broad lawns and narrow minds"), we would come up with inaccurate measures of populations for both—the former underestimated and the latter overestimated. Thus the Valley of Oaxaca researchers (and this is true for all researchers creating measures for variables of interest) had to make sure their measure actually measured what they thought it did—population, in this case.

In addition to measuring what they thought it did, the Valley of Oaxaca researchers had to make sure their measure of population was reliable. **Reliability** means that measurements taken of the same thing will provide the same data time and again, whether those measurements are taken by different people, taken under different conditions, or taken in different locations each time. Since the population measure was based on the area of habitation, the Valley of Oaxaca researchers had to certify that each person collecting data was trained in the same way to measure habitation areas. To help this, the crews worked in teams (so that they could check each other's work) and used aerial photographs so that physical features on the ground (and visible on the photographs) became landmarks for defining the area of a site.[3]

Most measures in scientific research are developed with quite specific tasks in mind. They are designed to measure the variables of interest, the variables for which data are needed to answer the researcher's question. We call the process of turning variables into valid and reliable measures **operationalization**. The example we have been using throughout this section, that of population as determined by habitation area, is a good example of operationalization in practice. The researchers had a question and needed specific data to answer it—population data. They knew there existed well-established relationships between habitation area and population, and well-established means of measuring habitation area. Not all measures are as clearly operationalized as this one, but regardless of what is being measured, operationalization follows this same basic process: finding a way to validly and reliably gather data to measure variables of interest.

3.1.3 Units of Analysis

In addition to figuring out how to measure variables, archaeologists also have to decide what things are appropriate to measure. We need a unit to base our measurements on, a **unit of analysis**. We might assume that the site is the basic unit for archaeological research, but that is not really the case. Units of analysis are varied, and indeed they change over time even in the same project. In the work I am doing at Bjorklunden the unit of analysis right now is the site, but as work progresses and we find activity areas or other types of features, I may decide that it makes more sense to use those as the basis of data collection and analysis. Similarly, at Tell es-Sweyhat the site is far too large to be a useful unit of analysis, so we use houses, rooms in houses, and features in rooms as the basis of data collection and analysis.

Finally it seems that we are at the point where we can get some data. We have measures. We have determined that they are both reliable and valid. We know what units we are going to use for data collection and analysis. So now we can go get data, right? Not quite. We have one final problem. There is no way we can ever hope to collect data for every possible unit of analysis out there. At the Bjorklunden site, for example, I can't even tell where the site boundaries are and, if I could, it would be impossible for me to reasonably excavate the whole area, particularly since the new conference center sits atop at least part of the site. Because archaeologists can almost never collect data for all of the possible units of analysis, sampling from those units is an important part of the data collection process.

3.2 HOW DO ARCHAEOLOGISTS SAMPLE
FROM THE ARCHAEOLOGICAL RECORD?

Sampling refers to methods used to select cases from a specified **target population** (sometimes also called a *sampling universe*). If, for example, we take a can of mixed nuts and select a handful to eat while watching TV, we are essentially choosing a sample of nuts from the can. If we simply stick our hand in and grab a fistful of nuts, it is very likely that the "sample" of nuts we grabbed will not accurately represent the target population of all the nuts in the can. That is, the proportion of peanuts, Brazil nuts, cashews, almonds, and filberts in our hand will not be the same as that in the can. Sampling methods are designed to ensure (within varying ranges of error) that the sample taken accurately represents the relative proportions of cases in a given target population. Of these methods, random sampling is the only method that completely assures that an unbiased sample of the target population will be selected.

3.2.1 Random Sampling

Random sampling means one thing: that every case in the target population has the same likelihood of being chosen. That's it. No mystery. Every unit has the same likelihood of being chosen. The trick is achieving that. In our can of nuts example, you might think that sticking your hand in and grabbing a sample would provide a random assortment of nuts in the can, but you'd be wrong. In fact, such grab-bag sampling (yes, that's actually the name it's given) provides relatively biased samples. For example, in the can of nuts the heavier nuts will likely have moved to the bottom of the can, the lighter nuts to the top. Thus a grab into the can will likely yield a biased sample of lighter nuts. So how do we choose random samples? Several methods have been devised.

The most basic method of random sampling is called **simple random sampling**. Unfortunately, it often isn't all that simple. Simple random sampling requires, first, that all cases in the target population be known. Second, it requires that each case be given a unique identifier (usually a number). Third, it requires a computer to generate a list of random numbers or the researcher to consult with a standard random number table in order to select the cases in the sample. Since sampling is based on selecting cases from a list of random numbers, this method absolutely assures an unbiased sample. But it is a cumbersome and time-consuming method. A simpler method than simple random sampling is called *systematic random sampling*.

Systematic random sampling relies on only two random numbers, a random starting number and a random interval number. As with simple random sampling, all cases in the target population must be identified and numbered. The sampler then chooses one number at random, identifying a starting case. The sampler next chooses an interval number at random, identifying the next case chosen. From there, the sampler simply selects cases using the same systematic interval (there's a lot of alliteration in that sentence, isn't there?). For example, if we took all the nuts out of our can and laid them out on the table in a line we could easily do a systematic sample. We would choose a random number, let's say 15, and then an interval number, let's say 4. We would count down the line to the fifteenth nut, then select the fourth nut after it as the first case in our sample. We'd then select the fourth nut after that, the fourth nut after that, and so on until we had a sample the size we need.

Both theoretical and empirical studies demonstrate that systematic random sampling provides samples that are nearly as good as ones collected by simple random sampling.[4] However, there is one problem to watch out for. If your target population has a regular, periodic pattern to it, systematic random sampling may, by chance, systematically hit or miss those periods and thereby provide a really terrible sample. In one archaeological case (perhaps mythical), a group of excavators used systematic random sampling to excavate a village site. They found much less material than they expected, and no houses. Two years later a work crew digging a drainage ditch through the site encountered literally dozens of houses. What had happened was that the town was laid out in a regular pattern, along linear streets and with houses at regular intervals. The systematic sampling had selected, at random, units between the houses![5]

3.2.2 Stratified Sampling

One of the drawbacks of random sampling is that researchers may be more interested in certain kinds of cases than others, yet random sampling treats every case the same. Researchers have devised **stratified random sampling** as a way of obtaining both a representative sample of the target population and a sample containing at least some of those cases of special interest. The way this is done is that the target population is divided into several distinct categories or "strata," and random samples are taken from each. For example, in an archaeological survey I conducted along the Tippecanoe River in Indiana one summer, I divided the survey area into floodplain and uplands and chose survey areas from each using random sampling. Why? Because I knew that prehistoric settlements in the floodplain differed from those in the uplands, and I wanted to make sure sites from both regions were well represented in my sample.

3.2.3 Cluster Sampling

Actually, the survey I used in the Tippecanoe River valley was a clustered stratified random sample. Clustering solves another problem faced by archaeologists using random sampling. When a random sample is chosen, the cases are often not contiguous, and that can be a problem for archaeologists. When doing a survey, we don't want to survey an area in one part of a county, then drive to the other side of the county to do the next area just because that was the survey location that came up from random sampling. That wastes a lot of time! It would be much better to have survey areas near one another. And that is what clustering does. In **cluster sampling** researchers select a case by random sampling but include contiguous cases as part of the sample. Cluster sampling does not provide as good a representative sample as purely random sampling, but it does make data collection easier, and it provides a far better sample than nonrandom methods of sampling.

3.2.4   Nonrandom Sampling

There are very few instances where nonrandom sampling can be justified. One would be where an entire known population is analyzed, as in some studies of rare objects. But where a large target population is known or is anticipated, nonrandom sampling will almost certainly select a nonrepresentative set of cases from the sample. If nonrandom sampling can be avoided, it should be. We discussed the most common form of nonrandom sampling—grab-bag—earlier when I gave the example of grabbing a fistful of nuts from a can of mixed nuts. But several more sophisticated methods are used in archaeology.

When archaeologists begin excavating a site and find a feature of interest, then follow that feature to others, and follow those to others, they are practicing snowball sampling. As the name implies, snowball sampling selects cases based on previous cases which in some way "point" to the next case as a good one to include in an analysis. Obviously this is a very good method for getting a lot of data quickly, but we have to worry that the data are biased. For example, an excavation strategy that follows interesting features will undoubtedly miss open areas—plazas, animal pens, and the like—on the site. The excavations will not offer a full picture of what the site was like, but rather one biased by what the excavators find interesting or important.

The other nonrandom sampling method that is used with some frequency in archaeology is called opportunistic sampling. Cases are chosen in opportunistic sampling simply because they are readily available. I have had students use a local collection of projectile points for research projects, for example, simply because the collection is large, well organized, and accessible. It is not, however, a random sample of the whole population of projectile points from northeast Wisconsin. It is clearly biased toward larger and "more beautiful" points—the old, worn-down points we often find in archaeological excavations are not represented. Thus the research done by my students cannot be said to directly apply to all projectile points in northeast Wisconsin, but only to this sample. And those conclusions may or may not hold up well when the whole population of interest is taken into account, which is the fundamental problem with nonrandom sampling.

3.3   SUMMARY

In the introduction to his book *The Raw and the Cooked,* anthropologist Claude Lévi-Strauss said, "The scientific mind does not so much provide the right answers as ask the right questions."[6] Lévi-Strauss is right, of course, which is why I have already said a lot about asking questions. However, it is not questions alone that provide the "right answers"; data are needed as well, and appropriate data at that. Archaeologists obtain data through a process of measurement. Measurement involves developing ways to collect accurate data to answer our question of interest (operationalization), and archaeologists can make measurements that produce one of three distinct types of data: nominal, ordinal, and interval. It is vital in making these measurements that archaeologists ensure that measures are both valid and reliable. Measurement also involves selecting appropriate units from which to take measurements (units of analysis), and selecting an appropriate sample of those units, since we rarely can measure all the units in existence. Several methods of sampling are used in archaeology, including stratified, cluster, and nonrandom ones, but random sampling is always the preferred method if it is possible to use it.

SUGGESTED READINGS

Aldenderfer, Mark, ed. 1987. *Quantitative Research in Archaeology: Progress and Prospects.* Newbury Park, CA: Sage. A remarkably well-written and cohesive collection of articles on quantitative approaches to archaeological analysis. Several of the chapters offer good introductions to sampling and measurement in archaeology.

Bernard, H. Russell. 1994. *Research Methods in Anthropology* (2nd ed.). Thousand Oaks, CA: Sage. My students call this the "blue bible," and for good reason—it is the single most useful book on anthropological research methods ever written.

Drennan, Robert. 1996. *Statistics for Archaeologists: A Commonsense Approach.* New York: Plenum. A clearly written and comprehensive introduction to archaeological applications of statistics, with a strong emphasis on sampling.

Nance, Jack. 1983. "Regional Sampling in Archaeological Survey," *Advances in Archaeological Method and Theory* 6:289–356. A discussion of how sampling is applied to archaeological survey. A somewhat difficult but very useful article.

Pelto, Pertti, and Gretel Pelto. 1970. *Anthropological Research: The Structure of Inquiry.* Cambridge, UK: Cambridge University Press. A classic introduction to the process of social science research that seems to only get better with age.

NOTES

1. See the chapter on methodology in Richard Blanton et al., *Monte Albán's Hinterland, Part 1.* (Ann Arbor: University of Michigan, Museum of Anthropology, Memoir 7, 1982).

2. Ibid.

3. Ibid.

4. Peter Peregrine, David Drews, Amy North, and Melissa Slupe, "Sampling Techniques and Sampling Error in Naturalistic Observation: An Empirical Evaluation," *Cross-Cultural Research* 8 (1993):232–246.

5. Kent Flannery, ed., *The Early Mesoamerican Village* (New York: Academic Press, 1976), pp. 49–50.

6. Claude Lévi-Strauss, *The Raw and the Cooked* (New York: Harper and Row, 1969).

4

Survey Methods and Strategies

OVERVIEW

4.1   How Do Archaeologists Find Sites?

    4.1.1   Literature Search

    4.1.2   Landowner and Collector Interviews

4.2   What Is Archaeological Survey?

    4.2.1   Pedestrian Survey

    4.2.2   Probing and Testing

    4.2.3   Remote Sensing

    4.2.4   Aerial Photography and Imagery

4.3   How Do Archaeologists Conduct Surveys?

    4.3.1   "Top-Down" Surveys

    4.3.2   "Bottom-Up" Surveys

    4.3.3   "Shotgun" and Predictive Surveys

4.4   Summary

In the 1970s archaeology went through a transition from asking largely descriptive questions to asking more theoretical ones. The "new archaeology" that grew out of this transition led to the more scientific research process I am trying to present in this book. It also led to a recognition that archaeology, at least in terms of its theoretical frameworks, must be tied to anthropology and the other social sciences. One of the prominent figures in the new archaeology movement was Lewis Binford, who argued that archaeology is not a discipline independent of anthropology but rather is a method or set of techniques for collecting and analyzing a particular type of anthropological data.[1] In the last two chapters we looked at archaeology's particular types of data—artifacts, ecofacts, and features. In the next few chapters we'll look at how archaeologists go about collecting those data.

4.1 HOW DO ARCHAEOLOGISTS FIND SITES?

The first question usually asked by novice archaeologists is: "How do you find a site?" A basic way is through archaeological survey, which we will discuss in the next section. An equally important way to find sites, though often not obvious to nonarchaeologists, is to look at the results of other researchers through literature searches and interviews.

4.1.1 Literature Search

A good place for archaeologists to begin looking for data is in the reports of other archaeologists. After all, we don't want to duplicate the efforts of other researchers. When Lawrence University's president asked me to examine the Bjorklunden property for archaeological sites, the first thing I did was to go to my office and check the site files in our laboratory to see if there had already been sites reported on the property. I also checked with the state archaeologist's office to see if there were any reported sites that were not duplicated in our files. Site files like those I checked are typically held in a central location, like a state museum, a department of natural resources, or the office of the state archaeologist. In Wisconsin there are several sets of site files: a primary set in the office of the state archaeologist, subsets in regional archaeology centers, and subsets in other institutions where professional archaeologists work, such as Lawrence University. Most states' site files are organized in a similar way.

Site files usually consist of a set of forms filled out by archaeologists describing the location, cultural affiliations (if known), physical features, state of preservation, and other basic information about a site. When archaeologists file these reports they obtain a site number to identify the site they've found. If the site has already been reported, then the existing number is used, and the archaeologists update the information already in the file. Site numbers in the United States have been standardized using the following format:

State Number-County Abbreviation-Site Number

So the Bjorklunden site is now known as 47-DR-421. The first number, 47, refers to Wisconsin (the forty-seventh state in alphabetical order in the continental United States), the letters are the abbreviation for Door County, and the last numbers identify the Bjorklunden site as the 421st recorded site in the county. Having standardized site numbers like this ensures that each site is uniquely identified and recorded.

In addition to the official state files, there are usually sets of "unofficial" documents that archaeologists need to check before collecting new data. Learning what these unofficial documents are is a large part of learning the practice of archaeology in a specific region. For Wisconsin there is the journal *The Wisconsin Archaeologist* in which most archaeological investigations in Wisconsin are reported, at least in part. There are also several older works, including an 1855 volume called *The Antiquities of Wisconsin*[2] and an 1894 volume called *Report on the Mound Explorations of the Bureau of American Ethnology*,[3] both of which contain important information about Wisconsin archaeological sites. There are also files and collections of previous archaeologists whose research never made it into the published literature. At Lawrence University, for example, we have collections from many sites that have only been partially analyzed and published. This is one of the ongoing issues facing archaeology—the need to do fieldwork to salvage endangered sites and the need to publish what has already been recovered. There has never been enough time or money to do both, and the situation remains a problem. But we'll discuss that later.

The continual need to salvage archaeological sites facing destruction has created a growing "grey literature" consisting of unpublished archaeological reports and analyses produced by commercial archaeological firms under contract to federal, state, or local governments, and by professional archaeologists and their students performing salvage operations not directly connected with ongoing research. My work at Bjorklunden falls into the latter category, and I have already produced one grey report on the site. This two-page

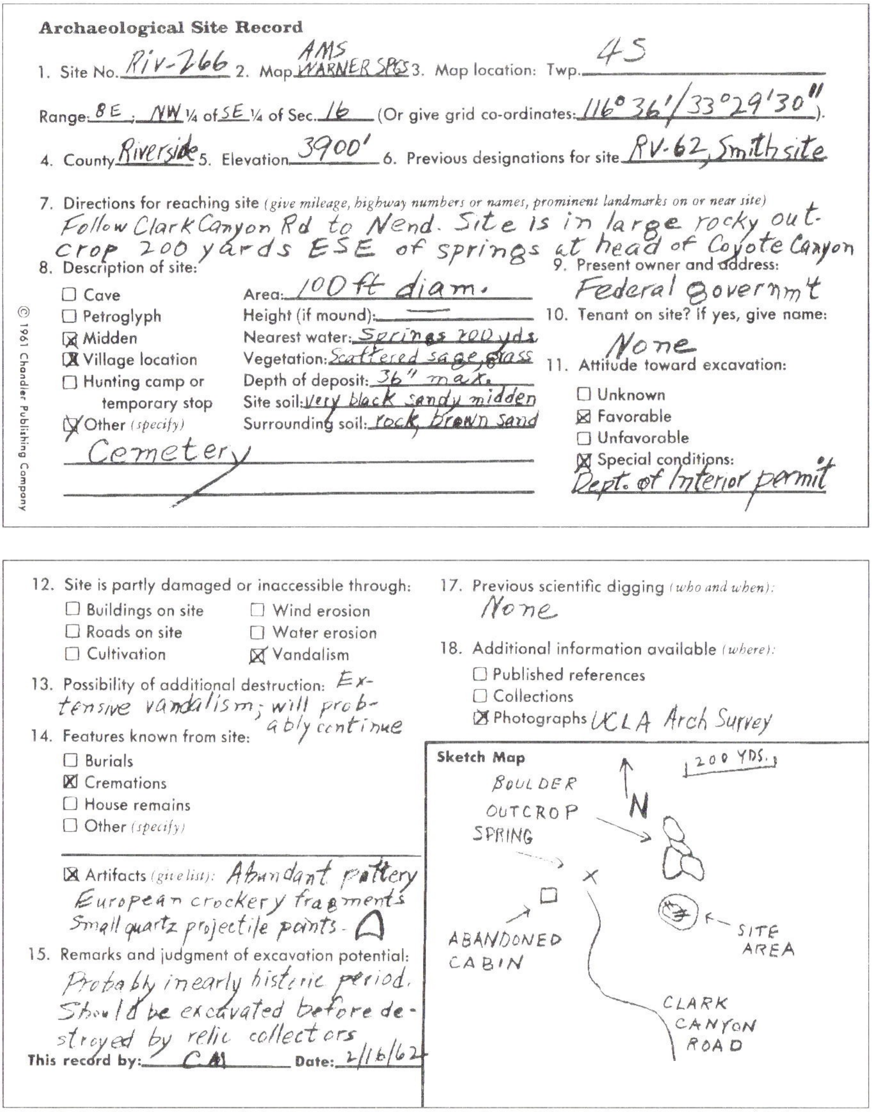

Archaeological Site Record

1. Site No. _Riv-266_ 2. Map _WARNER SPGS_ _AMS_ 3. Map location: Twp. _4S_

Range: _8E_ ; _NW_ ¼ of _SE_ ¼ of Sec. _16_ (Or give grid co-ordinates: _116°36'/33°29'30"_).

4. County _Riverside_ 5. Elevation _3900'_ 6. Previous designations for site _RV-62, Smith site_

7. Directions for reaching site (give mileage, highway numbers or names, prominent landmarks on or near site)
Follow Clark Canyon Rd to Nend. Site is in large rocky out-crop 200 yards ESE of springs at head of Coyote Canyon

8. Description of site:

- ☐ Cave
- ☐ Petroglyph
- ☒ Midden
- ☒ Village location
- ☐ Hunting camp or temporary stop
- ☒ Other (specify)
  Cemetery

Area: _100 ft diam._
Height (if mound): _____
Nearest water: _Springs 200 yds._
Vegetation: _Scattered sage, grass_
Depth of deposit: _36" max._
Site soil: _very black sandy midden_
Surrounding soil: _rock, brown sand_

9. Present owner and address:
Federal government

10. Tenant on site? if yes, give name:
None

11. Attitude toward excavation:

- ☐ Unknown
- ☒ Favorable
- ☐ Unfavorable
- ☒ Special conditions:
  Dept. of Interior permit

12. Site is partly damaged or inaccessible through:

- ☐ Buildings on site   ☐ Wind erosion
- ☐ Roads on site   ☐ Water erosion
- ☐ Cultivation   ☒ Vandalism

13. Possibility of additional destruction: _Extensive vandalism; will probably continue_

14. Features known from site:

- ☐ Burials
- ☒ Cremations
- ☐ House remains
- ☐ Other (specify)

☒ Artifacts (give list): _Abundant pottery European crockery fragments Small quartz projectile points._

15. Remarks and judgment of excavation potential:
Probably in early historic period. Should be excavated before destroyed by relic collectors

This record by: _C.M._ Date: _2/16/62_

17. Previous scientific digging (who and when):
None

18. Additional information available (where):

- ☐ Published references
- ☐ Collections
- ☒ Photographs _UCLA Arch Survey_

Sketch Map   _200 YDS._
BOULDER OUTCROP SPRING   N
ABANDONED CABIN
SITE AREA
CLARK CANYON ROAD

Figure 4.1 A standard site form.

Source: From The Archaeologist's Notebook by Clement Meighan, copyright © 1961. Chandler Publishing Company.

document on file in our laboratory and in the University's business office states what I found in the area where the new conference center was being built and my conclusion that important archaeological remains would not be destroyed by the construction. Tens of thousands of such documents exist in filing cabinets around the country. Thousands of larger and more detailed reports are on the shelves of state and local government archives.[4] Most of these reports are not catalogued anywhere and exist in only a few copies. The only way to access this literature is to know the archaeologists working in a given area and to know where to hunt for the reports they may have produced. Again, this is a large part of learning to do archaeology in a particular region, but it is also a significant problem, and one we will return to later.

4.1.2 Landowner and Collector Interviews

Professional archaeologists—those developing site files, journal articles, and contract reports—are not the only ones doing archaeology in the United States or elsewhere in the world for that matter. There are thousands of amateur archaeologists pursuing archaeology, too. Many times the amateurs are more knowledgeable about the archaeological record in their specific areas than are professional archaeologists in the region. The reason for this is that the amateurs usually live in the area where they collect artifacts, they know the landscape well, they are in close contact with other amateur archaeologists working in neighboring areas, and they have worked in the area for many years. Talking with amateur archaeologists can often provide more detailed information about the archaeological record in an area of interest than anything in the published or even grey literature. One word of caution: A small, unscrupulous minority among amateur archaeologists want to keep the archaeological record for themselves. In my experience (albeit not in Wisconsin) they have been purposely misleading in order to prevent scientific investigations of "their" sites. Again, we'll talk more about this later.

In a manner similar to amateur archaeologists, landowners often have a detailed knowledge of the archaeological record on their land. This knowledge comes from years of observing the landscape, its characteristics, and the places where archaeological remains have been found. Landowners can be hesitant to talk to archaeologists, and understandably so. Who would want a bunch of students tromping over their land digging holes (an image that is often what comes to mind when landowners initially hear of an archaeological survey of their land)? But public outreach and education are part of all archaeologists' job, and discussions with landowners, particularly before trying to obtain permission to work on their land, is a great way both to gain information about the archaeological record and to help educate the landowners about the archaeological research process.

Once the existing literature has been examined, amateur archaeologists have been interviewed, and landowners have been contacted and talked with and their permissions obtained, new archaeological work can begin. The first step in conducting any archaeological data collection project is survey.

4.2   WHAT IS ARCHAEOLOGICAL SURVEY?

Just as the phrase suggests, **archaeological survey** refers to methods of examining an area to determine if archaeological deposits are present. The simplest and most widely used method is pedestrian survey, though more sophisticated methods have been developed and are also widely used in some areas of the world.

4.2.1   Pedestrian Survey

There is nothing sophisticated about **pedestrian survey**; it just requires walking along and scanning the surface of the ground for artifacts. An example of a standard pedestrian survey is one I directed in the Tippecanoe River valley in Indiana. The area we were surveying was almost completely under cultivation, so the surface of the ground was easily visible. Using the rows of cornstalks as guides, my students and I walked the field, following a row to its end, then moving to a row not yet surveyed and starting back in the opposite direction. In this way we walked back and forth across the field until the entire area had been examined.

As we walked, we watched the ground. When we saw something that looked like an artifact (in this case, chert flakes, pottery fragments, bones, "fire-cracked" rock, or stone tools) we would take one of the survey flags we carried (orange or blue plastic flags on long wire sticks) and mark the location.

Figure 4.2   Pedestrian survey in progress.

Then we'd pick up the artifact to see what it was. If it indeed was an artifact (and it's amazing how often bird plop looks like a white chert flake!), we would put it back next to the flag and keep walking. We didn't collect anything until after we had walked the entire field. When we were done walking the field we went to a high area near the field boundary and looked back at what we had surveyed. What we saw were small clumps of orange and blue flags, and that is exactly what we hoped to see. Those small clumps were archaeological sites—concentrations of artifacts on the surface reflecting the presence of subsurface deposits.

Using a surveyor's transit and measuring tapes we determined the geographical location and size of each site and outlined them on a topographic map. We then collected the artifacts in each site, keeping the materials from the various sites separate. We, of course, also picked up the flags. By the end of the day, we had a good idea of the archaeological sites in the area we had surveyed. Our end products were a map of the sites, collections from each site (including several "diagnostic" artifacts we could use to date the sites), and a better knowledge of the topography and physiography of the area. And that is the purpose of archaeological survey—to locate and identify archaeological deposits.

From this example it should be clear that there is a fundamental assumption underlying pedestrian survey: that artifacts visible on the surface of the ground accurately reflect subsurface archaeological deposits. Obviously this

Figure 4.3   Mapping a site after pedestrian survey.

assumption is often violated—in river floodplains, for example, where annual buildup of silt may deeply cover archaeological deposits. Similarly, in forests and fields with grass the ground surface is often obscured, so while artifacts may be present on the surface of the ground, they won't be visible. Because of these problems several other methods of archaeological survey have been developed.

4.2.2   Probing and Testing

On the Bjorklunden property we are unable to do pedestrian survey. The new lodge is situated in a pine forest and the ground is covered by a thick mat of needles. So how can we find sites? Well, there are a variety of techniques for surveying where the ground is obscured, and the one we are using is called shovel testing. In **shovel testing** a standard volume of dirt (in our case one bucket) is removed from a single location and sifted through a screen to separate the dirt from the artifacts, after which the materials found are recorded. Usually the locations of the shovel tests are predetermined by random sampling or by some standard method (we took shovel tests every 5 meters along established lines at Bjorklunden). The basic theory behind shovel testing is to make the ground surface visible, at least in one location, to determine if subsurface deposits might be present. Thus it is not much different from standard pedestrian survey. It is, however, much more time consuming and difficult than pedestrian survey, and obviously only a tiny portion of the ground surface is seen.

Mechanical methods have sometimes been used to increase the area of ground surface exposed through testing. One common method involves using a bulldozer or road grader to scrape several inches of soil off the ground surface over a large area to expose a clean, unobscured surface. Archaeologists then walk the exposed surface and examine it for artifacts, just as in pedestrian survey. In cases where archaeologists believe there may be deeply buried deposits, as in the floodplain of a river, a backhoe might be brought in to dig a series of trenches through accumulated soil deposits with archaeologists following along behind, examining the walls of the trenches for artifacts. This again is really much like standard pedestrian survey, but in this case the surface is the vertical wall of the trench, rather than the horizontal surface of the ground.

A less invasive method of archaeological survey in places where the ground surface is obscured is called *probing*. **Probing** involves the use of one of several instruments to explore beneath the ground surface for archaeological deposits. One kind of instrument, called a *soil probe*, is a hollow tube connected to a long steel rod. When pushed into the ground and removed, the hollow portion brings with it a sample of the soil it has moved through. By examining the recovered soil, archaeologists might find artifacts or soil changes that indicate a buried site. Another kind of probe is simply a long steel rod with a small knob or ball on the tip and a T-handle on the other end. It can be inserted like a needle into the soil. Experienced users can feel subtle changes in soil consistency and density that might indicate a buried site. If lucky, they might hit a piece of pottery or stone tool. It sounds almost incredible, but in the hands of experienced users, a probe like this can be an extremely effective surveying tool.

4.2.3 Remote Sensing

In recent years a wide variety of powerful, noninvasive methods of archaeological survey have been introduced from the field of geophysical prospecting. These techniques are ones geologists use to locate oil deposits, ores and minerals, and the like. In the hands of archaeologists, they can be used to locate archaeological sites and even archaeological features within sites. There are two broad categories of **remote sensing** techniques (the generic name given to these geophysical techniques): passive and active. Passive techniques measure inherent properties of the natural world, such as magnetism and gravity, to identify disturbances or anomalies that may indicate an archaeological deposit. Active techniques affect the natural world in some way—by sending sound waves or electric current into the soil, for example, again to identify disturbances or anomalies that may indicate an archaeological deposit.

Figure 4.4   How a magnetometer works.

Source: From *Introduction to Geophysical Prospecting* by P. Kearey and N. Brooks, copyright © 1984, Blackwell Science, p. 192. Reprinted by permission of Blackwell Science, Ltd.

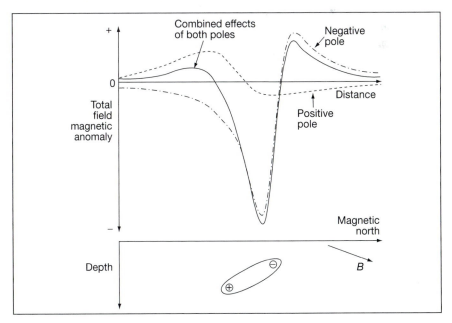

One of the most widely used, and most effective, passive remote sensing techniques is **geomagnetic surveying**. By using a magnetometer to take precise measurements of the earth's magnetic field over a large area, archaeologists can delineate anomalies indicating the presence of archaeological deposits from the surrounding soil. The reasons for this are complicated, but they come down to this: Many archaeological materials have a magnetic character different from undisturbed soil. For example, organic materials, like those discarded in garbage pits, can undergo a chemical process during decomposition that gives them a magnetic character quite different from nonorganic soils. Similarly, burned soil, like that in an oven or hearth, may have a strong magnetic character called *thermoremnant magnetism* that is caused when atoms in soil heated above its melting point all turn to point toward magnetic north. When the soil cools, the atoms remain pointed to magnetic north and, hence, the soil itself gains a strong magnetic character. Of course, many metals have a magnetic character, too, and these can easily be sensed during geomagnetic surveying.[5]

At Tell es-Sweyhat we have been extensively surveying the city's outer town to determine, without excavating, how the town was organized. Over the course of two field seasons we have done geomagnetic surveys over roughly one-quarter of the outer town and have been able to identify houses, pottery production areas, and defensive works, among other things. We began by making sure that geomagnetics would work. We surveyed eight 20-meter square units, which we called "grids," collecting data at various levels of res-

Figure 4.5   Geomagnetic surveying at Tell es-Sweyhat.

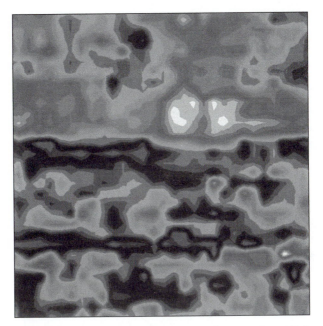

Figure 4.6 The results of geomagnetic surveying at Tell es-Sweyhat. Note the parallel lines at the top of the image. These are the buried foundations of the ancient fortification wall.

olution and using several different survey techniques. After examining the data and testing the anomalies through test excavations, we found we could use magnetic surveying to identify lots of subsurface features. We then began surveying large contiguous areas in order to determine how much of the ancient city plan we could see.[6] This ability to see below the ground surface without excavating is one of the most remarkable facets of remote sensing. As we'll learn in the next chapter, excavation is extremely destructive, costly, and time consuming, and most archaeologists (surprisingly) avoid it except when necessary. Remote sensing offers a unique alternative that, when the conditions are right, can offer an excellent picture of subsurface features.

A widely used active remote sensing technique is **soil resistivity surveying**. Like geomagnetic surveying, the basic idea behind soil resistivity surveying is to locate areas with an anomalous electromagnetic character when compared with surrounding areas. Unlike geomagnetic surveying, soil resistivity surveying is done by sending an active electric current through the ground and measuring changes in the resistivity of the soil the current passes through. To accomplish this a series of metal stakes is placed in the ground in two long lines, called *arrays*. One array is used to send the current from a

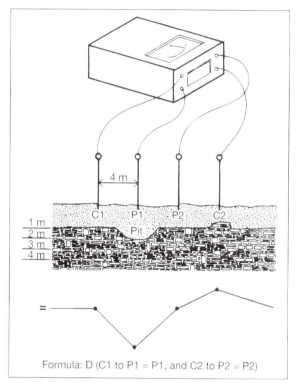

Figure 4.7　How a soil resistivity array works.

Source: Reprinted with the permission of Simon & Schuster from *A Complete Manual of Field Archaeology* by Martha Joukowsky. Copyright © 1980 by Martha Joukowsky.

power source into the ground. The other array measures the current sent from the first array. Depending on the character of the intervening soils, more or less current will reach each of the stakes in the second array, and from these differences a map of the resistivity of the soil can be made. Soil resistivity is affected by human presence in many ways, just as soil magnetic characteristics are, and thus a wide variety of archaeological deposits can be located and identified using soil resistivity.[7]

James Adovasio and his colleagues provide a good example of the utility of soil resistivity survey in their work on the Howarth/Nelson site in western Pennsylvania.[8] The site is a very large and well-preserved settlement with habitations dating from A.D. 1000 into the historic period. The site was threatened with destruction by the construction of a natural gas pipeline, and the archaeologists had only a limited time to investigate it. Following pedestrian survey and test excavation, a soil resistivity survey was conducted over the entire site area in order to establish the size and layout of the settlement. In combination with artifact distribution data from the pedestrian survey, the soil resistivity data provided a clear picture of where important subsurface deposits were located. This information allowed the archaeologists to develop an excavation strategy to maximize data recovery in the short time available.

Two other active remote sensing techniques are becoming increasingly popular: soil interface radar and electromagnetic survey. In **soil interface radar** an electromagnetic pulse is sent into the ground from an antenna and the time it takes for reflection of that pulse to reach back to the antenna is recorded. Thus, it works just like radar does tracking storms or airplanes, but in this case, the radar pulse is sent into the soil. Instead of an airplane or storm cloud reflecting the pulse back to the antenna, soil interfaces do. Soil interface radar, under the right conditions, can give a remarkably detailed picture of soil layers, features, architecture, and the like, even deeply buried.[9]

Jeanne Arnold and her colleagues have been using soil interface radar to explore complex late prehistoric Chumash sites in the Santa Barbara Channel Islands.[10] These sites have multiple house structures and a variety of storage and refuse pits, as well as hearths, burials, and other cultural features. Because

Figure 4.8   A soil interface radar survey in progress at Chaco Canyon, New Mexico.

the sites are so complex, the logistics of excavation are also complicated, and excavation strategies need to be carefully planned. Arnold and her colleagues hoped that remote sensing techniques would provide the information they needed to effectively plan excavations of these complex sites. They found that the soil interface radar data provided useful information about the location of houses, pits, and other features, especially when combined with other data sources—particularly geomagnetics—and that these data significantly helped in planning excavation strategies.

In **electromagnetic survey** an electromagnetic field is created and the soil reaction is observed. Where geomagnetic surveying passively measures variation in the earth's magnetic field, electromagnetic surveying actively imposes a magnetic field on the soil so that anomalous effects can be determined.[11] An interesting application of electromagnetic survey was carried out by Rinita Dalan at the Cahokia site in East St. Louis, Illinois.[12] Cahokia is the largest pre-Columbian settlement in the United States, covering an area of roughly 15 square kilometers and containing a number of "precincts" or "neighborhoods" within it. Prominent among these is an "elite precinct" in the center of the settlement that was surrounded by palisade wall. Dalan was interested in mapping the location of this wall, but as this central palisade had an estimated length of 5 kilometers in total, only a small portion of which had been excavated, she decided that an electromagnetic survey would provide the data needed to trace its outline. She conducted a large-scale survey over several areas of the site that were suspected to contain the central palisade and was able to readily map several long sections of the palisade using the electromagnetic data.

There are also other, less widely used techniques that can be effective in the right circumstances. At Tell es-Sweyhat, for example, we used **gravity surveying** to locate hollow tomb chambers below the ground. We measured the very subtle variations in the earth's gravitational field to locate the large, hollow voids of the tombs buried deep beneath the ground surface. Some archaeologists have had success using **seismic surveying**. This technique sends a seismic wave through the ground and measures how it is affected by the soil, in much the way resistivity surveying sends an electric current through the soil and identifies disruptions. Much success has been had in finding sites through measuring **soil chemistry** because humans tend to add significant amounts of phosphates to soils where they live. Still other techniques are under development.[13]

Remote sensing is a burgeoning field with exciting possibilities for aiding archaeological survey. Remote sensing is clearly not a substitute for excavation, but these techniques do allow archaeologists to locate buried features and in many cases to identify their type. This information is extremely valuable in assessing the extent of archaeological deposits, their state of preservation, and, to some extent, their significance. It is particularly important information for planning excavation strategies, especially in situations where excavations must be carried out quickly.

4.2.4   Aerial Photography and Imagery

In addition to ground-based remote sensing techniques, a variety of aerial remote sensing techniques have been successfully used in archaeological survey. In fact, almost as soon as the airplane was invented the utility of **aerial photographs** for archaeological reconnaissance was recognized.[14] In England, for example, early pilots not only saw the great stone circles of Stonehenge, Avebury, and the like, but also saw what we call "crop marks" today—areas where crops have grown either better or poorer than surrounding crops because of what is beneath them. On aerial images from Avebury you can clearly see not only the stone circle that is visible on the surface today, but also the remains of more ancient stone circles that are now buried. Why are these visible? Well, it's because stone does not absorb water; grass growing above the circles gets less water than surrounding grass and therefore appears brown in comparison.

In addition to aerial photographs, **digital imagery**, often from satellites, has proven useful to archaeologists.[15] In one of the more famous examples, satellite-derived radar images allowed archaeologists to locate and map ancient river courses in the Egyptian desert. Similarly, satellite images helped archaeologists in the southwestern United States follow ancient road networks used by prehistoric Puebloan groups. For large features satellite imagery can be useful, but for smaller features it isn't. Why not? Because the resolution of

Figure 4.9   Aerial image over Avebury with crop marks showing ancient features.

the imagery only allows features larger than about 10 square meters (at best—with some imagery you need even larger features) to be seen. New techniques of image processing and enhancement are always being developed, however, and some forms of satellite imagery (radar, for example) can actually achieve rather high resolution. Future archaeologists may be able to use aerial imagery more broadly than we can today.[16]

4.3   HOW DO ARCHAEOLOGISTS CONDUCT SURVEYS?

Regardless of the survey method being used (surface, remote sensing, and so on) by archaeologists, they have a choice of how to conduct a survey; that is, archaeologists have a choice of survey strategies. By strategy I mean the way in which the survey methodology is employed to gain information about the archaeological resources in a given area.

4.3.1   "Top-Down" Surveys

The most scientifically (or at least statistically) appropriate survey strategy is what I call "top-down." An archaeologist employing a **top-down strategy** uses random sampling to select areas to survey and usually attempts to cover a large area, generally ignoring previous knowledge or intuitive knowledge about the area. Such a survey should provide a statistically valid sample of sites in the area of interest and should include sites of all types and from all environments. Thus a top-down strategy is particularly useful when archaeologists want to understand variation in prehistoric settlement or wish to test a particular hypothesis that requires a representative sample of sites of all kinds.

Lynn Goldstein recently used a top-down strategy in her work on a large late prehistoric site called Aztalan in southeastern Wisconsin.[17] Aztalan is an unusual site because it appears to be a cultural outpost of Mississippian peoples in an area otherwise inhabited by Oneota peoples. Goldstein wanted to understand why this site was there and whether it was indeed an isolated Mississippian outpost. In order to answer those questions she developed a stratified random sample of 170 40-acre survey units within a roughly 70-square-mile area around Aztalan. Goldstein and her team surveyed these units and were able to infer that the area was sparsely inhabited during the time Aztalan was, and that the only Mississippian settlement in the area was Aztalan itself.

4.3.2   "Bottom-Up" Surveys

Perhaps the most common survey strategy is what I call "bottom-up." Archaeologists employing a **bottom-up strategy** start at an established site and work

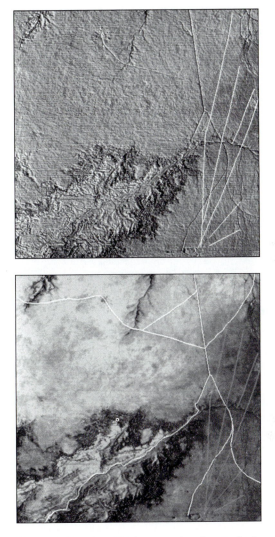

Figure 4.10   Satellite images showing ancient roads (top) and current roads (bottom) in the southwestern United States. The current roads follow typography and the path of least resistance in construction. The prehistoric roads are strikingly linear.

outward from it, attempting to find related sites. A bottom-up strategy makes a lot of sense in a situation where archaeologists are interested in finding sites neighboring the one they are working on, in defining the boundaries of a large

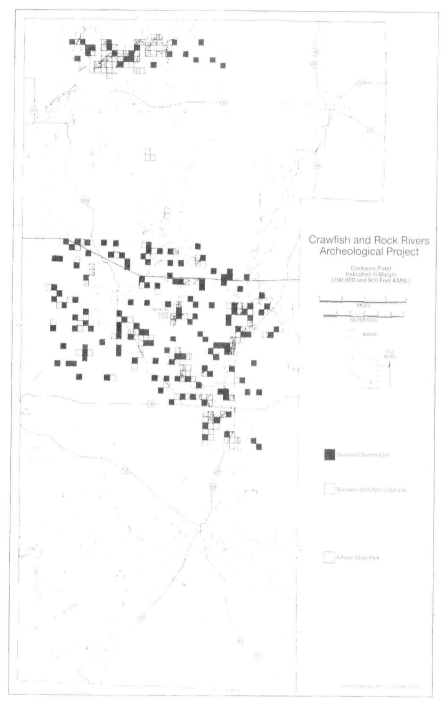

Figure 4.11   The locations of Goldstein's Aztalan survey grids.

Source: Lynn Goldstein. 1997. "Exploring Aztalan and Its Role in Mississippian Societies," in *Research Frontiers in Anthropology*, ed. Carol R. Ember, Melvin Ember, and Peter N. Peregrine. Upper Saddle River, NJ: Prentice Hall.

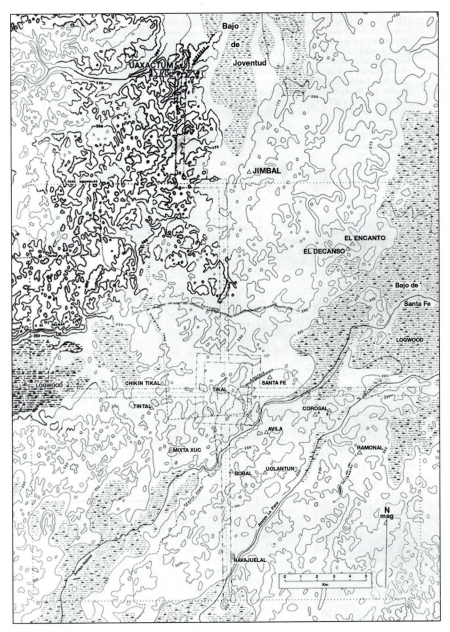

Figure 4.12 The locations of Puleston's Tikal survey strips.

Source: From *The Settlement Survey of Tikal* (Tikal Report, Number 13) by Dennis Puleston, copyright ©
1983, The University Museum, University of Pennsylvania. Reprinted by permission.

settlement area, or in better understanding a local settlement system. In some ways it may seem that Goldstein employed a bottom-up strategy in her survey of the area around Aztalan; after all, she wanted to know other sites in the region surrounding the site. But another example should help make the difference between top-down and bottom-up strategies more clear.

One of the first major archaeological surveys to be undertaken in the dense jungles of the Mayan region was carried out by a team led by Dennis Puleston in 1965 and 1966.[18] The main objectives of the survey were to find the limits of the ancient city of Tikal and to better understand the nature of extramural settlement around Mayan cities like Tikal. To accomplish these objectives Puleston and his team surveyed four 250-meter-wide, 12-kilometer-long strips radiating out from the center of Tikal, one strip following each of the cardinal directions. Thus Tikal was the established site that formed the "bottom" of the survey, and the survey itself moved out to find other related sites. Given their objectives, this "bottom-up" strategy made sense and yielded important results.

4.3.3 "Shotgun" and Predictive Surveys

A third strategy, which I call "**shotgun survey**," uses archaeologists' intuitive knowledge of prehistoric settlement and landscape to focus survey on places likely to have sites. In Goldstein's Aztalan survey, for example, it became clear that sites in the northern survey area were all located on high ground surrounded by low, swampy areas. After surveying some of the low areas and finding nothing, Goldstein decided to limit survey to the high ground.[19] Future archaeologists going into adjacent areas to do survey might simply decide, based on this previous knowledge, to survey only high ground. That seems a reasonable strategy, but there is one rather significant problem—the "self-fulfilling prophecy." If you start with the assumption that sites are on high ground and then only survey high ground, guess what you'll find: Sites are only on high ground! I hope you can see that's not much of a revelation, is it? By surveying all areas, both those where sites are expected and those where they aren't, archaeologists can make nontrivial statements about where people were living and where sites can be expected to be found.

Falling completely in the self-fulfilling prophecy trap, and indeed wholly based on it, is predictive surveying. **Predictive surveying** uses existing literature and background knowledge about prehistoric settlement in a given region to anticipate where sites will be located. Survey is then focused on those predicted areas. Clearly this is a very limited strategy where archaeologists will, by the nature of the strategy itself, find only what they expect to find. Why use predictive or shotgun surveying? The primary reason is time. Predictive and shotgun surveying save a tremendous amount of time that would otherwise be spent surveying areas unlikely to contain sites. So if finding sites alone—and not learning about past settlement systems, preferences, variations, and the like—is the goal of the survey, then predictive and shotgun strategies are appropriate. Once again, it is important to remember that all archaeological research begins with a question. If that question relies solely on sites being found, then these strategies are great timesavers.

The utility of predictive survey was illustrated in the Delaware coastal plain example of Jay Custer and his colleagues, who developed a predictive model of site location using satellite imagery.[20] They took site data from existing surveys and combined site location information with information on the site's environment based on satellite imagery. The use of satellite images in this way is somewhat complicated. Basically different soils and vegetation reflect light in different ways, and therefore the unique characteristics of the light reflected at a particular location on the ground match its unique environmental characteristics. What Custer and his colleagues did was to identify the kind of environment that sites tended to be located in by examining the light reflected in areas containing known sites. Then they used a computer to find all the other locations in their area of interest that had similar light reflection characteristics. They predicted these would be areas with a high probability of containing sites. Follow-up pedestrian survey upheld their prediction. However, they caution that a predictive model should only be used to guide research—areas defined as having a low probability of sites may in fact contain sites. But as an aid in planning a survey strategy, predictive modeling can be extremely helpful.

4.4 SUMMARY

Archaeologists find sites through a variety of methods. Two of the more important are literature searches and interviews with landowners and collectors. These two methods allow archaeologists to determine what other researchers have found before going through the effort of archaeological survey. Archaeological survey is the primary method for finding sites. In pedestrian survey archaeologists simply walk along, scanning the ground for artifacts that might suggest the presence of buried archaeological deposits. Probing and testing the soil can also be used to determine if buried archaeological deposits exist. A variety of remote sensing techniques, including geomagnetics, soil resistivity, soil conductivity, and soil interface radar, might also be used not only to locate but also to map buried deposits. Aerial imagery, including photographs from airplanes and even digital images from spacecraft, can aid in the location of archaeological features.

Regardless of the survey methods employed, archaeologists choose one of several strategies to conduct their surveys. Top-down strategies use random sampling or another statistically appropriate sampling method to choose areas to survey. Bottom-up strategies begin at a known site and work out from it in order to locate neighboring and related sites. Shotgun and predictive strategies use archaeologists' knowledge of a region or a predictive model of settlement location to select survey areas that are highly likely to contain sites. This is a useful strategy for finding lots of sites quickly, but only those kinds of sites archaeologists are specifically looking for.

SUGGESTED READINGS

Ball, Steven. 1998. "The Discovery of Archaeological Sites," in Carol R. Ember, Melvin Ember, and Peter N. Peregrine, eds. *Research Frontiers in Anthropology*. Upper Saddle River, NJ: Prentice Hall. A comprehensive and highly readable introduction to archaeological survey, covering all the methods discussed here.

Clark, Anthony. 1996. *Seeing beneath the Soil: Prospecting Methods in Archaeology*. London: Batsford. A bit dated but still very useful introduction to remote sensing methods of archaeological survey. Clark does a wonderful job of simplifying rather difficult discussions of how these methods work.

Feder, Kenneth. 1997. "Site Survey," in Thomas Hester, Harry Shafer, and Kenneth Feder, eds. *Field Methods in Archaeology* (7th ed.) Mountain View, CA: Mayfield. Perhaps the best single overview of archaeological survey available.

Fish, Suzanne, and Stephen Kowalewski. 1990. *The Archaeology of Regions: A Case for Full Coverage Survey*. Washington, DC: Smithsonian Institution. A collection of essays on survey strategy, with a focus on comprehensive survey of large areas.

McManamon, Francis P. 1984. "Discovering Sites Unseen," *Advances in Archaeological Method and Theory* 7:223–292. A comprehensive but sometimes difficult overview of archaeological survey methods and strategies.

Schiffer, Michael, Anne Sullivan, and Thomas Klinger. 1978. "The Design of Archaeological Surveys," *World Archaeology* 10(1):1–28. A brief but thorough discussion of archaeological survey strategies.

Schollar, Irwin, A. Tabbagh, A. Hesse, and I. Herzog. 1990. *Archaeological Prospecting and Remote Sensing*. Cambridge, UK: Cambridge University Press. A masterful overview of remote sensing in archaeology. Difficult at times, but mandatory reading for those seriously interested in archaeological remote sensing.

NOTES

1. Lewis Binford, "Archaeology as Anthropology," *American Antiquity* 28 (1962):217–225; also "Archeological Perspectives," in *New Perspectives in Archaeology*, ed. L. R. Binford and S. R. Binford (Chicago: Aldine, 1967), pp. 5–32.

2. Increase Lapham, *The Antiquities of Wisconsin: As Surveyed and Described by I. A. Lapham* (Washington, DC: Smithsonian Institution, 1855).

3. Cyrus Thomas, *Report on the Mound Explorations of the Bureau of American Ethnology* (Washington, DC: Bureau of American Ethnology, Twelfth Annual Report, 1894).

4. An impressive demonstration of the vastness of this literature can be found in the four-volume *Archeological Literature of the South-Central United States*, ed. W. Fredrick Limp, Ellen Zahn, and James P. Harcourt (Fayetteville, AR: Arkansas Archeological Survey Research Series, No. 36, 1989). More than 5,000 references are listed, and these only cover the south-central United States!

5. For a good overview, see Ralph von Frese, "Archaeomagnetic Anomalies of Midcontinental North American Archaeological Sites," *Historical Archaeology* 18 (1984):4–19.

6. Our preliminary report was published, with color images, in *Expedition* 38 (1996):14–35.

7. The best single overview of soil resistivity surveying is probably Christopher Carr, *Handbook on Soil Resistivity Surveying* (Evanston, IL: Center for American Archaeology, 1982).

8. James Adovasio and Ronald Carlisle, "Some Thoughts on Cultural Resource Management in the United States," *Antiquity* 62 (1988):72–87.

9. Anthony Clark, *Seeing beneath the Soil* (London: Batsford, 1996), pp. 118–120.

10. Jeanne Arnold, Elizabeth Ambos, and Daniel Larson, "Geophysical Surveys of Stratigraphically Complex Island California Sites: New Implications for Household Archaeology," *Antiquity* 71 (1997):157–168.

11. Anthony Clark, *Seeing beneath the Soil* (London: Batsford, 1996), pp. 99–117.

12. Rinita Dalan, "Electromagnetic Reconnaissance of the Central Palisade at the Cahokia Mounds State Historic Site," *The Wisconsin Archaeologist* 70 (1989):309–332.

13. See, for examples, Anthony Clark, *Seeing beneath the Soil* (London: Batsford, 1996), pp. 118–123.

14. Leo Deuel, *Flights into Yesteryear: The Story of Aerial Archaeology* (New York: St. Martin's Press, 1969).

15. A general overview is James Wiseman, "Wonders of Radar Imagery," *Archaeology* (September/October 1996), pp. 14–17.

16. See Irwin Scollar, A. Tabbagh, A. Hesse, and I. Herzog, *Archaeological Prospecting and Remote Sensing* (Cambridge, UK: Cambridge University Press, 1990).

17. Lynn Goldstein, "Exploring Aztalan and Its Role in Mississippian Societies," in *Research Frontiers in Anthropology*, ed. C. R. Ember, M. Ember, and P. N. Peregrine (Upper Saddle River, NJ: Prentice Hall, 1998).

18. Dennis Puleston, *The Settlement Survey of Tikal*, Tikal Report, No. 13, (Philadelphia: University Museum, University of Pennsylvania, 1983).

19. Lynn Goldstein, "Exploring Aztalan and Its Role in Mississippian Societies," in *Research Frontiers in Anthropology*, ed. C. R. Ember, M. Ember, and P. N. Peregrine (Upper Saddle River, NJ: Prentice Hall, 1998).

20. Jay Custer, Timothy Eveleigh, Vyautas Klemas, and Ian Wells, "Application of LANDSAT Data and Synoptic Remote Sensing to Predictive Models for Prehistoric Archaeological Sites: An Example from the Delaware Coastal Plain," *American Antiquity* 51 (1986):572–588.

5

Excavation Methods and Strategies

OVERVIEW

5.1 What Techniques Do Archaeologists Use to Excavate Sites?

    5.1.1 Horizontal Controls

    5.1.2 Vertical Controls

5.2 What Strategies Do Archaeologists Use to Excavate Sites?

    5.2.1 Standard Excavation Strategies

    5.2.2 Special-Case Excavation Strategies

5.3 What about the Digging Itself?

5.4 Summary

The shabby tweed jacket alone suggested he was a scholar. The horn-rimmed reading glasses and tousled piles of coffee-stained papers completed the picture. He sat under a dim reading light flipping vaguely through a massive folio of antediluvian age. Dust filtered lightly between his face and the lamp as he turned the pages. I had only watched him a few moments when I saw him quickly take up a pen and furiously write in a tattered spiral notebook. He put down the pen as quickly as he had taken it up, reached to the top of the page, and tore it from the folio in one rapid motion. He proceeded to take a silver Zippo out of the side pocket of his jacket and light the bottom corner. He held the burning page over a wastebasket until it was fully engulfed, then dropped it in and turned back to the book.

In shock I hurried to the librarian's carrel. "That man just tore a page out of a book and burned it!" I exclaimed.

The librarian looked up slowly. "Hum," he said, looking enigmatically past me at the man.

"Aren't you going to do anything?" I asked, puzzled at the librarian's disinterested response.

"Oh, it's OK," he said, looking back at me. "He's an archaeologist."

Uh-oh, Peregrine's gone crazy. What in the world is this story about? Well, it's intended to illustrate one of the truly odd facts about archaeological research. Here the librarian is unconcerned about the archaeologist's seemingly bizarre and destructive behavior because he knows that fact. What is it? That archaeologists destroy their data as they collect it. When we excavate, we destroy the very site we are studying. We destroy the very context of the artifacts, ecofacts, and features we want to examine. When we excavate, we act precisely as the scholar in the story—we read the record of the past and then destroy it. All that we have in the end are our notes. And that makes excavation a dangerous activity and a necessarily cautious, time-consuming, and precise one that no archaeologist wants to undertake without good reason.

What are good reasons to excavate? The most common one is threat of site destruction without excavation. All archaeological sites are in a constant process of decay, but farming, construction, erosion, and the like can accelerate the decay process, even bring about an instantaneous destructive change (as when a backhoe digs through a site). If a site is threatened, it makes sense to excavate it and salvage as much information as possible. A second good reason to excavate is to recover specific information to test a hypothesis, information that is not otherwise obtainable. It is never appropriate to excavate simply to recover artifacts, although before World War II that was rather common (as the Indiana Jones movies make clear). Why is this? Largely because the focus and purpose of archaeological excavation is not to recover artifacts but rather to recover the relationships among and between artifacts, ecofacts, and features.

5.1   WHAT TECHNIQUES DO ARCHAEOLOGISTS USE TO EXCAVATE SITES?

The techniques of archaeological excavation and (as we will learn in the next chapter) recordkeeping are designed to recover and record, in as much detail as possible, the relationships among and between artifacts, ecofacts, and features—what archaeologists call **context**. At the conclusion of a well-executed excavation, any archaeologist should be able to take the excavator's records and the materials recovered and reconstruct the context of those materials as they were before the site was excavated. In essence, the end product of an excavation is a three-dimensional picture, drawn in words, maps, tables, and the like, of the archaeological site before excavation began. How is this accomplished?

In order to reconstruct context, we need to know the precise location where each artifact, ecofact, or feature was found and record that location so that each item excavated can be put back in place, analytically at least, through the excavator's records. The techniques of archaeological excavation are designed to accomplish this by maintaining well-defined horizontal and vertical controls on the spatial location of material recovered. **Horizontal controls** refer to techniques used to locate and record artifacts, ecofacts, and features in horizontal (north-south, east-west) space. **Vertical controls** refer to techniques used to locate and record artifacts, ecofacts, and features in vertical (up-down) space.

5.1.1   Horizontal Controls

Test pits, soundings, and trenches are the basic horizontal units of excavation. **Test pits** are usually square units of 1 meter, 2 meters, or 5 meters on a side. Horizontal control is maintained by keeping all the material from a test pit together in a single, uniquely defined collection. Thus the resolution of the horizontal control can be adjusted by changing the size of the test pit. Test pits are used to locate subsurface deposits and are usually combined into larger excavation units as deposits are identified and followed. When a test pit is very deep it is called a **sounding**. Soundings are useful for the initial identification of archaeological strata and for finding sterile soil (where archaeological deposits cease). **Trenches** are basically long test pits. They are used like soundings to identify archaeological strata, often in large and very complex sites where a single sounding would be uninformative.

A good example of how test pits and trenches can be effectively used comes from Kent Flannery's excavations at Guilá Naquitz, a cave site with evidence for early agriculture in the Valley of Oaxaca, Mexico (oh no, not the Valley of Oaxaca again!).[1] Flannery and his colleagues were searching for a site with well-preserved plant remains dating to the Archaic and Formative periods. How to find such sites? Test them! At Guilá Naquitz, Flannery initially excavated several small test pits and found the site was a candidate for his research project. After testing other sites in the area, Flannery returned to the cave to begin formal excavations. At this point, he began a trench. Why? To establish the stratigraphy of the cave and from that to establish the vertical control (cultural strata) for excavation—but we'll get to that later. Once the conditions of the archaeological record were established (through test pits) and the stratigraphy determined (through trenching), Flannery began full-scale excavation of the cave, using 1-meter by 1-meter excavation units laid out in 64-unit grid covering the whole site.[2]

Excavation units are larger units of horizontal control. Excavation units are generally made up of test pits joined or expanded to follow archaeological deposits of interest. They differ from test pits in that their location and size are driven by what is found below the ground surface. In the case of Guilá Naquitz, Flannery wanted to excavate as much of the habitation area as

Figure 5.1   Map of the Guilá Naquitz excavation units.

Source: Figure from *Guilá Naquitz: Archaic Foraging and Early Agriculture in Oaxaca, Mexico* by Kent Flannery, copyright © 1986 by Academic Press, reproduced by permission of the publisher.

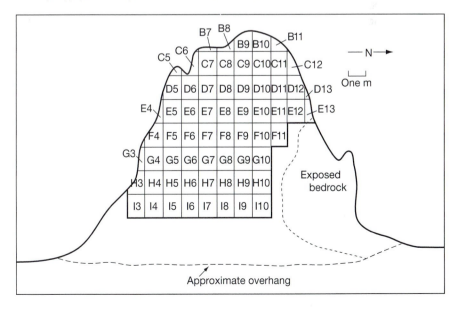

possible. He expanded the excavation outward from the original trench until the edges of the habitation area were reached. Thus, Flannery exposed the whole living area of the cave site and was able, by examining material by each stratigraphic level, to reconstruct the pattern of habitation through time.[3] The stratigraphy in Guilá Naquitz was not very complicated. In cases where stratigraphy is very complicated or where sites are very deep, a thin (usually 10- to 25-centimeter) wall of unexcavated soil, called a **balk**, can be left between the test pits that make up the excavation unit. Flannery didn't need to use balks, but we'll examine later some cases where they were used.

Architecture is the most common unit of horizontal control in some parts of the world. Rooms or buildings are used to horizontally define the archaeological excavation. One of the great architectural finds in recent years is the Early Bronze Age palace at Tell Mardikh (ancient Ebla) near Hama, Syria. Excavations at Tell Mardikh began in 1964 under the direction of Paolo Matthiae of the University of Rome. Matthiae and his team chose Tell Mardikh because they were interested in understanding the beginnings of urban life in northern Mesopotamia, and the site appeared to be a very early, and very large, urban settlement.[4] As is often the case when investigating such large sites, it took ten years before significant deposits from the early city came to light, but when they did, they were spectacular.

Perhaps the most spectacular find at Tell Mardikh was a preserved palace complex dating from the late Early Bronze Age, roughly 2250 B.C. Even though only a small portion of the place has been excavated, its architecture is complex. Matthiae and his crew had to carefully determine how to maintain horizontal control over this large, complex building. What they did was to divide the building into **loci**, giving each room and each major feature a separate locus number and collecting materials from each locus separately. Thus all the materials coming from a particular room were kept separately from all other materials. In this way the architecture itself formed the basic unit of horizontal control. Why was this palace so well preserved? Apparently because it was destroyed by Naram-Sin of Akkad and abandoned.[5] The mud-brick buildings collapsed and were covered with wind-blown soil, creating a mound upon which a new palace was built in the Middle Bronze Age, some 300 years later. So rapid and complete was the palace's destruction that the entire royal archives—more than 15,000 clay tablets—were left in place, on their shelves, and buried.[6]

5.1.2 Vertical Controls

Cultural levels or **strata** are the primary vertical control for excavation. Each layer of cultural deposit defines a unique occupation or range of occupation that is kept separate for analysis and interpretation. **Stratigraphy**—working out the relationships between and among strata—is a major part of archaeological research in areas where archaeological deposits are very deep. As I said earlier, the stratigraphy at Guilá Naquitz was not complex, but it did

Figure 5.2   The Bronze Age palace at Ebla.

show a clear sequence of occupation in the cave. Flannery defined five major occupations, ranging from roughly 8000 B.C. to A.D. 700, each identified by a different stratum of soil.[7] Each stratum had a different color, consistency, and, of course, vertical location below ground.

How do strata like these form? Why are they different from one another? The answer is complicated and is unique to each site, but in all cases it has to do with the behavior of the people using the site. At Guilá Naquitz, the earliest clear occupation stratum, Zone D (dated at roughly 8000 B.C.), was dark compared to other strata because the people using the cave at the time that stratum was created had brought large numbers of oak leaves into the cave and these had burned at some point, creating a dark mix of decomposing leaves and ash.[8] Following their use of the cave, dirt blew in, rock and grit fell from the cave roof, and the stratum was covered. The next stratum, Zone C (dated at roughly 7400 B.C.) was much like Zone D. It too was composed of burnt leaves and ash but was clearly separated from Zone D because the burnt leaves formed a clear line of demarcation between the two.[9] The next stratum, Zone B (dated at roughly 6700 B.C.), containing many hearths and work areas, was

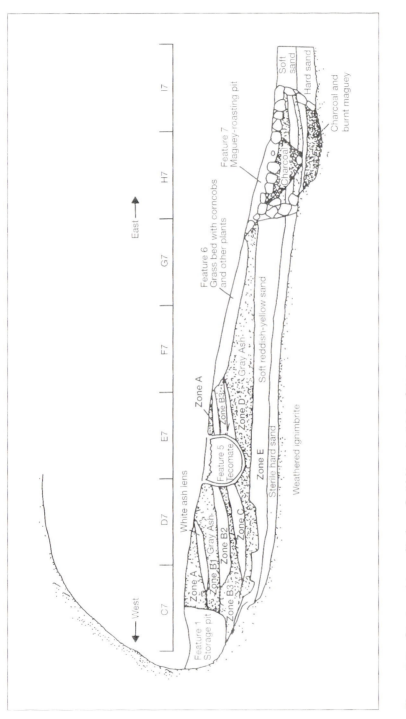

Figure 5.3 Stratigraphic profile from Guilá Naquitz (Units C7 to I7).

Source: Figure from *Guilá Naquitz: Archaic Foraging and Early Agriculture in Oaxaca, Mexico* by Kent Flannery. copyright © by Academic Press. reproduced by permission of the publisher.

much more complicated than the other strata. It represented many repeat occupations of the cave, each occupation depositing a layer of ash from the fires the people used. Thus, Zone B was light in color and ashy in texture compared to the darker and more organic Zones C and D.[10]

Not all sites have the clear stratigraphy Guilá Naquitz had. In fact, on many sites the differences between occupations are so brief, and the ways of life so similar, that archaeologists cannot distinguish strata in the occupation. In such cases **arbitrary levels**, usually 10 centimeters in depth, are used to give vertical control to the excavation. In fact, they were even used by Flannery at Guilá Naquitz in the test pits he dug before the stratigraphy of the cave was known. The logic behind arbitrary levels is that by keeping materials together in small vertical divisions (like 10 centimeters), actual cultural divisions might be found later during analysis. That is, a regular difference in ceramics, lithics, or other artifacts might be identified between the arbitrary levels once analysis is begun, and a sequence of occupation might then be reconstructed based on those differences. Clearly, this is not as good a method as using actual cultural strata, but in many cases it is all archaeologists can do.

Features (including architecture) are sometimes used for vertical control when they can be assumed to have been used during only one time period, stratigraphically defined. In fact, features are one of the things that often make defining stratigraphy difficult. Why? Because when people dig pits, foundations, postholes, or the like, they tend to dig down through earlier occupations, and, in so doing, mingle their material debris with that of earlier peoples. For this reason, later features often intrude into earlier cultural strata, mixing everything up. When this happens it is important to use the feature itself as the unit of vertical control rather than the strata, because the strata become meaningless when a feature intrudes through them. This is particularly true when the strata being used for vertical control are actually arbitrary levels. What happens if archaeologists are using arbitrary levels and don't realize that a feature has intruded into an earlier deposit? A puzzle. But dealing with such puzzles is what the process of good recordkeeping and careful spatial analysis, which we will discuss in the next two chapters, are supposed to help solve.

5.2 WHAT STRATEGIES DO ARCHAEOLOGISTS USE TO EXCAVATE SITES?

When archaeologists combine a horizontal and a vertical control into an overall plan for uncovering an archaeological deposit, they are following a particular **excavation strategy**. There are a large number of excavation strategies, each with its own benefits and drawbacks. What leads archaeologists to choose a particular one? Well, remember once again that archaeological research begins with questions for which model answers are developed and evaluated. Archaeologists need to choose an excavation strategy that will provide the information needed to evaluate a particular model answer for a specific archaeological question. In addition, some strategies are better than others for excavating large features, deep deposits, or deposits with very complex stratigraphy. Let's look at some of the more common excavation strategies.

5.2.1   Standard Excavation Strategies

Step trenching is a strategy in which individual strata are exposed in a step-like fashion (with each step of a designated size, such as 5 meters by 5 meters) before being excavated across the entire length of the trench. Thus, a site with ten strata would have a trench placed across it composed of ten excavation units, the first exposing the bottom (tenth) stratum, the next exposing the ninth stratum, the next the eighth, and so on. Step trenching is useful in situations where deposits are very deep and where the stratigraphy is complex,

Figure 5.4   The primary step trench at Tell es-Sweyhat.

and it is particularly productive in excavating stratified mounds such as the large tells that are typical of ancient settlements in the Near East.

We've used step trenching extensively at Tell es-Sweyhat. Tell es-Sweyhat itself covers an area of roughly 11 hectares and is roughly 15 meters tall. Test pits or typical excavation units in such a large and deep mound would be impossible. You'd have to carry every bucketload of dirt up 15 meters of ladders to get it out of the unit, and you'd need electric lights at the bottom in order to see what you're digging! Step trenching solves both problems, as the stepped units allow easy access to deposits. More important, the vertical face of the stepped units provides excellent stratigraphy for maintaining vertical control.

Using **vertical face trenching** archaeologists expose a vertical face from the ground surface to sterile soil before excavating individual strata across the entire length of the trench. In some cases, once a single trench is finished, the long vertical faces are used to excavate outward from them. The advantage of this approach is the long vertical face it provides. Vertical face techniques are particularly practical where deposits are deep but the occupation is expected to be short term, that is, where there will not be a great need to separate out artifacts by vertical strata. The strata will tell more about the construction of the deposit or the deposition of materials that make it up than about temporal sequences of materials, for example, in the excavation of middens and burial mounds.

During the 1930s the Works Progress Administration (WPA) excavated a number of large burial mounds in the central and southeastern United States using a modified form of vertical face trenching. At the Hiwassee Island site, for example, the WPA crews excavated the mounds by quartering them. They

Figure 5.5 Vertical face trenching of a burial mound (Unit 42) at Hiwassee Island.

excavated a quarter of the mound, then used the exposed vertical faces to provide both stratigraphic control and information on how the mound was constructed. Once one quarter was completed, an adjacent quarter was excavated, leaving a balk wall between the two for vertical control. This sequence was repeated twice more, until the entire mound was excavated, and then the balk walls themselves were excavated. In this way, entire mounds were excavated, but both horizontal (by way of the quarters) and vertical (by way of the long stratigraphic profiles provided by the balk walls) were maintained until the very end of the excavation.[11]

The **isolated pit approach** is an excavation strategy that involves excavating many small test pits over a large area in locations defined by random sampling, either simple or systematic. This is one of the more common excavation strategies because it offers several advantages over others. First, it provides a good sample of the entire range of materials from the site. Second, only a small percentage of a site needs to be excavated in order to uncover a representative sample of materials. Third, it offers a view of the stratigraphy and occupational history of the whole site, not just a part of it. It is not all that useful if deposits are very deep (step trenching would likely be better), or if particular features or aspects of a site are the focus of interest (excavating those using an appropriate strategy would be better).

One of the best examples of the isolated pit approach is Robert Braidwood and Bruce Howe's excavation of Jarmo. Braidwood and Howe wanted to know where and when the first animals were domesticated in the Near East. They suspected this had occurred in the Zagros mountains where Jarmo was located, and they knew from the site's lithics that it dated to the time period they were interested in. However, little else was known about Jarmo or indeed about other sites from the time period. Thus, Braidwood and Howe needed to both gather basic information on the extent, organization, and makeup of the site and find faunal remains that might show evidence of animal husbandry. What could they do to achieve both? Place test pits in a systematic fashion across the entire site! Braidwood and Howe covered the site with a 1-meter by 1-meter grid of units and selected units for excavation using systematic random sampling. Not only did they achieve a good understanding of the site, they also found the evidence for early animal domestication they were looking for.[12]

Using the **block approach** archaeologists open a large area of soil at one time, excavating down across the whole block at once either by arbitrary levels or by cultural levels defined by a sounding. This is perhaps the most common excavation strategy used, because it provides the easiest data to interpret and offers a good picture of a site. The block approach does not work well where cultural strata are intermingled or very complex. It also does not work well on very large sites where a huge block would need to be opened to see a representative picture of the site. Opening a large area all at once requires a large crew. Working with smaller crews, archaeologists often employ a modified block approach, in which adjacent excavation units are excavated one after the other, uncovering and recording all the cultural strata in one unit before moving on to the next. This is what Flannery did at Guilá Naquitz.

An important benefit of using a block approach is that it allows intrasite patterns to be seen easily. Some of the finest examples of the block approach were undertaken as part of archaeological salvage work during the construction

Figure 5.6   Map of Jarmo excavation units.

Source: From *Prehistoric Investigations in Iraqi Kurdistan* by Rob Braidwood and Bruce Howe, copyright © 1960, The Oriental Institute of the University of Chicago, Studies in Ancient Oriental Civilization, No. 31, Fig. 6. Courtesy of the Oriental Institute of the University of Chicago.

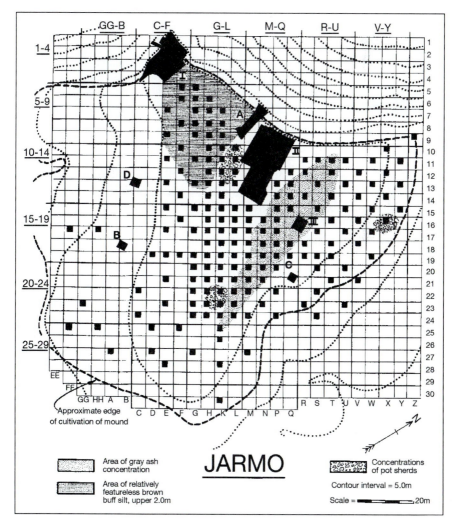

Figure 5.7   Large-scale surface stripping at the Range site.

of the Interstate 270 bypass around St. Louis, Missouri.[13] Large areas were opened on many of the sites (indeed, the entire highway right-of-way in some cases), with mechanized equipment such as road graders taking off the top layers of soil to expose archaeological deposits quickly. Archaeologists were to come in afterward to identify, map, and excavate those deposits. In this way entire villages were sometimes exposed, allowing the archaeologists to see how the village was organized and how that organization changed over time. At the Range site, for example, organization changed from a circular hut compound to a village of rectangular houses arranged linearly. Changes of this sort point to marked social and political changes that might otherwise go unrecognized.[14]

The ability of the block approach to expose settlement organization and change over time is one of its great strengths, but its weakness for investigating sites with complex stratigraphy would seem to limit this strength significantly. However, a modified form of the block approach, called the **Wheeler-Kenyon method** after its most famous users, Mortimer Wheeler and Kathleen Kenyon, opens large areas at a single time leaving balk walls to preserve stratigraphy at regular intervals. This solves the problem encountered in the standard block approach when very complex stratigraphy is excavated. The balks allow continuous stratigraphic profiles to be maintained while at the same time opening large blocks of the site. Parts of Tell Mardikh were excavated in this way. Tell Mardikh had a long and complex occupational history. The lower town has superimposed remains of numerous Bronze Age houses.

Figure 5.8 Wheeler-Kenyon method excavations at Ebla.

Separating these occupations required careful stratigraphic analysis, yet the occupied area is so large that only a block excavation could reveal a large enough section of the settlement to provide useful information. The combined need for clear stratigraphic records and broad areal exposure is precisely the situation where the Wheeler-Kenyon method works well, and that is why it was used in the lower town at Tell Mardikh.[15]

5.2.2 Special-Case Excavation Strategies

Burials are an important type of archaeological deposit because they are, at once, an assemblage of artifacts, ecofacts, and features. They also give archaeologists the only contact they have with the actual people being studied. However, these very facts often make archaeologists reticent to excavate burials. Why? Because if the excavation is done poorly, an enormous amount of information will be lost, and if it is done at all, the remains of another human being must be disturbed. Indeed, many nations (including the United States) have laws regulating the excavation of burials, and some formally prohibit the disturbance of human remains. Today, most human remains are excavated only when they are accidentally discovered during the course of ongoing excavations, or where they are threatened with destruction. No matter how they are discovered, the excavation of burials is a specialty that should only be performed by well-trained archaeologists.

The excavation of burials is usually done using brushes, bamboo sticks (which are hard enough to dig in the soil but softer than metal), and dental instruments. One strategy common to almost all burial excavations is **pedestalling**, where burial items and the bones themselves are left in place (in

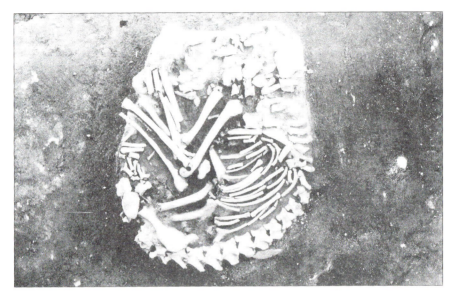

Figure 5.9   A pedestalled dog burial.

situ) on columns of soil until the entire burial feature is excavated. This allows the excavator to see the relationships between the artifacts, ecofacts, and features of the burial clearly. Conservation of the burial is often performed on the bones once the whole burial and associated funerary objects are exposed, in order to avoid damaging them during removal. A chemical mixture called *polyvinyl acetate* is frequently brushed on the bones to consolidate and protect them. Soil samples are often removed during the process of excavation, in order to recover floral and faunal remains that might provide information about burial rites, season of burial, or even foods the person had eaten before dying! Careful notes are always kept during burial excavation, and photographs are taken regularly in order to ensure that a complete record of the burial is made.[16]

Features are also important for they preserve an assemblage of artifacts in context. Indeed, features are so important that in some "salvage" projects where archaeological deposits are threatened with immediate destruction, only features are excavated. Features are sometimes excavated as whole units, sometimes in levels (arbitrary or stratigraphic, if they are present), but most often they are excavated by sectioning. In sectioning a feature archaeologists cut the feature in half, remove the soil in one half of the feature as a whole unit, then use the preserved section to determine whether cultural strata exist in the feature.

Superimposed architecture presents another special case. Excavating where walls and floors interfere with one another requires a combination of the block approach (usually within rooms), pedestalling (to leave walls or

Figure 5.10   Superimposed architecture in the excavations at Tell es-Sweyhat.

other features intact as lower architectural features are uncovered), and step trenching (required where architectural features are too big to pedestal). These kinds of excavations, which lead to multilevel excavation units with complex stratigraphic profiles, are extremely difficult to analyze and interpret. Such excavations are performed only by the most experienced archaeologists.

5.3   WHAT ABOUT THE DIGGING ITSELF?

You are right in noticing that I haven't said much about how archaeologists actually *do* excavation, that is, how they physically dig sites. That's because there simply isn't that much to it. Digging holes is digging holes. Archaeologists dig holes more carefully and slowly than you might if you were, say, planting a tree, but they are digging holes just the same. The important thing—and the thing I have focused on in this chapter—is how archaeologists decide where to put the holes they dig and what strategy they use to dig them. The

Figure 5.11   Troweling an excavation unit.

physical digging just isn't that important (and, if the truth be known, it is usually not done by trained archaeologists anyway, but by students, volunteers, and paid workers). Having said that, I would like to briefly discuss a few digging techniques are unique to archaeology.

Troweling is perhaps the digging technique most commonly identified with archaeology. When troweling, archaeologists use a standard mason's pointing trowel (usually a 5-inch or shorter one) with sharpened edges to carve thin slices of dirt from the floor or face of an excavation unit. Troweling allows archaeologists to both find artifacts in situ (in place) and feel soil changes that might identify a feature or cultural strata. Thus troweling is used when archaeologists are trying to uncover small artifacts in situ or when trying to find features or strata that are not obvious in color or composition. It is also used to clean profiles and features for photographing or drawing. Troweling is not used when it does not have to be, because it is an extremely slow digging technique.

Shovel scraping is another common digging technique. Archaeologists use a shovel with a sharpened edge to carve thin slices from the floor of an excavation unit. Shovel scraping allows larger artifacts to be found in situ and permits archaeologists some feel for changes in soil texture. It is less sensitive than troweling and does not allow for small artifacts to be found in situ; thus it is most often used in combination with **screening** to find small artifacts. Shovel scrapings are placed in a bucket, then carried to a screen and sifted through. The coarseness of the screen mesh is dependent on the size of the artifacts archaeologists want to recover. Shovel scraping in combination with screening is a common digging technique because it both allows for fairly rapid excavation and provides fairly good recovery of artifacts.

The fastest digging technique is **picking**. A small metal pickaxe, usually with a 5- to 7-inch pick, is used to loosen soil, which is then shoveled out of the excavation unit, usually to be screened. Only the largest artifacts are found in situ when picking, but if soils are very solid or a site is very large and deposits very deep, picking may be the only viable digging technique.

5.4 SUMMARY

Excavation is a very destructive method of data collection because the context of artifacts, ecofacts, and features is lost when archaeologists excavate a site.

Figure 5.12 Shovel scraping an excavation unit.

For that reason archaeologists have developed excavation techniques that allow them to record with precision the horizontal and vertical position of everything they find, allowing sites to be put back together through notes, maps, and photographs once the excavation is completed. Horizontal control is maintained through excavation units or trenches; vertical control is maintained by keeping track of cultural strata or by excavating a site by standard levels which mimic cultural strata. By putting together particular types of horizontal and vertical control methods, archaeologists develop an excavation strategy. Among the more common excavation strategies are step trenching, vertical face trenching, the isolated pit approach, and the block approach. Each has its own benefits and drawbacks but is chosen by archaeologists primarily for its ability to obtain the information the archaeologists need to answer their question of interest.

SUGGESTED READINGS

Barker, Philip. 1993. *Techniques of Archaeological Excavation* (3rd ed.). London: Batsford. A comprehensive textbook on archaeological excavation, replete with examples and insights. By far the best single source on excavation.

Brothwell, Don. 1981. *Digging Up Bones*. Ithaca, NY: Cornell University Press. An excellent overview of the excavation, conservation, and analysis of human burials.

Hester, Thomas. 1997. "Methods of Excavation," in Thomas Hester, Harry Shafer, and Kenneth Feder, *Field Methods in Archaeology* (7th ed.). Mountain View, CA: Mayfield, pp. 69–112. A concise yet complete overview of excavation methods.

Joukowsky, Martha. 1980. *A Complete Manual of Field Archaeology*. Upper Saddle River, NJ: Prentice Hall. An excellent introduction to large-scale excavation, particularly of the kind done in the Near East.

Purdy, Barbara. 1996. *How to Do Archaeology the Right Way*. Gainesville: University Press of Florida. A clearly written and easy to understand introduction to archaeological excavation and field methods.

NOTES

1. Kent Flannery, ed., *Guilá Naquitz: Archaic Foraging and Early Agriculture in Oaxaca, Mexico* (New York: Academic Press, 1986).
2. Ibid., pp. 65–80.
3. Ibid., pp. 80–95.
4. Paolo Matthiae, *Ebla: An Empire Rediscovered* (Garden City, NY: Doubleday, 1981), pp. 40–47.
5. Ibid., pp. 58–64.

6. Ibid., pp. 150–158; also Giovanni Pettinato, *Ebla: A New Look at History* (Baltimore: Johns Hopkins University Press, 1986), pp. 51–58.

7. Kent Flannery, ed., *Guilá Naquitz: Archaic Foraging and Early Agriculture in Oaxaca, Mexico* (New York: Academic Press, 1986), pp. 80–95.

8. Ibid., pp. 81–82.

9. Ibid., pp. 82–85.

10. Ibid., pp. 85–89.

11. Thomas Lewis and Madeline Kneberg, *Hiwassee Island: An Archaeological Account of Four Tennessee Indian Peoples* (Knoxville: University of Tennessee Press, 1970/1946), pp. 21–22.

12. Robert Braidwood and Bruce Howe, *Prehistoric Investigations in Iraqi Kurdistan* (Chicago: Oriental Institute of the University of Chicago, Studies in Ancient Oriental Civilization, No. 31, 1960).

13. Charles Bareis and James Porter, *American Bottom Archaeology* (Urbana: University of Illinois Press, 1984).

14. John Kelly, Andrew Fortier, Steven Ozuk, and Joyce Williams, *The Range Site: Archaic through Late Woodland Occupations* (Urbana: University of Illinois Press, 1987); also see John Kelly, Steven Ozuk, and Joyce Williams, *The Range Site 2: The Emergent Mississippian Dohack and Range Phase Occupations* (Urbana: University of Illinois Press, 1990); also see Peter Peregrine, "Social Change in the Woodland-Mississippian Transition: A Study of Household and Community Patterns in the American Bottom," *North American Archaeologist* 13 (1992):131–147.

15. Paolo Matthiae, *Ebla: An Empire Rediscovered* (Garden City, NY: Doubleday, 1981).

16. See Don Brothwell, *Digging Up Bones* (Ithaca, NY: Cornell University Press, 1981).

Recordkeeping

OVERVIEW

6.1 How Do Archaeologists Record Context?

6.2 What Types of Records Do Archaeologists Keep?

6.2.1 Excavation Records

6.2.2 Accession Records

6.2.3 An Example: Kaminaljuyu

6.3 Summary

In the last chapter I made the point that archaeology is like doing research in a library where you burn each page after you read it—all you have left is your notes. In this chapter we will learn what kinds of notes archaeologists take when they excavate a site. There are two key points to archaeological recordkeeping: recording context and redundancy. Recording context is the most important job archaeologists have. As I have tried to explain several times, an artifact or ecofact without context is often meaningless, and several standard systems have been devised to ensure that the context of all artifacts and ecofacts on a site is preserved.

6.1 HOW DO ARCHAEOLOGISTS RECORD CONTEXT?

The **point-plot system** is the most basic method of recording context. With it every artifact or ecofact is individually recorded (or point-plotted) in terms of its horizontal and vertical location. Contextual relationships are thereby reconstructed when all the point-plotted artifacts are mapped together. While this is by far the most accurate system available, it is also the most labor intensive and cumbersome and is only used where extreme accuracy is essential. One case is the Lower Paleolithic site of Cagny-l'Epinette in northern France. The site's excavator, Harold Dibble, was interested in testing how extensively natural processes disturbed living floors on very early habitation sites. Dibble was bothered by the fact that most scholars assumed that patterns found on early sites reflected human activity and not redeposition from natural processes. In order to examine the effects of natural processes on the patterning of artifacts, Dibble decided he had to point-plot everything found on the site. Point-plotting allowed Dibble and his colleagues to examine the site in three dimensions using computer modeling and to demonstrate that, at least at this one Lower Paleolithic site, natural processes significantly impacted artifact patterning.[1]

For most excavations, point-plotting is unnecessary, and many archaeologists use a simple **lot system** to record context. In the lot system all artifacts and ecofacts found together in a single horizontally and vertically defined unit are combined into one group (or lot) for the purposes of collection and analysis. Often individual types of artifacts or ecofacts, such as bone, stone, ceramics, and so on, are given separate lots within each horizontally and vertically defined unit. New lot numbers are usually assigned each day if work done in

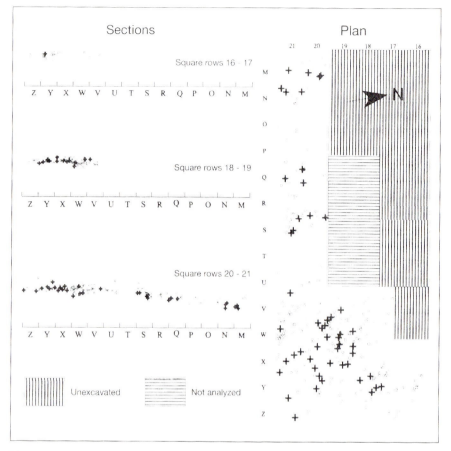

Figure 6.1   Map showing the horizontal and vertical disturbance of bone fragments in Bed II at Cagny-l'Epinette.

Source: From "Testing the Reality of a 'Living Floor' with Archaeological Data" by Harold Dibble, Philip Chase, Shannon McPherron, and Alain Tuffreau. Reproduced by permission of the Society for American Archaeology, from *American Antiquity* 62 (4) 1997.

a single horizontally and vertically defined unit takes place over the period of several days. If large amounts of material are being uncovered, archaeologists may even change lot numbers several times a day.

I have always found it useful to use as many lots as reasonable, and I usually change lot numbers at lunch, and sometimes also at morning and afternoon breaks. Why? Because I learned the hard way that lots can always be combined, but a single lot cannot be easily separated. I was excavating a rather uninteresting site in Lafayette, Indiana one summer, and since we were finding very little material I was using only a single lot a day. One day after lunch, we started finding more material than we had been. Toward the end of the day we began to find small pieces of charcoal. The next morning the charcoal continued, and then we found some rather large pieces of ceramics. After lunch, the material stopped, and we found less and less the rest of the day. When we finished the unit and started looking at our notes, the profiles, and the materials we had found, it became clear we had cut right though the corner of a burned prehistoric house! Lack of experience and a preconceived idea that there was nothing of importance on the site led me to miss the house, but if I had been more diligent in changing lots regularly, I could easily have pulled those lots out which we collected when, in retrospect, we were excavating the house, and thereby kept the house material in context.

Another common system archaeologists use to record context is called the **lot-locus system**. This system adds a secondary horizontally and vertically defined unit (the locus) to the lot system, such that each locus has artifacts and ecofacts found in it collected in separate lots. In other ways it is just like the lot system. Cultural strata, buildings, or rooms within buildings are often used as loci in the lot-locus system. We use such a system at Tell es-Sweyhat. We assign each location or feature we think might be significant its own locus number and collect lots from each locus daily. So lots from cultural strata, rooms, cultural strata within rooms, features, and so on are kept separate from one another because they were collected from separate loci. This is obviously a more complicated system than the simple lot system, but it has the advantage of maintaining all collections in rather specific horizontal and vertical context. In situations where horizontal and vertical context is complex, the lot-locus system is the only way to go.

Regardless of the recording system archaeologists use, all archaeologists record context through photographs and maps. Indeed, photographs and maps are perhaps the most important tools used to record context. Why? Primarily because context is a spatial phenomenon, and while words and numbers can describe spatial relationships, photographs and maps can do so much better and indeed do it more accurately. Archaeologists typically photograph the floor of each cultural strata in each unit, all features found both before and after their excavation, and at least one stratigraphic profile for the unit. Maps are typically made of the floor of each cultural strata in each unit and of at least one stratigraphic profile in the unit. Thus photographs and maps end up being largely redundant, and that is typical of archaeological records—most of them overlap significantly and purposely with other records.

6.2 WHAT TYPES OF RECORDS DO ARCHAEOLOGISTS KEEP?

Two basic types of records are kept by archaeologists: excavation records and accession records. **Excavation records** catalog the process of excavation itself,

Field Record

Date _____   Area/ plot ____ Square ____   Unit/ level ____   Locus ____

Depth from _____ at beginning = _____ m   Supervisor _____

Closing depth from _____ m

Soil description _____

_____

Munsell readings _____   Wentworth scale _____

Full description and comments _____

_____

_____

_____

_____

Associated features _____

_____

_____

_____

Description of finds and provenance = Associated artifacts
Serial number   Description   Measurements   Catalog No.

Other
Pottery container: No. _____   label _____

Stone container: No. _____   label _____

Photo: Roll no. _____   Frame _____

Conclusions _____   Contact prints

_____

_____

_____

_____

Figure 6.2   A typical level record form.

Source: Reprinted with the permission of Simon & Schuster from *A Complete Manual of Field Archaeology* by Martha Joukowsky. Copyright © 1980 by Martha Joukowsky.

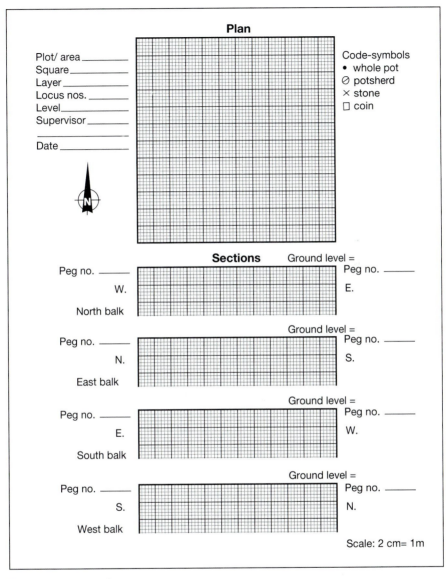

Figure 6.2 (cont.)

while **accession records** list what was found. In both cases redundancy in recordkeeping is explicit. By recording information in several forms and in several different places, archaeologists hope to ensure that nothing is missed, and that in fact small nuances they might otherwise not see can be teased out of the records.

6.2.1   Excavation Records

Daily logs are journals written by all members of an excavation crew explaining exactly what work they performed, the conditions of work, what they found, and any other observations or insights the crew members want to add. Daily logs are meant to provide a narrative, informal portrait of what happened on the site, what was found, and what work was done on a given day. A typical daily log begins with a description of the weather, in order to give readers a sense of the working conditions that day, and any factors (for example, intense heat, light rain, and so on) that might affect visibility or the workers' concentration. The log then describes where the crew members are working, what they are doing, and whom they are working with. As the day goes on, crew members are expected to keep a continuing record of the work they are doing, whom they are doing it with, and what they are finding. Sketch maps of unit floors and features should be included, as should a list of all lots collected and what materials were included in them. Notes should be made of any interesting or unusual finds, of features, of changes in soil conditions— really anything that might be useful to know later on. All crew members are expected to do this so that there will be several overlapping sets of similar notes. This redundancy is purposeful, for by recording the perspectives of all crew members, archaeologists gain a variety of perspectives on the excavation. In addition, someone might note a piece of information that later is crucial to interpreting a unit.

Level records are more formal records completed for each level (arbitrary or stratigraphic) in each unit. They are meant to provide detailed information on how a given level was excavated and what was found in it. A typical level record describes how the level was excavated, who excavated it, when the excavation was performed, and any interesting or unusual features or artifacts recovered. It is important that the individuals who excavated the level and the days they worked are noted, because that information allows archaeologists to go back to those crew members' daily logs for additional information about the excavation of the level. Level records typically also list all lots collected in the level, all photographs taken, all features excavated, and any stratigraphic profiles drawn. In a sense, level records are a sort of summary and index pointing to crew members' daily logs, to feature records, and to lots and photographs from the level (see pp. 90–91).

It is important to distinguish level records from stratigraphic records, which are produced whenever stratigraphy needs to be recorded and are always produced in association with unit and feature records (which I will describe shortly). **Stratigraphic records** depict, describe, and provide an initial interpretation of the stratigraphy (layers) at a given location on the site. In a sense, stratigraphic records force archaeologists to interpret the stratigraphy based on what they know at the time. Stratigraphic records are therefore usually imperfect, because later information may change the interpretation.

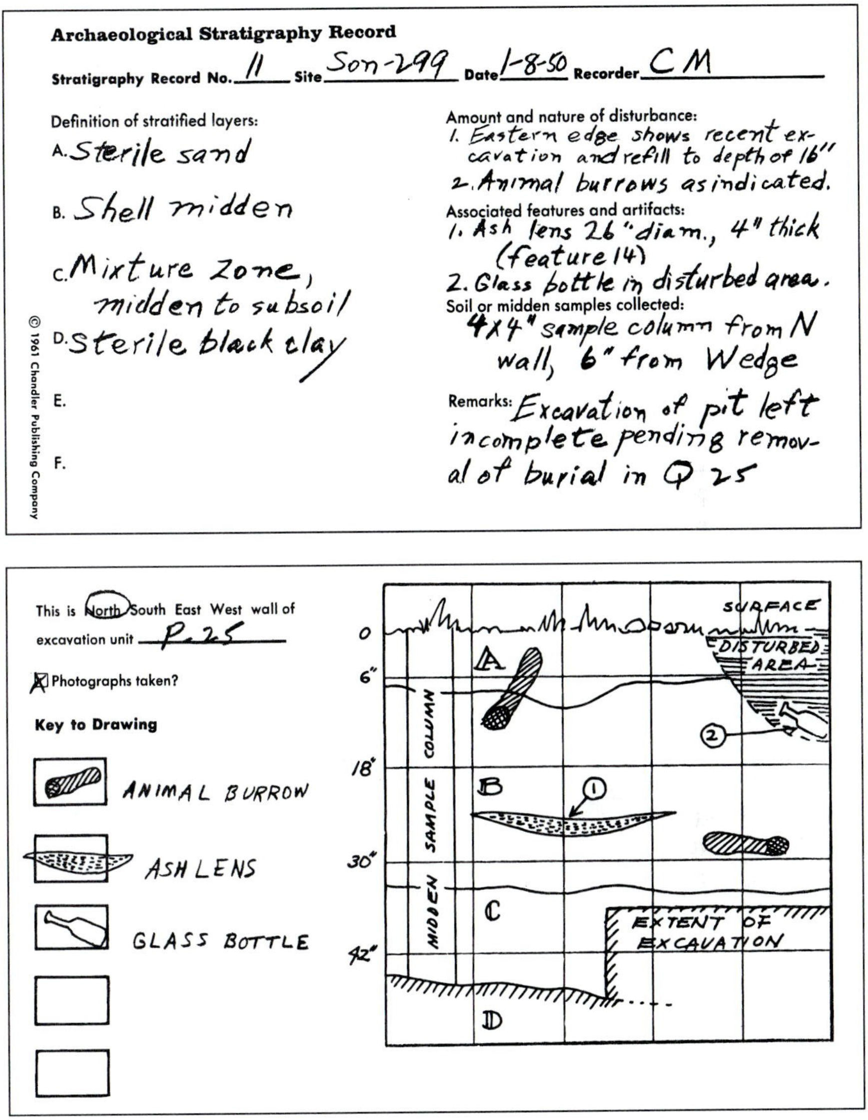

Archaeological Stratigraphy Record

Stratigraphy Record No. *11* Site *Son-299* Date *1-8-50* Recorder *CM*

Definition of stratified layers:

A. *Sterile sand*

B. *Shell midden*

C. *Mixture zone, midden to subsoil*

D. *Sterile black clay*

E.

F.

Amount and nature of disturbance:
1. Eastern edge shows recent excavation and refill to depth of 16"
2. Animal burrows as indicated.

Associated features and artifacts:
1. Ash lens 26" diam., 4" thick (feature 14)
2. Glass bottle in disturbed area.

Soil or midden samples collected:
4 x 4" sample column from N wall, 6" from Wedge

Remarks: *Excavation of pit left incomplete pending removal of burial in Q 25*

© 1961 Chandler Publishing Company

This is North/South East West wall of excavation unit *P.25*

☒ Photographs taken?

Key to Drawing

ANIMAL BURROW

ASH LENS

GLASS BOTTLE

SURFACE
DISTURBED AREA
EXTENT OF EXCAVATION

SAMPLE COLUMN
MIDDEN

Figure 6.3 A typical stratigraphic record form.

Source: From *The Archaeologist's Notebook* by Clement Meighan, copyright © 1961, Chandler Publishing Company.

The purpose of the stratigraphic record is to force the excavator to record information as excavation is ongoing, not to provide a final interpretation of that information. That final interpretation is left for feature and unit records.

Feature records are completed each time a feature is excavated. They are meant to be comprehensive and detailed summaries of how a given feature

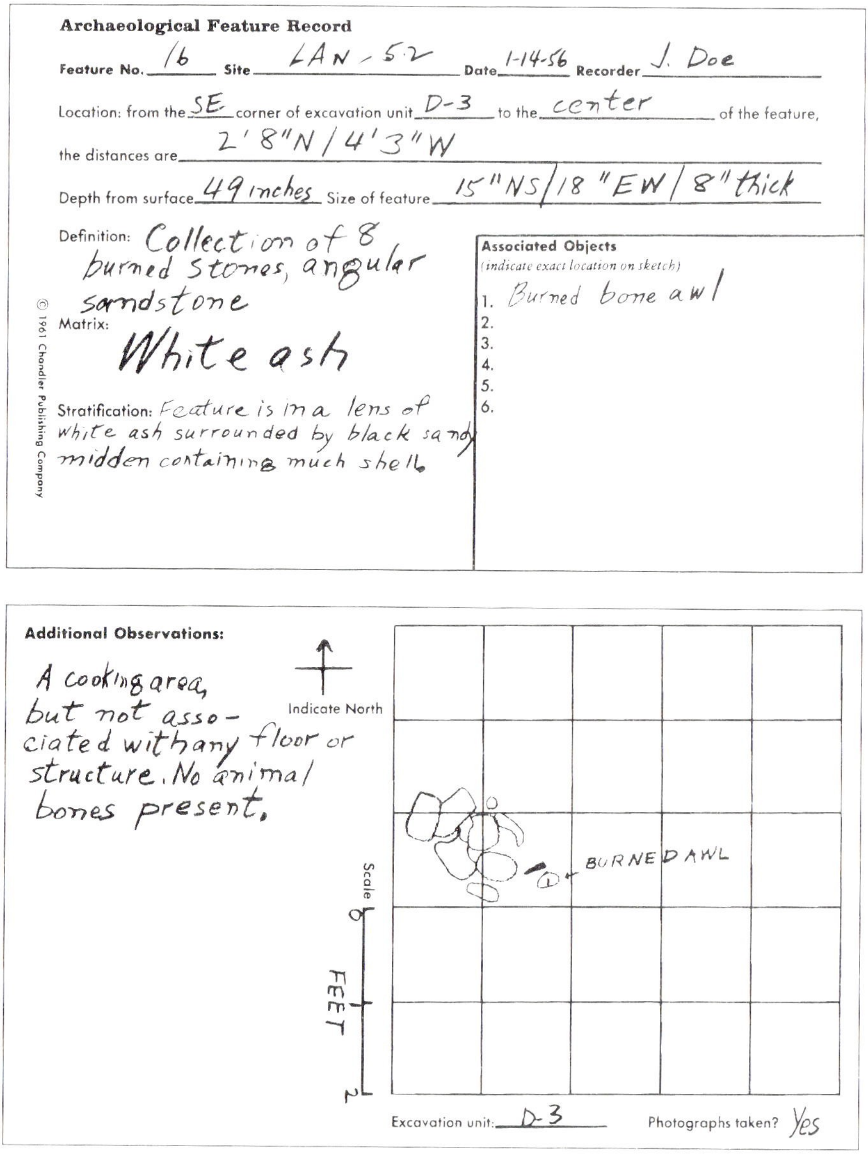

Archaeological Feature Record

Feature No. _16_ Site _LAN-52_ Date _1-14-56_ Recorder _J. Doe_

Location: from the _SE_ corner of excavation unit _D-3_ to the _center_ of the feature,

the distances are _2'8"N / 4'3"W_

Depth from surface _49 inches_ Size of feature _15"NS / 18"EW / 8" thick_

Definition: _Collection of 8 burned stones, angular sandstone_

Matrix: _White ash_

Stratification: _Feature is in a lens of white ash surrounded by black sand midden containing much shell_

Associated Objects
(indicate exact location on sketch)

1. _Burned bone awl_
2.
3.
4.
5.
6.

© 1961 Chandler Publishing Company

Additional Observations:

A cooking area, but not associated with any floor or structure. No animal bones present.

Indicate North

Scale

FEET

BURNED AWL

Excavation unit: _D-3_   Photographs taken? _Yes_

Figure 6.4   A typical feature record form.

Source: From *The Archaeologist's Notebook* by Clement Meighan, copyright © 1961, Chandler Publishing Company.

was excavated, accounts of what was found in it or associated with it, and interpretations of what the feature represents. Typical feature records include not only all the "who, what, when" sort of information in level records but also a formal map of the feature and a detailed description of what was found in it. Feature records, then, serve two purposes: They provide an index pointing to other records (unit, level, daily logs, and so on), but they also form the primary description and interpretation of the feature. A special type of feature record, the burial record, does the same, but may even include information from laboratory analyses of the skeleton or associated grave goods. Another special type of feature record, the architectural record, may be rewritten several times as new units expose previously unexcavated portions of a building. Thus feature records are seen as primary documents both describing and interpreting the features found on a given site.

Unit records are produced each time a unit is completely excavated. These are meant to be comprehensive descriptions of the work done in a given unit and the archaeological deposits found there. Like feature records, they are at once both indices pointing to other records and primary descriptions and interpretations of the unit and what was found in it. They are perhaps the most important records developed, as they are meant to be the excavator's best interpretation of the unit at the time of excavation. They may be revised and updated later as analysis of artifacts, ecofacts, and features brings new information to light, but they are important enough that most archaeologists will spend one or more entire days in the field completing a unit record, checking the information against other records and against the unit itself, and making sure that everything has been recorded before "closing" the unit.

6.2.2 Accession Records

Lot books are used in the field to record the lots or point-plotted artifacts collected each day. They are typically just a list with each line giving information on a different lot and noting the lot number, the unit and level it comes from, what is in it, and who collected it. With that information the lot can be tied to daily logs, level records, and unit records, and thus the materials in the lot can be put back into context.

Photographic records define the location, direction, and subject of each photograph taken, both in the field and in the lab. They typically are lists, like lot books, with each line giving information on a specific photograph. The information included is usually the number of the roll of film, the number of the photograph on the roll, the subject of the photograph (unit and level or the like), who took the photograph, and when it was taken. Again, this allows the photograph to be linked with other records and thus put back into context.

Accession catalogues are used in the lab after artifacts and ecofacts are initially processed (washed and conserved) and provide the numbers (called *accession numbers*) with which artifacts and ecofacts are marked for storage. The accession catalogue is the primary record for all materials after excavation. It links an artifact to a lot, to a unit, to a level, to photographs, to maps, and to the daily logs of the individuals who excavated it. Once an artifact is accessed

Kaminaljuyu Project:
Daily Field Record

Attached documents (please check)

_____ 1. Grid paper
_____ 2. Feature record
_____ 3. Burial record
_____ 4. Photographic record
_____ 5. Radiocarbon record
_____ 6. Stratigraphy record

Recorder _____   Date _____   Zone _____   Area _____
Sector _____

Squares worked

Square _____   Excavated from _____ to _____ cm BD
Objects found (only items of special interest)

Square _____   Excavated from _____ to _____ cm BD
Objects found

Square _____   Excavated from _____ to _____ cm BD
Objects found

Square _____   Excavated from _____ to _____ cm BD
Objects found

Square _____   Excavated from _____ to _____ cm BD
Objects found

Square _____   Excavated from _____ to _____ cm BD
Objects found

Figure 6.5   Kaminaljuyu daily field record form.

Source: From Joseph Michaels, ed., _Settlement Pattern Excavations at Kaminaljuyu, Guatemala._ University Park: The Pennsylvania State University Press, 1979, pp. 17–18. Copyright © 1979 by The Pennsylvania State University. Reproduced by permission of the publisher.

Daily Field Record (cont.)

Feature(s) worked   Designation   Description

Artifact and/or feature associations: Note and describe any and all cluster-
ings of artifacts and/or features, giving dimensions, distances, spatial relationships, and types of artifacts and/or features. Plot all artifacts and/or features in
face view, giving field number(s) and BD(s) for each artifact and/or artifact cluster.

Observation, inferences and interpretations: Evidence for and type of distribution, if any; note also the lack of disturbance; give an interpretation of the cultural significance (activities performed) of the artifactual and/or feature remains.

and marked with a formal number, the number can be used to place it back
in context through the web of records surrounding it—no matter where it
goes—and that is what archaeological recordkeeping is all about.

6.2.3   An Example: Kaminaljuyu

I find it hard to understand an overview like this without a concrete example,
so here's one: the recordkeeping system used for the settlement excavations
at Kaminaljuyu, an ancient Mayan city in the central highlands of Guatemala.[2]
The settlement excavations at Kaminaljuyu were designed to map the pattern
of occupation through time at the site, and the excavations themselves were
performed using a combination of random sample test pitting and trenching.[3]
    The first Kaminaljuyu form we'll look at is the "Daily Field Record,"
which is basically a standardized form of the daily log.[4] The information
recorded here includes the date, the location on the site where work was performed (as designated here by Zone, Area, and Sector), and the specific units
in that location that were worked on. In each unit excavators note the depth
"below datum" (BD) that was excavated and any objects of special interest
that were encountered, including features. What all this information is meant
to do is provide a basic "who, what, where" framework for the work that was
performed on a given day. Future archaeologists can use this information to
reconstruct who was working where on a given day, whom they were working

---

Kaminaljuyu Project:
Feature Record

Document No. 2

Zone _____   Area _____   Sector _____

Date _____   Square(s) _____   Feature # _____

Exposed by _____   Recorded by _____

Provenience

a. Horizontal (distance of center point of feature from N & W walls):

     N _____

     W _____

b. Vertical (BD to top and bottom of feature):

     Top _____

     Bottom _____

Dimensions

a. Maximum length _____   Orientation _____ from North

b. Maximum width _____   Orientation _____ from North

Description

a. Shape (face view) _____

_____

b. Shape (profile view) _____

_____

c. Material (texture, condition, color) _____

_____

Matrix (soil texture, condition, color, etc.) _____

_____

Figure 6.6   Kaminaljuyu feature record form.

Source: From Joseph Michaels, ed., *Settlement Pattern Excavations at Kaminaljuyu, Guatemala.* University Park: The Pennsylvania State University Press, 1979, pp. 20–22. Copyright © 1979 by The Pennsylvania State University. Reproduced by permission of the publisher.

Feature Record (cont.)

Stratigraphy (present/absent; if present draw, describe, and label) _____

_____

_____

Feature comments (stone, ceramics, bone, perishables, charcoal, ash, etc.)

Quantity   Description   Field Number(s)

Matrix comments (stone, ceramics, bone, perishables, charcoal, ash, etc.)

Quantity   Description   Field Number(s)

Artifact and/or feature associations: Note and describe any and all cluster-ings of artifacts and/or features, giving dimensions, distances, spatial relation-ships, and types of artifacts and/or features. Plot all artifacts and/or features in face view, giving field number(s) and BD(s) for each artifact and/or artifact cluster.

Observation, inferences and interpretations: Evidence for and type of distri-bution, if any; note also the lack of disturbance; give an interpretation of the cul-tural significance (activities performed) of the artifactual and/or feature remains.

---

with, what they were working on, and what they found. The second page of the form allows excavators to offer insights or observations about the work performed that day. This kind of information can often be the most valuable recorded. It is not formally recorded elsewhere but with it future archaeolo-gists might be able to answer some particular question or problem with a par-ticular feature or artifact.

A second Kaminaljuyu form we'll examine is the "Feature Record."[5] Here again we see basic locational and personnel information presented first—the "who, what, where, when" identification. Next comes information about the specific location of the feature, its dimensions, and its physical character-istics. Sketch maps would likely be attached to this form to offer a better visual

---

Kaminaljuyu Project:
Photographic Record

Document No. 4

Note: Each photograph shall include, in clear view, a north arrow, a standard unit of measure, and a plaque with the following information:

Zone _____   Area _____

Sector _____   Date _____

Level _____   BD _____

Subject _____

Excavator _____

Photographer _____

Facing _____

Recorder _____   Date _____   to _____   Site _____

Excavation Unit _____

#	Camera	Film & ASA	Level	BD	Subject	Neg #

Figure 6.7   Kaminaljuyu photographic record form.

Source: From Joseph Michaels, ed., *Settlement Pattern Excavations at Kaminaljuyu, Guatemala,* University Park: The Pennsylvania State University Press, 1979, p. 26. Copyright © 1979 by The Pennsylvania State University. Reproduced by permission of the publisher.

of the feature, and photographs would also probably be taken of it. The second page of the form lists the materials found and their lot numbers (called "Field Numbers" here). These first two pages, then, provide basic information on the feature and form an index pointing to specific materials (artifacts and ecofacts) and other documents (daily field records, maps, photographs) that hold more specific information. The last page provides excavators the opportunity to add observations and insights about the feature and to provide an "on-the-spot" interpretation of it.

A third form we'll take a look at is a little different from the previous ones, as it is primarily an index: the "Photographic Record."[6] The photographic record doesn't catalog any primary data itself but rather indicates where that primary data, in the form of a photograph, can be found. Notice that all the basic "who, what, when, where" information is not recorded on the form but individually on a plaque visible in each photograph. All the basic information is carried with the photograph, right on the negative, and can therefore never be lost. The rest of the details add to what is recorded on the photograph itself and provide enough basic information to allow archaeologists to find particular photographs of interest without having to physically look at each photograph and the information recorded on it. So we see that the roll number, camera number, film type, and ASA are all recorded first. This may not seem that important, but it may turn out that a particular roll of film or a particular camera was defective, and the information may help future archaeologists make a useful image from a problematic negative. Next the level, depth below datum, and subject are listed. This information will allow other researchers to find photographs of interest quickly and easily. Finally, the negative number—the unique identifier for that particular image—is given.

Finally, let's look at the Kaminaljuyu "Stratigraphy Record."[7] This form is more of a primary data form than an index or interpretative description. Its purpose is to define the strata in a given unit. Here, then, the "where" information is presented first, but information on "who" performed the excavation of the unit and "when" it was performed are not presented at all. The only "who" and "when" here concern when the form was filled out and by whom. The focus is on the definition of the strata, not on the excavation of the unit. So almost the entire first page of the form provides space to define strata based on soil texture, condition, and color. The second page provides recorders a place to describe disturbances to the strata (from tree roots, rodent holes, or the like). These parts of the form, then, formally identify and define the strata in a given unit. In a sense, they create information through these definitions. The last part of the form is an index, where recorders are expected to note the lot numbers (again, here called "Field Numbers") of materials associated with each of the strata just defined.

Kaminaljuyu Project:
Stratigraphy Record

Zone _____   Area _____

Sector _____   Square(s) _____

Number of layers excavated _____

Recorder _____   Date _____   Site _____

Definition of stratified layers: Define soil texture, condition, and color, and give BDs (top and bottom of each layer); provide a detailed profile view of each stratigraphic section, indicating the layer designation of each stratum as defined below, and place on appropriate graph paper and attach to form.

	Soil sample collected	
1.	❑ Yes	No ❑
2.	❑ Yes	No ❑
3.	❑ Yes	No ❑
4.	❑ Yes	No ❑
5.	❑ Yes	No ❑
6.	❑ Yes	No ❑
7.	❑ Yes	No ❑

Amount and nature of disturbances (if any):

Figure 6.8   Kaminaljuyu stratigraphic record form.

Source: From Joseph Michaels, ed., *Settlement Pattern Excavations at Kaminaljuyu, Guatemala.* University Park: The Pennsylvania State University Press, 1979, pp. 29–30. Copyright © 1979 by The Pennsylvania State University. Reproduced by permission of the publisher.

Stratigraphy Record (cont.)

Artifact and/or feature associations: List all artifacts and/or features found in each stratum by field number. Include in profile drawings of stratigraphic sections all features actually observed, giving their field numbers and a brief descriptive name for each.

Quantity   Description   Layer   Field Number(s)

6.3 SUMMARY

Archaeological recordkeeping focuses on two main tasks: (1) recording context and (2) providing redundancy. The first is the primary job of all archaeologists, as excavation destroys context as it proceeds. Thus archaeological recordkeeping must record context as excavation destroys it. Redundancy performs two important roles. First it ensures that important information will be maintained even if some records are lost or damaged. Second, redundancy makes it more likely that all information is recorded at least once. Excavation records are the basic tools used to record context. They include daily logs, level records, feature records, and unit records, in addition to more specific or focused records. Excavation records also provide information on who did what when and where during the course of an excavation, as well as formal and informal indices to the materials and information collected. Accession records are used to keep track of materials collected. The overall goal of archaeological recordkeeping is to provide the information necessary for other archaeologists to put a site back together as it was before excavation and then go through the whole process of excavation in detail.

SUGGESTED READINGS

Feder, Kenneth. 1997. "Data Preservation: Recording and Collecting," in Thomas Hester, Harry Shafer, and Kenneth Feder, *Field Methods in Archaeology* (7th ed.). Mountain

View, CA: Mayfield, pp. 113–142. A short but complete summary of archaeological recordkeeping.

Joukowsky, Martha. 1980. *A Complete Manual of Field Archaeology.* Upper Saddle River, NJ: Prentice Hall. A brief overview of the recordkeeping system used in large, complex excavations.

Meighan, Clement. 1961. *The Archaeologist's Notebook.* San Francisco: Chandler Publishing. Contains a very short introduction to archaeological recordkeeping and a large number of generic forms for archaeologists to use and adapt in their projects.

NOTES

1. Harold Dibble, Philip Chase, Shannon McPherron, and Alain Tuffreau, "Testing the Reality of a 'Living Floor' with Archaeological Data," *American Antiquity* 62 (1997):629–651.

2. See Joseph Michaels, ed., *Settlement Pattern Excavations at Kaminaljuyu, Guatemala* (University Park: Pennsylvania State University Press, 1979).

3. James Fitting, "Research Design," in *Settlement Pattern Excavations at Kaminaljuyu, Guatemala,* Joseph Michaels, ed. (University Park: Pennsylvania State University Press, 1979), pp. 1–30.

4. Ibid., pp. 17–18.

5. Ibid., pp. 20–22.

6. Ibid., p. 26.

7. Ibid., pp. 29–30

7

The Analysis
of Spatial Patterns

OVERVIEW

7.1   What Is Point-Pattern Analysis?

    7.1.1   Quadrat Methods

    7.1.2   Distance Methods

    7.1.3   Dispersal Methods

7.2   What Is Regional Analysis?

    7.2.1   Central Place Theory

    7.2.2   Network Methods

    7.2.3   Relational Methods

7.3   What about Context?

7.4   Summary

I have been harping throughout this book on the importance of context in archaeological research. But how do archaeologists actually analyze context? That's the question we are going to consider in this chapter. It is interesting, given archaeology's focus on context, that formal analysis of spatial patterns has not been given that much attention.[1] Many archaeologists are satisfied with interpretations of spatial patterns based solely on the subjective assessment of excavators, not on the more rigorous analytical techniques I will describe here. In fact, a chapter like this—on objective and quantitative approaches to the analysis of spatial patterns—is somewhat rare in books on archaeological research and methods. Spatial analysis, in my opinion, is one of the places where archaeology still needs to grow.

There are two basic logics of spatial analysis: (1) point-pattern and (2) regional. In **point-pattern analysis** archaeologists examine deviations from random patterns to identify concentrations of material, trends in artifactual deposition, and the like. In **regional analysis** archaeologists attempt to examine how behaviors structure a settlement system. Obviously a model of behavior is required before this can be done, and regional analysis becomes, in essence, a test of a particular model of behavior against the observed pattern of materials in the archaeological record. Confused? Well, let me explain these two logics in more detail.

7.1   WHAT IS POINT-PATTERN ANALYSIS?

Point-pattern analysis is the simpler of the two logics of spatial analysis and the more broadly useful. The fundamental assumption in point-pattern analysis is that artifactual material will be deposited randomly on a site or in a region in the absence of human behavior or influence. Deviations from a random pattern, then, are assumed to be caused by human behavior or influence. Most forms of point-pattern analysis do not require archaeologists to hypothesize what those behaviors or influences are, but rather simply to define variations from a random pattern, which they are free to interpret as they please. Let's take a look at some of the more common methods of point-pattern analysis.

7.1.1 Quadrat Methods

If you haven't heard the term before, a **quadrat** is simply a rectangular area used for data collection or analysis. Quadrat methods are based on these rectangular areas, employing them as the basic units of data analysis and interpretation. The first step in all quadrat methods, then, is to divide the area of interest into equal rectangular (or square) units. In archaeology this is often easy since excavation units can be used as quadrats (in fact, this ease of transition from data collection into spatial analysis is one reason quadrat methods are among the most widely used in archaeology). The next step is to determine if items of interest are randomly distributed among those units and, if they are not, to ascertain whether comprehensible patterns are present. How do we do this? Well, there are a variety of statistics out there to use, but the most basic one is the chi-squared statistic. In fact, most of the other statistics are just variations on chi-squared developed to make them more applicable to unique cases or types of data.

The chi-squared statistic is formally defined by the equation $\chi^2 = \Sigma(O - E)^2/E$, where O is the observed value of some material of interest in a quadrat and E is the value expected in that quadrat if the distribution of material were random (there is another mathematical formula you use to determine the expected value, but we needn't go into that here). What you have, then, is the squared difference between the observed value and the expected value for a given quadrat divided by the expected value for that quadrat, and the resulting values for all the quadrats summed together. If there are big differences between the observed and expected values, then the squared difference will be large and will be divided by a smaller number; the resulting value will be large. If there are not big differences, the opposite will be true; the resulting value will be small. When all are summed up, a big value suggests there are big differences from a random pattern, a small value suggests there are not. How big the value of chi-squared has to be in order to show a significant deviation from a random pattern is dependent on how many quadrats there are, but standard tables can tell you how likely it is that the value of chi-squared you got was the result of a random pattern.

Michael Dacey used the chi-squared statistic to see whether the artifacts found at the site of Sde Divshon in the Negev desert were randomly distributed. He started (not surprisingly) by dividing the site using the excavator's original 1-square-meter units as his quadrats. He then used artifact counts from each unit to see if those observed values of artifacts were randomly distributed on the site. He found that none of them were. Let's take a look at the observed counts for end-scrapers (that is, stone tools designed for scraping meat off skin and bones). Dacey found that the value of chi-squared for this set of quadrats is 87, which suggests that the observed distribution of end-scrapers would occur by random processes less than two times in one hundred, and that's pretty unlikely.[2]

Tool type	Cell count map	Frequency array		Moments	
		Number of tools	Number of cells	Mean	Variance
End-scrapers	1 1 0 1 0 2 0 2 0	0	16	1.87	2.59
	0 0 2 2 0 0 0 4 3	1	14		
	0 1 3 1 0 1 2 2 4	2	13		
	1 2 1 1 1 0 4 3 3	3	7		
	0 0 0 1 5 2 2 4 3	4	9		
	2 1 2 0 4 5 4 3 2	5	3		
	1 4 4 4 5 1 2 6 3	6	1		
		Σ	63		

Figure 7.1   Observed counts of end-scrapers from Sde Divshon.

Source: From "Statistical Tests of Spatial Association in the Locations of Tool Types" by Michael Dacey.
Reproduced by permission of the Society for American Archaeology from *American Antiquity* 38 (2), 1973.

So Dacey found a big chi-squared value. What did he do with it? All it really told him was that the observed pattern deviated from random. He had to go back to the data themselves, identify where the deviations occurred, and determine what those deviations might mean. This is one of the drawbacks of quadrat methods—they can tell you if a deviation from random occurs, but they can't tell you what that deviation means. Several other statistics can identify if a deviation forms a linear pattern through the quadrats, or if there are empty quadrats in the observed data, but even those require a lot of interpretation. What Dacey did was to examine the co-occurrence of several artifact types; that is, he looked at whether different types of tools tended to deviate from random in the same way. From that he hoped to be able to identify activity areas on the site. Unfortunately, those co-occurrences didn't appear in the data, and he was left with the simple knowledge of variance from a random pattern, not with a good understanding of what that variance meant. Fortunately, several other methods of point-pattern analysis provide more clearly objective information about variations from random patterns.

7.1.2   Distance Methods

Distance methods of point-pattern analysis measure distances from items of interest to all other items of interest and use statistical tests to determine whether the items are distributed randomly. The primary statistic used is the nearest neighbor statistic, which is defined by the equation $C = (R_o - R_c)/\sigma R_c$, where R_o is the observed average distance to the nearest neighbor, R_c is the expected average distance, and σR_c is the standard deviation of the expected

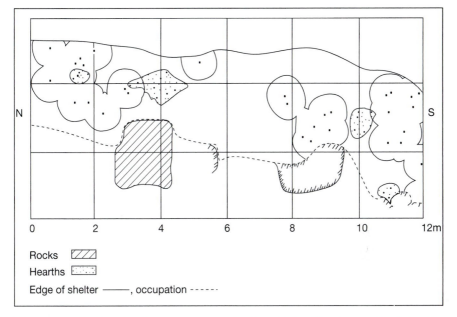

Figure 7.2   Distribution of end-scrapers on the Upper Paleolithic level of Abri Pataud, defined by drawing circles with radii equal to a calculated cut-off point around each item.

Source: From "Spatial Analysis of Occupation Floors II: The Application of Nearest Neighbor Analysis" by Robert Whallon. Reproduced by permission of the Society for American Archaeology from *American Antiquity* 39 (1) 1974.

distances to all the nearest neighbors (that is, the average amount by which the expected distances vary from one another). What we have in this equation, then, is the difference between the observed average distance and the expected average distance, divided by the expected amount of variance in the distances. If the difference between the observed and expected distances is either much bigger or much smaller than the expected variance, then it suggests that the items of interest are, respectively, much farther away from one another or much closer together than expected.

Robert Whallon provided a useful introduction to nearest neighbor analysis in his examination of the French Upper Paleolithic cave site of Abri Pataud.[3] Whallon conducted nearest neighbor analyses on end-scrapers, worked bone, retouched blades (stone blades that had been reworked after manufacture, often to resharpen them), and backed blades (stone blades with one dull side). He found that for all four types of artifacts the average nearest neighbor distances were significantly less than would be expected from a random distribution and, thus, that all four types of artifacts tended to cluster together. But what did Whallon do with this information? Once variation from random is found, how does one identify and make sense of the variations? Whallon used a simple cut-off distance to define clusters of artifacts, but he noted that there are more sophisticated analyses that could be performed on the data.

Indeed, one of the more valuable things about distance methods is that, once variation from random is shown, additional statistical tests can be performed on the distances between items of interest, and these can identify unique patterns or clusters. Some statistics which can do this include discriminant analysis, which uses scores on a set of variables to classify items sharing similar scores into discrete categories, and cluster analysis, which charts the degree of similarity between items on a branching diagram, called a dendrogram, based on the items' scores on a set of variables. Both these techniques are far too complicated to describe in detail here, but it is important to recognize that they produce *objective* groupings of items based on their spatial relationships, rather than simply pointing out that differences from a random pattern exist and leaving the identification of where those differences occur up to archaeologists. An interesting twist on this idea can be seen in what I call dispersal methods.

7.1.3   Dispersal Methods

Dispersal methods of point-pattern analysis attempt to determine whether (1) the patterning of items of interest can be explained by random dispersal from a given point or (2) they have been clustered during dispersal. In a sense, this method works backwards from the other two we have discussed. Instead of

Figure 7.3   Two examples of random walks from a point source.

Source: From *Spatial Analysis in Archaeology* by Ian Hodder and Clive Orton, copyright © 1976, Cambridge University Press. Reprinted by permission of Ian Hodder.

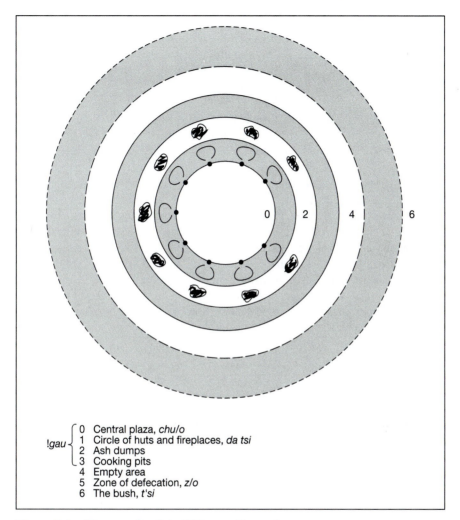

Figure 7.4 Diagram of an "ideal" !Kung settlement.

Source: Figure from *The Dobe !Kung* copyright © 1984 by Holt, Rinehart and Winston, reprinted by permission of the publisher.

taking the observed pattern as a starting point, dispersal methods start with a set of hypothesized patterns and attempt to see if an observed pattern matches any of them. Primary techniques are regression analysis, which measures the degree of linear (or curvilinear) association between two or more continuous variables, one of which might be distance from an item's source; **random walks**, which are used to predict a random pattern of dispersal from a point source; and **trend surface analysis**, which fits equations for relationships among three continuous variables to contour maps. All of these are more complex than we need to go into here, but they illustrate the basic idea of dispersal methods: Create a model of a dispersal pattern and see if the observed data match it. If they do, then you have a good idea of how the observed pattern was created. If such a pattern can be found (and in many cases it can't), you have a powerful vision of the behaviors that shaped the context of artifacts.

An interesting twist on the application of dispersal methods in archaeology was offered by Susan Gregg and her colleagues in an article testing the validity of intrasite spatial analysis techniques.[4] Instead of using random walks to create a dispersal model to test against the archaeological record, they used them to simulate a set of archaeological sites in order to test the sensitivity of spatial analytical techniques. Beginning with an ethnographically described !Kung (a group of nomadic hunter-gatherers in the Kalahari region of southwestern Africa) campsite, Gregg and her colleagues used random walks to artificially "disturb" the deposited material in the campsite. They then applied cluster analysis both to the original ethnographically described campsite and to the simulated "disturbed" campsite and found that, regardless of the level of disturbance, cluster analysis was still able to identify most of the unique household and activity areas present in the actual ethnographically described camp (see Figure 7.4).

7.2   WHAT IS REGIONAL ANALYSIS?

Regional analysis is similar to dispersal methods in many ways. Primarily, it is based on the same basic method of developing hypothetical models of patterning and testing to see which fits the archaeological record the best. Unlike the methods of point-pattern analysis (including dispersal methods), methods of regional analysis assume that the whole region of interaction (a site, a group of sites, and so on) is known and that data are available for the whole of that region. In addition, almost all methods of regional analysis focus on intersite relationships rather than intrasite ones, and most assume active interaction, making the application of these methods to inert objects, like most artifacts, impossible. Because of this limitation, and because the assumption that a whole region is known is often impossible to meet with archaeological data, regional analysis, while powerful, is not used as often as might be expected.

7.2.1   Central Place Theory

One of the earliest, and still one of the most influential, methods of regional analysis is central place theory. **Central place theory** was developed by Walter Christaller in the 1930s as a way to model a "perfect" settlement system given interactions between settlements based on a known set of principles.

Central place theory is complex in its logic and models, but it is founded on a basic "mini-max" principle—that people will minimize the energy they need to expend to get things done or, on the other hand, maximize efficiency. Under this basic principle, Christaller hypothesized that a perfect settlement system would be based on a set of hierarchically nested hexagons with primary settlements in the center of the hexagon and secondary settlements located on either the edges or the corners of the hexagons, depending on the "logic" of the settlement system (whether it is transport oriented, market oriented, administratively oriented, and the like). This may seem a bit bizarre, but even stranger is that it works! For example, G. William Skinner showed that central place theory accurately modeled settlement distribution in rural China.[5] Skinner's work was eye opening to a lot of archaeologists who had assumed that central place theory was only applicable to modern nations; it demonstrated that central place theory was applicable to non-Western, noncapitalist political economies.

In the years following Skinner's publication there have been a number of influential applications of central place theory in archaeology. Perhaps the most influential to date was Gregory Johnson's study of Early Dynastic settlement in a portion of lower Mesopotamia called the Diyala plains. Johnson began by creating a model "lattice" of nested hexagons, based on the administrative and transport structures which most scholars believed characterized Early Dynastic settlement. After adjusting the hypothetical model for variations in landscape and location (for example, those on the edges of the model might be linked into other settlement systems), Johnson found that the model fit the settlement data well and thus provided support for the existing understanding of the processes that shaped settlement in the region.[6] It is interesting, given the analytical power central place theory possesses, that it has not been more widely employed in archaeology. It does have stringent

Figure 7.5 Diagram showing "classic" nested central place hierarchies according to the (a) market, (b) transport, and (c) administrative principles of organization.

Source: From *Spatial Analysis in Archaeology* by Ian Hodder and Clive Orton, copyright © 1976, Cambridge University Press. Reprinted by permission of Ian Hodder.

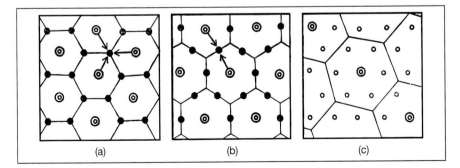

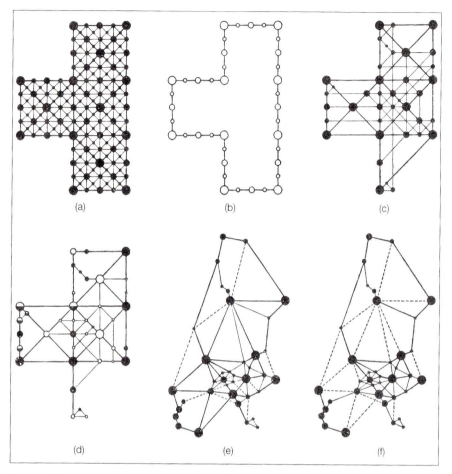

Figure 7.6   Johnson's central place modeling of Early Dynastic settlement: (a) shows the basic lattice, (b) and (c) show adjustments for boundaries and topography, (d) the corrected lattice, and (e) and (f) applications of the model to the actual Early Dynastic settlement.

Source: From *Spatial Analysis in Archaeology* by Ian Hodder and Clive Orton, copyright © 1976, Cambridge University Press. Reprinted by permission of Ian Hodder.

data requirements, and it does take a lot of time and effort in model building and testing, but its potential results far outweigh those drawbacks.

7.2.2   Network Methods

Other methods of regional analysis based on formal models are network methods. **Network methods** are based on hypothesized relationships of communication or interaction between settlements in a settlement system. The hypothesized relationships are translated into a graphical model, with the relationships themselves represented by lines and the settlements linked through them represented by connecting points or nodes. In this way, the hypothesized relationships between and among a group of settlements are represented by a graph. This graph can be used as is to simply describe interactions between settlements in a system, but it can be used in much more sophisticated ways as well. A set of powerful mathematical procedures known collectively as **graph theory** can be applied to discern unique properties of individual points or of the graph as a whole. Used in conjunction with graph theory, a graph of interactions between settlements can provide predictions of settlement patterns based on a particular set of assumptions, or it can allow for predicted relationships to be compared with actual settlement patterns.

I have used graph theory extensively in my work on Mississippian societies in the late prehistoric eastern United States. The Mississippians were unusual among prehistoric societies in the region because they built very large, walled towns in riverine settings. Most scholars suggested that these communities were built because of access to prime agricultural land. I hypothesized that they were built to take advantage of riverine trade. If that were so, I posited, they should be located in places where riverine trade could be most easily undertaken and controlled. Graph theory provided a way to identify those locations. Using rivers as the lines in my graph, and river junctions

Figure 7.7   Network model of the Mississippi River drainage.

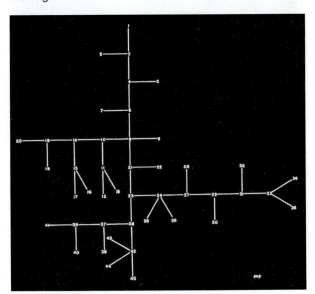

as points, I identified those locations that would have been most suited to controlling riverine trade. I then compared those locations to the locations of known Mississippian towns. I found a strong relationship, which I interpret as supporting the idea that riverine trade was important to Mississippian town location.[7]

7.2.3   Relational Methods

Relational methods of regional analysis are somewhat different from both network and central place methods because they are not based on a preexisting hypothesis or theory. **Relational methods** examine the relationships between settlements based on a particular characteristic, often size. They differ from point-pattern analyses because they don't assume a random pattern, and yet

Figure 7.8   Map of the central Mississippi River drainage showing the "zone of centrality" and major Mississippian period sites.

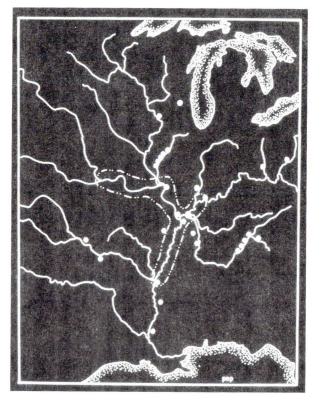

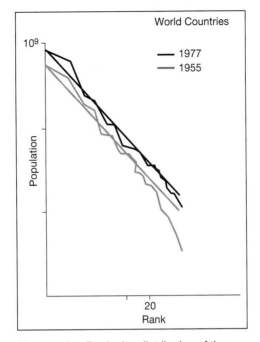

Figure 7.9   Rank-size distribution of the world's fifty most populous countries.

Source: Reprinted from "The Evolution of Primate Regional Systems" by Stephen Kowalewski, copyright © 1982, from *Comparative Urban Research* 9, Fig. 1, p. 72. Reprinted by permission of Transaction Publishers.

they do predict a "standard" pattern from which individual settlements might be seen to vary. In addition, while all of the point-pattern methods can be used on both artifacts and settlements, relational methods only make sense when applied to settlements. The most common relational methods of settlement pattern analysis include rank-size analysis, gravity analysis, and Thiessen polygon analysis.

Archaeologists conducting a **rank-size analysis** attempt to determine whether any settlements vary from a predicted linear pattern of rank versus size. To start, they graph (on a log-log scale) the size of a settlement (in number of people) against its rank (in terms of size) in a settlement system to see if there is variation from a linear relationship. Why a linear relationship? Well, in organized settlement systems a linear relationship is what is found. It is not entirely clear why, but a linear rank-size graph demonstrates a tightly integrated, organized settlement system. Any variation, such as one site being much larger than expected (known as a *primate distribution*), suggests something unique about the settlement system and may help archaeologists understand how

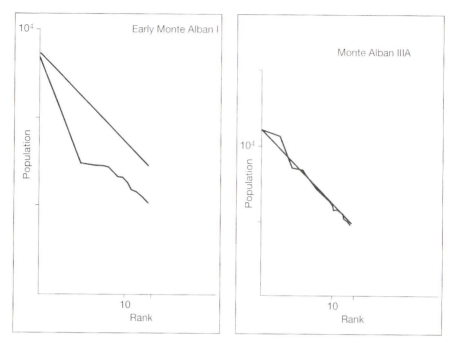

Figure 7.10   Rank-size distributions for the Valley of Oaxaca during the (a) Monte Albán Early I and (b) Monte Albán IIIA periods.

Source: Reprinted from "The Evolution of Primate Regional Systems" by Stephen Kowalewski, copyright © 1982, from *Comparative Urban Research* 9, Figs. 5, p. 7, and 8, p. 74. Reprinted by permission of Transaction Publishers.

the system operates. For example, a primate rank-size distribution was present in the Valley of Oaxaca from the time of the first settled communities (ca. 1500 B.C.) until about A.D. 250. What happened to change the settlement system at that time? Stephen Kowalewski argues that as the Monte Albán state became stronger and more stable, the whole settlement system became more integrated and unified, and thus the primate rank-size distribution, which had been dominated by Monte Albán, was replaced by a more linear one, with the Monte Albán state integrating other sites in the Valley of Oaxaca, allowing them to flourish and grow in size.[8]

Similarly, **gravity analysis** explores variations from a predicted level of interaction between settlements based on the equation $M_{ij} = P_i P_j (D_{ij})^{-2}$, where M is the predicted interaction, P is some measure of the "mass" of the settlements (often population size is used), and D is the distance between the two settlements. Those of you who have had physics might recognize this as the standard equation for the attraction between objects, or the "inverse square rule," and it is. It might seem a bit odd to apply a standard model for inanimate objects to human settlements, but again, it works. Its main utility in

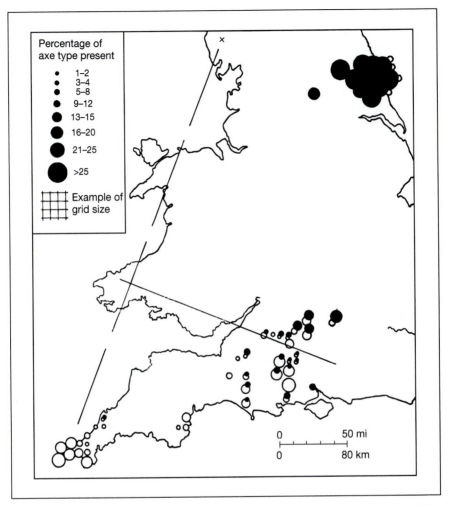

Figure 7.11 Map showing Hodder's drop-off point for Neolithic axe distribution. The dark circles represent Group VI axes and the open circles Group I axes. The size of the circles represents the percentage of each axe type.

Source: From *Spatial Analysis in Archaeology* by Ian Hodder and Clive Orton, copyright © 1976, Cambridge University Press. Reprinted by permission of Ian Hodder.

archaeology is to find deviations from expected patterns, that is, places where the level of interaction between settlements seems to be significantly different from what the mass of the settlements would predict. However, it has also been used to confirm patterns that seem to be apparent in the archaeological record. In one classic example from southern England, Ian Hodder demonstrated that the location where Neolithic axes from one production facility stopped being common and those from another started being common was precisely the location where the stronger level of "attraction" from one production facility to the other also shifted.[9]

Finally, Thiessen polygons have proven to be very useful in archaeological spatial analysis. **Thiessen polygons** are imaginary polygons that surround a site and demarcate that site's sphere of influence. They are constructed by drawing lines between settlements and then bisecting those lines, creating polygons. These polygons can be used to predict the region of political or economic control for the settlements in a system, and they seem to be effective in doing so. One interesting example is the work of Norman Hammond on the

Figure 7.12   Thiessen polygons drawn around residential plazas at Lubaantun.

Source: From *Models in Archaeology.* edited by David Clarke. Copyright © 1972, Methuen, Fig. 20.19, p. 775. Reprinted by permission of Taylor & Francis Books Ltd.

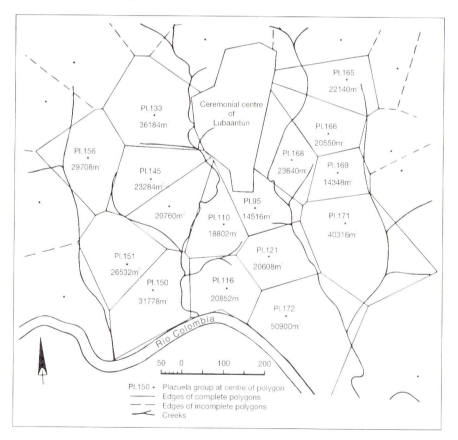

settlement system around the Classic Maya site of Lubaantun. Lubaantun, while containing a large ceremonial district, was clearly the center of a larger region of smaller "plaza groups," that is, small residential groupings that surrounded the larger ceremonial center. Hammond wanted to understand the relationships among these small settlements and the larger center. Were they tightly linked to the center, or did each function as an independent "home base"? One avenue Hammond used to investigate this question was to draw Thiessen polygons around all of the plaza groups, excluding the main ceremonial center of Lubaantun. What he found was that each plaza group appeared to control an area of about 25,000 square meters—much too small to be independent. He also extended this analysis to surrounding ceremonial centers and found they each controlled an area of roughly 1,600 square kilometers. Based on this information, Hammond was able to develop testable hypotheses about the population of Lubaantun, the spread of that population along the adjacent Colombia river, and the extent of the territory of Lubaantun polity.[10]

7.3 WHAT ABOUT CONTEXT?

I started this chapter talking about context and how spatial analysis allows archaeologists to examine it. I've discussed a number of methods for doing spatial analysis, but what does it all mean? Where is context in all this? Everywhere. The spatial relationships between and among artifacts or sites *is* context, and spatial analysis provides a set of tools for examining those relationships in an objective and quantitative way. Spatial analytical techniques are not the only tools archaeologists bring to the study of context; in fact, most examinations of context are simple visual inspections. Interpretations are often based on intuition or experience, not quantitative methods, and there is nothing wrong with that. Archaeologists' knowledge and experience are the most important things they bring to the examination of context and should not be dismissed (as some do) for not being purely objective. The point I want to make here is that spatial analysis can help archaeologists examine context by providing different ways of looking at the archaeological record and different tools for finding patterns. Remember that, when it comes right down to it, there are no right or wrong answers in archaeology, just better and poorer ones. We can never get back to the real past as it actually happened; all we can do is interpret the effects of that past on the material world and hope to interpret those effects in a reasonable way. Spatial analysis is one set of tools archaeologists have to help them do that, and to date I don't think they have been used all that effectively.

7.4   SUMMARY

The analysis of spatial patterning is a central feature of archaeology, and it is surprising that subjective and informal interpretations seem to be more common than objective and quantitative ones. Objective methods of spatial analysis used by archaeologists fall into two primary forms: point-pattern analysis and regional analysis. Methods of point-pattern analysis are generally based on finding deviations from a random pattern and include quadrat methods, distance methods, and dispersal methods for determining what a random pattern should look like. Methods of regional analysis are generally based on a theory of site location and are applied by imposing a model of site location on the archaeological record in order to see similarities and differences. Common methods used to create models of settlement location include central place theory, network methods, and relational methods. All are important, for all provide different views of the archaeological record and different insights to bring to the main task: examining and interpreting context.

SUGGESTED READINGS

Carr, Christopher. 1984. "The Nature of Organization of Intrasite Archaeological Records and Spatial Analytic Approaches to Their Investigation," *Advances in Archaeological Method and Theory* 7:103–222. An important and comprehensive, but very difficult, overview and evaluation of spatial analysis techniques applied to the examination of intrasite artifact patterns.

Haggett, Peter. 1966. *Locational Analysis in Human Geography*. London: Edward Arnold. This is the "bible" of spatial analysis and provides an introduction to all of the methods noted here, and many others. It was revised and expanded in 1977 but is, unfortunately, now out of print. If you are interested in spatial analysis, however, you'll need to find a copy and read it—nothing else is as detailed or complete.

Hodder, Ian, and Clive Orton. 1976. *Spatial Analysis in Archaeology*. Cambridge, UK: Cambridge University Press. An application of Haggett to archaeology, full of excellent examples and clear explanations. Another piece of required reading for anyone interested in spatial analysis.

Paynter, Robert. 1982. *Models of Spatial Inequality: Settlement Patterns in Historical Archaeology*. New York: Academic Press. A good introduction to regional analysis in archaeology, illustrated with interesting examples taken from historic archaeology in New England.

NOTES

1. See the discussion in the first chapter of Ian Hodder and Clive Orton, *Spatial Analysis in Archaeology* (Cambridge, UK: Cambridge University Press, 1976).

2. Michael Dacey, "Statistical Tests of Spatial Association in the Locations of Tool Types," *American Antiquity* 38 (1973):320–328.

3. Robert Whallon, "Spatial Analysis of Occupation Floors II: The Application of Nearest Neighbor Analysis," *American Antiquity* 39 (1974):16–34.

4. Susan Gregg, Keith Kintigh, and Robert Whallon, "Linking Ethnoarchaeological Interpretation and Archaeological Data," in *The Interpretation of Archaeological Spatial Patterning*, ed. Ellen Kroll and T. Douglas Price (New York: Plenum, 1991), pp. 149–196.

5. G. William Skinner, "Marketing and Social Structure in Rural China, Part I," *Journal of Asian Studies* 23 (1963):3–43.

6. Gregory A . Johnson, "A Test of the Utility of Central Place Theory in Archaeology," in *Man, Settlement, and Urbanism*, ed. P. J. Ucko, R. Tringham, and G. Dimbleby (London: Duckworth, 1972), pp. 769–785.

7. Peter N. Peregrine, "A Graph-Theoretic Approach to the Evolution of Cahokia," *American Antiquity* 56 (1990):66–75.

8. Stephen Kowalewski, "The Evolution of Primate Regional Systems," *Comparative Urban Research* 9 (1982):60–78.

9. Ian Hodder, "A Regression Analysis of Some Trade and Marketing Patterns," *World Archaeology* 6 (1974):172–189.

10. Norman Hammond, "Locational Models and the Site of Lubaantun: A Classic Maya Centre," in *Models in Archaeology*, ed. David Clarke (London: Methuen, 1972), pp. 757–800.

8

Ceramic Analysis

OVERVIEW

8.1   What Are Ceramics Made From?

8.2   How Are Ceramics Made?

8.3   How Do Archaeologists Analyze Ceramics?

8.4   What Can Archaeologists Learn from Ceramic Analysis?

8.5   Summary

"**M**ore than any other category of evidence, ceramics offers archaeologists the most abundant and potentially enlightening source of information on the past."[1] So states archaeologist Charles Redman in his foreword to *Approaches to Archaeological Ceramics*. Most archaeologists would accept Redman's statement as right on the money. Ceramics are clearly one of the most important—if not the most important—artifactual materials recovered. Why? Well, first, because they survive well in the archaeological record, and so where ceramics are used, archaeologists can pretty well count on their being recoverable. Second, people regularly change the forms and designs of the ceramics they make, so ceramics are a very useful tool for dating archaeological deposits. Third, people use ceramics to carry and ship items, so they may be invaluable markers of trade. Finally, where ceramics are used to cook and store food they become necessary for life, and political authorities have frequently latched onto this knowledge by establishing control over ceramic production and distribution. Hence ceramics can, in some cases, be useful tools for investigating political organization. In short, ceramics have the potential to provide archaeologists with information about the age of an archaeological deposit and with information on the social, economic, and political organization of the people who used them. Pretty good for something that is basically just dirt, eh?

8.1 WHAT ARE CERAMICS MADE FROM?

Ceramics are made from clay, which, in turn, is basically fine-grained soil that becomes plastic when wet. That's the short answer. The longer answer is that ceramics are made from what archaeologists call **paste**. It consists of the soil itself and both the natural and potters' inclusions and additions to the soil. The determination of the paste composition itself usually requires sophisticated chemical analysis. In recent years archaeologists have even been able to use trace elements in ceramics to identify the specific sources of individual pastes.

Most potters add some form of **tempering** to the paste to give it properties it does not naturally have and often simply to make it hold together better. Tempering can usually be seen with a hand lens and is often used as a proxy for defining the type of paste used in creating a ceramic object. There are four common types of tempering: (1) fiber tempering, where small pieces

Grain classification	Limiting dimensions (mm)	Sieve opening nearest to largest particle	Number of meshes per cm	Sieve number
Granules	2–4	4.00	2.0	5
Very coarse sand	1–2	2.00	3.5	10
Coarse sand	1/2–1	1.00	7.0	18
Medium sand	1/4–1/2	0.50	13.0	35
Fine sand	1/8–1/4	0.25	24.0	60
Very fine sand	1/16–1/8	0.125	47.0	120
Silt	less than 1/16	0.062	93.0	230

Figure 8.1   Wentworth's Size Classification Scale.

Source: Reprinted with the permission of Simon & Schuster from *A Complete Manual of Field Archaeology* by Martha Joukowsky. Copyright © 1980 by Martha Joukowsky.

of plant material are added; (2) grog tempering, where small pieces of crushed ceramic are added; (3) grit tempering, where small pieces of rock or sand are added; and (4) shell tempering, where small pieces of crushed shell are added.

When examining ceramic pastes, archaeologists examine the chemical structure of the paste and the type of tempering. They often combine these two into what they call the texture of the paste. **Texture**—basically whether the paste itself is uniform or irregular—can usually be determined with a hand lens. The uniformity of the paste can usually be defined by examining the largest granules in the paste and relating them to a standard classification scale, such as the Wentworth Size Classification Scale shown in Figure 8.1.

Archaeologists also examine the color and hardness of the paste, as both directly relate to its chemical makeup and its tempering. The color of the paste is measured using the Munsell color chart, a standard set of colors used by soil scientists to define soil types. The paste's color can reflect both the physical material it is made from and the conditions in which it was fired. High-temperature firing usually produces a white or grey paste, and overfiring produces a greenish-grey paste. Firing in a reduced atmosphere (in the absence of oxygen) often leads to a black paste. Hardness is basically a measure of whether the paste is more or less likely to break and is usually measured with the Moh's scale, an index of hardness based on the ability of an item to be scratched by increasingly hard minerals. The chemical structure of a paste, its tempering, and how it was fired can all influence the hardness of the resulting ceramic.

It should be clear that a lot of factors can influence the physical properties of a ceramic. Potters have a range of choices in clay, in tempering, and in

1. *Talc* (can be crushed by a fingernail)
2. *Gypsum* (can be scratched by a fingernail)
3. *Calcite* (can be scratched by an iron nail)
4. *Fluorite* (can be scratched by a glass)
5. *Apatite* (can be scratched by a penknife of ordinary steel)
6. *Orthoclase feldspar* (can be scratched by quartz)
7. *Quartz* (can be scratched by a steel nail)
8. *Topaz and beryl* (can be scratched by an emerald)
9. *Corundum* (can be scratched only by a diamond)
10. *Diamond*

Figure 8.2   The Moh's Scale.

Source: Reprinted with the permission of Simon & Schuster from *A Complete Manual of Field Archaeology* by Martha Joukowsky. Copyright © 1980 by Martha Joukowsky.

firing that all affect how the ceramic will turn out. How are these choices made? How are ceramics pieces themselves built from paste? Let's find out.

8.2   HOW ARE CERAMICS MADE?

The simplest way to make a ceramic item is by the pinch method. In the **pinch method** potters take a lump of clay and shape it by pinching it between their fingers. Related to the pinch method is the **slab method**, in which potters first make large flat slabs of clay that they then join and shape into the desired item. A more common, and perhaps somewhat more sophisticated, method of making ceramic items is through coiling. When using a **coiling method**, potters begin with long and often thick strands of clay that they coil to form the basic shape of the desired item. When working with any of these techniques, potters generally use one of two methods to finish the surface and interior of the item. In one method, called **smoothing**, potters smooth the surface of the object with a spatula of wood or ceramic or some other flat tool (indeed, even bare hands can be used). In the other, called the **paddle and anvil** method, potters use a paddle on the outside and an anvil on the inside of the ceramic object to "hammer" the surface into shape. Potters might also utilize a mold to shape the paste. The molding method is typically employed when many copies of a single form are desired, particularly if the form is very complicated. Wheel-made pottery is the most sophisticated method of making

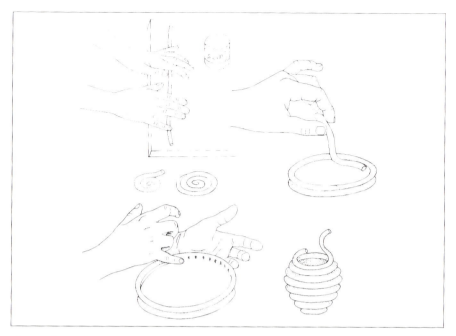

Figure 8.3   The coiling method of pottery construction.

Source: Reprinted with the permission of Simon & Schuster from *A Complete Manual of Field Archaeology* by Martha Joukowsky. Copyright © 1980 by Martha Joukowsky.

Figure 8.4   The paddle and anvil method of finishing pottery.

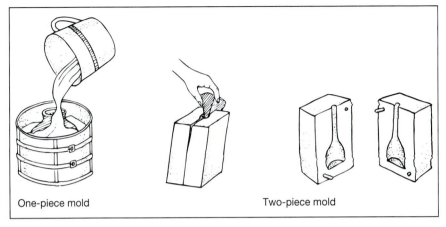

One-piece mold   Two-piece mold

Figure 8.5   The mold method of pottery construction.

Source: Reprinted with the permission of Simon & Schuster from *A Complete Manual of Field Archaeology* by Martha Joukowsky. Copyright © 1980 by Martha Joukowsky.

Figure 8.6   The wheel method of pottery construction.

Source: Reprinted with the permission of Simon & Schuster from *A Complete Manual of Field Archaeology* by Martha Joukowsky. Copyright © 1980 by Martha Joukowsky.

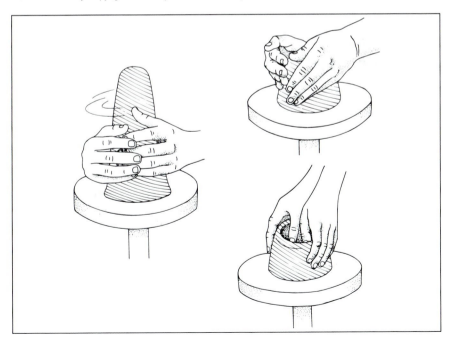

ceramic items. As the name suggests, wheel-made pottery is made on a potter's wheel. It is formed by using centrifugal force from the turning of the wheel in combination with the potters' fingers to "pull" the ceramic out of a lump of clay. It allows for complex, thin-walled designs that would be difficult or impossible with other techniques.

Once a ceramic item is formed, that is not the end of the work. Ceramics are subject to an enormous range of decoration, and indeed it is the rare pot that has no additional work put into it after it has been shaped. Potters might apply a **coating** to the surface of an item, that is, a slip, wash, or glaze that, after firing, will give the object's surface a particular texture or color. Potters might physically alter the surface of the ceramic through **incising and engraving** (cutting linear designs into the surface of the object), **stamping** (impressing designs into the surface of the object using a stamp or paddle of some kind), or **punctating** (pressing designs into the object using a pointed implement or even creating holes in it). Finally, potters might make additions to the surface of the object through **appliqueing** (applying additional paste or other material to the surface) or **incrusting** (impressing material into the surface).

Figure 8.7   Diagram illustrating incising, stamping, and punctating.

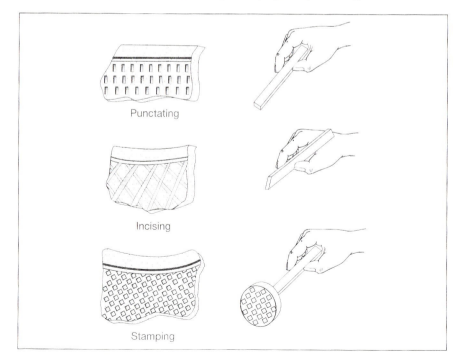

Punctating

Incising

Stamping

So, the ceramic is now formed. It has been decorated, perhaps with a glaze, some surface alteration, and perhaps even some surface additions. But the item is still not done! Next it has to be fired. **Firing** is the process of heating raw ceramics to a high temperature, driving all the water out of the paste, and—depending on the composition of the paste and tempering—causing new chemical bonds to form within the paste. There are two basic techniques of firing ceramics: pit firing and kiln firing. In **pit firing** the ceramics are fired by an open or exposed flame, often with the ceramics in a shallow pit underneath the open fire (hence the name pit firing). It is difficult to control temperature in pit firing, and pit-fired ceramics often have varying coloration, hardness, and even texture due to inconsistent temperatures and levels of oxygen that different parts of the item were exposed to during firing. In **kiln firing** the ceramics are

Figure 8.8   An updraft (a) and downdraft (b) kiln.

Source: From *Approaches to Archaeological Ceramics* by Carla Sinopoli, copyright © 1991, Plenum Publishing, Fig. 2.14, p. 32. Reprinted by permission of Plenum Publishing Corporation.

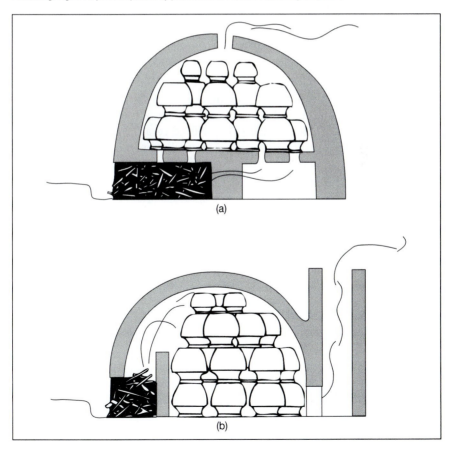

(a)

(b)

Figure 8.9   Polychrome and burnished ceramics.

exposed not directly to a flame but rather to the heat from a fire within an oven-like structure called a *kiln*. It is much easier to control temperature and oxygen content in a kiln, and hence kiln-fired ceramics are generally more uniform in color and hardness than are pit-fired ceramics.

Now the ceramic is finished, right? Wrong. Potters might still apply some postfiring decoration. The surface of the ceramic might be painted, often in one or two colors, but even in many colors, a decorative style which is called **polychrome** in the language of ceramic analysis. Or it might be polished to a high gloss by rubbing it with a smooth rock, which is called **burnishing**. Finally, potters might enhance the decoration through surface alterations or additions. Once these are all complete, the ceramic item is finally finished. Whew! That's a lot of work!

8.3   HOW DO ARCHAEOLOGISTS ANALYZE CERAMICS?

Now that we know how ceramics are made, we can start looking at how archaeologists go about analyzing them. There are four common foci for ceramic analysis: manufacture, form, decoration, and dimension. The focus of all four is really on typology, that is, who made the ceramic and when they made it. Once a ceramic is placed in a typology, it can start being used to answer questions like those we'll look at in the next section. But first, let's take a look at how archaeologists do ceramic analysis.

The analysis of ceramic manufacture has primarily to do with all the things we just finished talking about, that is, paste, construction technique, firing, and so on. Archaeologists have taken a wide range of approaches in order to analyze ceramic manufacture. At one end are approaches like those used by Anne Underhill, who studied contemporary potters in rural China in order to better understand how ancient potters might have manufactured ceramics.[2] Studies like Underhill's are typically called **ethnoarchaeological studies**, because they use ethnographic data to inform the examination of the archaeological record. Related to ethnoarchaeological studies are **experimental studies**, which attempt to replicate particular ceramic forms by experimenting with various production methods in order to understand how those particular ceramics were made. At the other end of this range are microscopic and chemical approaches, such as neutron activation analysis and thin section analysis, which employ state-of-the-art scientific techniques to examine ceramics at a molecular level.[3]

Formal analysis of ceramics, as the name suggests, focuses on the examination of ceramic forms. Archaeologists doing a **formal analysis** attempt to describe the overall shape of a ceramic item as objectively and with as much detail as possible. Archaeologists usually focus formal analysis on body shape, rim and lip stance, and secondary features. **Body shape** refers to the overall form of the object. Figure 8.10 offers one system an archaeologist might use to describe body shape. **Rim and lip stance** refers to the shape of the rim and lip of a ceramic vessel relative to the rest of the object, as illustrated in Figure 8.11. Why do archaeologists focus on the rim and lip? The answer is that they tend to be the most diagnostic. For example, the Oneota people who lived around Lawrence University in the late prehistoric period almost always shaped the rims of their pots like we do the edge of a pie crust—pinching it in regular intervals around the whole pot. When I see a rim with this pinching I know who made it, for it is diagnostic of northeastern Wisconsin Oneota. Figure 8.12 shows a set of rim profiles for northern Syria. Again, you can see that they are all fairly distinctive. This variety in vessel rims and lips is common around the world, hence archaeologists know rims and lips are something they can usually count on to be diagnostic. Finally, secondary features refer to things added to the main body of a ceramic item, such as handles, spouts, or legs, that make it distinctive. Like rims and lips, secondary features are often unique and diagnostic, and if present, archaeologists can usually rely upon them to help place a ceramic piece into a typology.

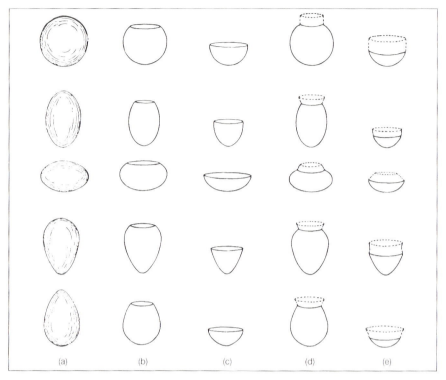

Figure 8.10   Ceramic body shapes.

Source: From *Ceramics for the Archaeologist* by Anna Shepard. Reprinted by permission of the Carnegie Institution of Washington.

Figure 8.11   Rim and lip stance. To gain the stance, turn the rim upside down; when no light appears under its finished edge, its proper stance is known.

Source: Reprinted with the permission of Simon & Schuster from *A Complete Manual of Field Archaeology* by Martha Joukowsky. Copyright © 1980 by Martha Joukowsky.

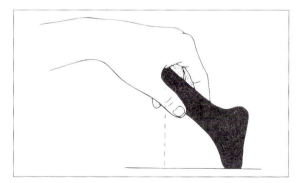

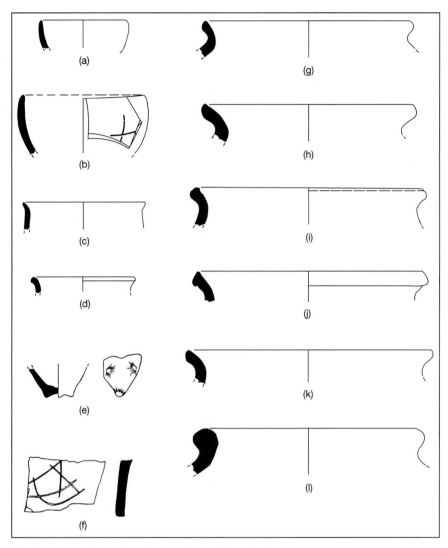

Figure 8.12 Some rim diagrams for northern Syria.

Source: From *Subsistence and Settlement in a Marginal Environment* by Richard Zettler, ed., Museum Applied Science Center for Archaeology, Vol. 14, copyright © 1997, University Museum, University of Pennsylvania, p. 33. Reprinted by permission of University Museum, University of Pennsylvania.

Metrical analysis is often done in combination with formal analysis, as both an aid to and an extension of formal analysis. Archaeologists doing a **metrical analysis** of a ceramic item basically take a set of designated measurements from the item and use those to aid in classifying it. Standard measurements include things such as maximum diameter, rim diameter, maximum height, rim

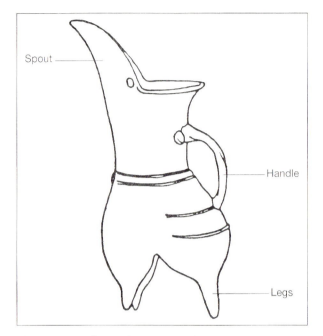

Figure 8.13   Secondary ceramic features.

thickness, and many others. Figure 8.14 shows some of the more common measurements. After taking these measurements, archaeologists would use them to
classify the item into a group with similar measurements. For example, Carla
Sinopoli was able to develop a complex and detailed typology for the ceramics at the site of Vijayanagara in India based on metric traits.[4] With this detailed
typology Sinopoli was able to identify subtle patterns in the archaeological
record, which we will discuss in more detail.

An object's design is the one focus of ceramic analysis that can often move
well beyond simple typology, although it is also a very useful tool for typology.
Design refers to the shapes, motifs, symbols, and the like added as decoration
to the surface of a ceramic object. At a basic level, design can be a great aid to
typology because designs, just like shapes, rims and lips, and other features of
ceramics, tend both to be unique to particular groups and to change regularly
over time. For example, in the southwestern United States a clear distinction can
be made in pottery from the Mogollon peoples and pottery from the Anasazi
peoples based solely on design. The Mogollon painted red designs on brown
unslipped pottery, while the Anasazi painted black designs on white slipped
pottery. Beyond typology, however, the study of design can also be used to
examine the world view of a people. For example, Timothy Pauketat and

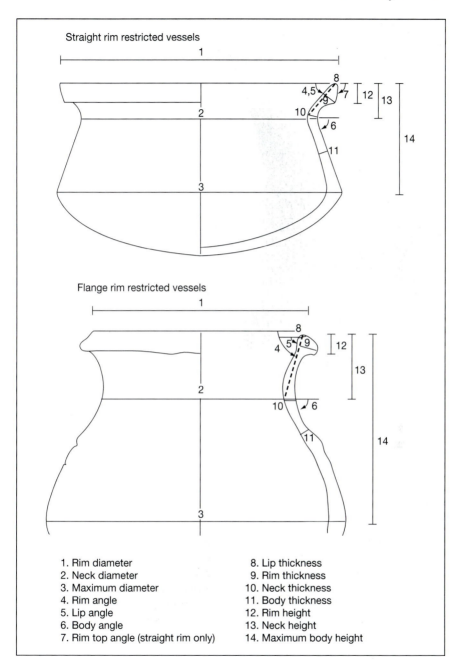

Figure 8.14 Metrical features and measurements of ceramics.

Source: Carla Sinopoli. 1998. "Learning about the Past through Archaeological Ceramics: An Example from Vijayanagara, India," in *Research Frontiers in Anthropology,* Volume I: Archaeology, edited by Carol R. Ember, Melvin Ember, and Peter N. Peregrine. Prentice Hall, Upper Saddle River, NJ, Fig. 2.

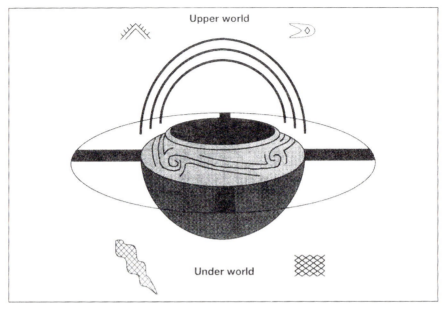

Figure 8.15   Ramey Incised pottery, showing the suggested upper world/under world decorative division.

Source: Reproduced by permission of the American Anthropological Association from *American Anthropologist* 93:4, December 1991. Not for further reproduction.

Thomas Emerson recently suggested that the designs found on Ramey Incised pottery, a type of ceramic made almost exclusively in the American Bottom region, showed a division between earth and sky, a division that was meant to reinforce an existing political structure in part legitimized by the idea that the sky was sacred and the earth profane.[5] In this type of ideographic study, the examination of design becomes a field in and of itself and goes well beyond what I hope to introduce you to in this book (indeed, it is a primary focus of some entire disciplines, including large segments of art history).

8.4   WHAT CAN ARCHAEOLOGISTS LEARN FROM CERAMIC ANALYSIS?

To this point we have learned how ceramics are made and how archaeologists go about analyzing them. But what can archaeologists learn from ceramics? There is, in fact, quite a lot to learn through ceramic analysis, and I'd like to focus on four main areas: dating, trade, social organization, and political organization. Let's take a look at each.

Ceramics are most widely used to date archaeological deposits, and they are an extremely useful tool in this regard. As we have seen, potters have a lot of choice in how they create and decorate ceramics, but the choices individual potters make tend to follow culturally dependent, learned practices shared by all members of their culture. In other words, every culture has a set of norms to which it assumes ceramic items will conform. We eat soup, for example, out of shallow bowls with unrestricted rims. There's no reason we couldn't eat soup out of deep bowls or bowls with restricted rims (in fact, if you go to a fancy restaurant, you might get a restricted rim bowl with a lid for your soup), but we don't. Why not? Because that's not what we expect, and the people who produce our ceramics expect the same things we do, so we get shallow bowls for soup. The fact is, however, that we may not always follow this norm, and, in fact, dish-like bowls were the norm for soup in previous centuries. Norms change all the time, and thus ceramics change, too. By charting those changes through time, archaeologists can use ceramics to develop a highly accurate chronology for a locality or region.

Ceramics reflect cultural practices and norms and therefore reflect people in a particular place at a particular time. This fact, obviously, forms the basis for the use of ceramics for dating archaeological deposits. It also forms the basis for the use of ceramics for examining ancient trade. At its simplest, the examination of ancient trade is just a search for nonlocal ceramics within a particular archaeological assemblage. In more complex forms, the spatial patterning of whole ranges of ceramics can be analyzed to understand how they are moving between and among communities, often using the techniques of spatial analysis we discussed in Chapter 7. Perhaps the most dramatic examples come from studies of Roman ceramics. As the Roman empire expanded, trade between distant regions began to flourish. This trade is recorded in the ceramics in which materials were transported from one part of the empire to another. One focus of research is on amphorae—long, narrow, handled jars used for transporting a variety of liquids, from olive oil to wine, on ships. From the examination of amphorae, archaeologists have been able to reconstruct with great detail trade routes across the empire, to the point of being able to identify when trade originating in particular regions flourished or waned. In one remarkable example, J. A. Riley was able to use stamped inscriptions on amphorae to examine how products from a single Italian estate found their way across Europe, showing both the extent of this trade and the remarkable expansion of commerce.[6]

It may be less obvious how ceramics can help archaeologists understand social organization, but it is related, again, to the cultural patterns and norms that are reflected in ceramics. An excellent example is the work done by Carla

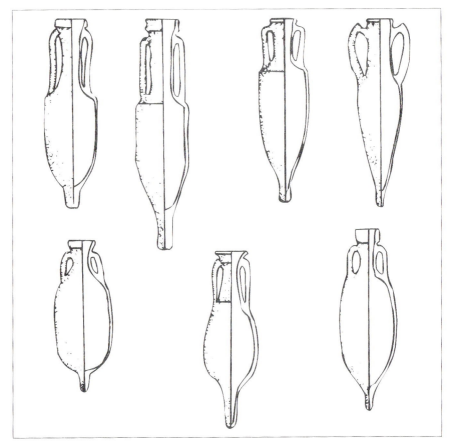

Figure 8.16   Roman amphorae.

Source: From Fig. 5.12, p. 113 in *Approaches to Archaeological Ceramics* by Carla Sinopoli (ed.). Copyright ©
1991 by Plenum Publishing Corporation. Reprinted by permission.

Sinopoli at the Iron Age site of Vijayanagara in southern India.[7] Previous excavations had identified three separate areas of the site: a "Noblemen's Quarter"
composed of elite residences of high-caste Hindus, an "Islamic Quarter" in
which Muslim mercenaries were housed, and the "East Valley," which was
thought to contain residences of lower-caste Hindus. Sinopoli wanted to see
if the ceramics could provide more information about social organization at
the site. She began by looking strictly at the ceramics in the "Noblemen's
Quarter" and found that there were distinct areas within the quarter where
ceramics seemed to be related to different tasks. From this information Sinopoli determined that not all the structures in the "Noblemen's Quarter" were

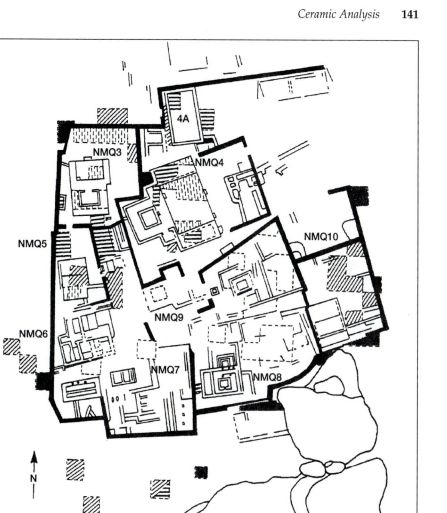

Figure 8.17   Activity areas in the "Noblemen's Quarter" at Vijayanagara.

Source: Carla Sinopoli. 1998. "Learning about the Past through Archaeological Ceramics: An Example from Vijayanagara, India," in *Research Frontiers in Anthropology,* Volume I: Archaeology, edited by Carol R. Ember, Melvin Ember, and Peter N. Peregrine. Prentice Hall, Upper Saddle River, NJ, Fig. 5.

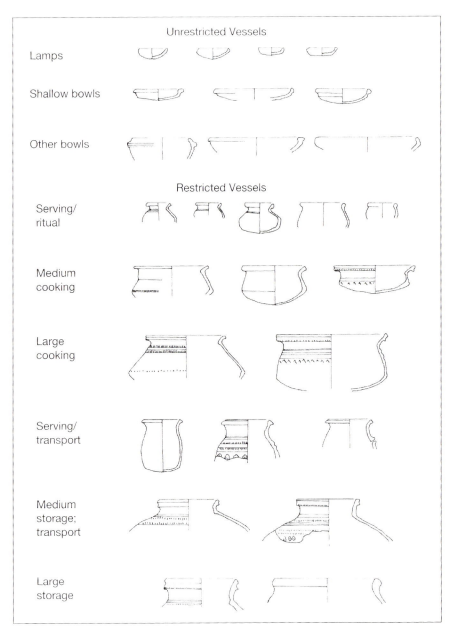

Figure 8.18　　Vessels from Vijayanagara. Those in the top three rows, primarily eating vessels, were found about twice as frequently in the "Islamic Quarter" when compared to other areas of the site.

Source: Carla Sinopoli. 1998. "Learning about the Past through Archaeological Ceramics: An Example from Vijayanagara, India," in *Research Frontiers in Anthropology.* Volume I: Archaeology, edited by Carol R. Ember, Melvin Ember, and Peter N. Peregrine. Prentice Hall, Upper Saddle River, NJ, Fig. 3.

elite residences. Some were apparently servants' residences, and some were administrative buildings. The "Noblemen's Quarter," then, was more than just an elite neighborhood; it was also the center of the town's administration. Sinopoli also compared ceramics across the three areas and found distinct differences. For example, the "Islamic Quarter" had significantly more eating vessels than either of the two other areas, a difference which Sinopoli interpreted as being related to Hindu restrictions on the use of ceramics for holding food. This example shows that ceramics can even inform archaeologists about such nonmaterial aspects of culture as religious beliefs!

Like social organization, it may be difficult to see how ceramics would reflect political organization, but let me offer one classic example as a demonstration. Gregory Johnson was interested in understanding the evolution and maintenance of Middle Uruk period states in the Susiana plains of southern Iran.[8] Ancient texts recorded a system of state-supported labor that required individuals to offer some of their time to state projects in return for rations of grain. Other scholars had suggested that a particular type of ceramic—bevel-rim bowls—might have been ration containers, and Johnson decided to test this idea. He found that bevel-rim bowls could be easily mass-produced, and that indeed mass-production sites were present in the archaeological record. Bevel-rim bowls were apparently created in three relatively standard volumes that would provide, respectively, a day's requirement of calories in grain down to roughly one-third of a day's requirement. These bowls were found on sites of all kinds in the area Johnson studied, suggesting that if they were used for rations, the state system was pervasive—it controlled some labor in settlements of all kinds. Thus Johnson was able to use ceramics to develop a complex picture of state-controlled labor in ancient Mesopotamia. His comments on this provide a nice ending to our discussion: "Preliminary demonstration of characteristics of an Uruk ration system does indicate the importance of such seemingly

Figure 8.19 Bevel-rim bowls.

Source: Carla Sinopoli. 1991. *Approaches to Archaeological Ceramics.* New York: Plenum, Fig. 7.3, p. 152.

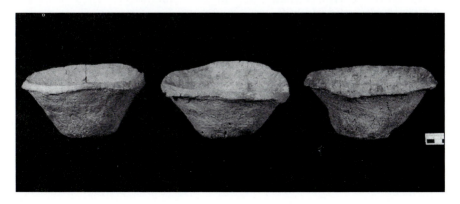

minor data as bevel-rim bowl measurements."[9] Thus, with careful analysis, even minor features of ceramics can provide important insights into ancient cultures.

8.5　SUMMARY

Ceramics are made from paste composed of clay and tempering. They are manufactured by a variety of methods, from simple pinching to the use of a potter's wheel. Ceramics can be decorated with even greater variety. Slips can add color, and modifications and additions of many kinds can be made to the item's surface. Once formed and decorated, ceramics are fired. The archaeological analysis of ceramics rests on examining the many choices potters make during this complex process of production. Potters' choices reflect culturally based preferences and norms as well as technological preferences and limitations. By carefully identifying the various manufacture and design characteristics of a ceramic, archaeologists can place the ceramic in a typology and, from that, determine its cultural affiliation and age. Information on form, manufacture, design, and dimension gained during this analysis can also be used by archaeologists to gain insights into the technology, trade relations, and social and political organization of ancient peoples.

SUGGESTED READINGS

Orton, Clive, Paul Tyers, and Alan Vince. 1993. *Pottery in Archaeology*. Cambridge, UK: Cambridge University Press. Perhaps the best overall introduction to ceramic analysis. Not as detailed as other sources, but with lots of information on how archaeologists actually do ceramic analysis.

Rice, Prudence. 1987. *Pottery Analysis: A Sourcebook*. Chicago: University of Chicago Press. A rich, encyclopedic overview of ceramic analysis methods. A must for anyone seriously interested in the subject.

Shepard, Anna. 1963. *Ceramics for the Archaeologist*. Washington, DC: Carnegie Institute of Washington (Publication 609). A classic and still useful introduction to ceramic analysis.

Sinopoli, Carla. 1991. *Approaches to Archaeological Ceramics*. New York: Plenum. A comprehensive and readable introduction to ceramic analysis, with an emphasis on the kinds of questions that archaeologists can answer using ceramics.

NOTES

1. Charles Redman, "Forward," in *Approaches to Archaeological Ceramics* by Carla Sinopoli (New York: Plenum, 1991), p. v.
2. Anne Underhill, "Investigating Craft Specialization during the Longshan Period of China, in *Research Frontiers in Anthropology, Volume I: Archaeology,* ed. Carol R. Ember, Melvin Ember, and Peter N. Peregrine (Upper Saddle River, NJ: Prentice Hall, 1998), pp. 411–434.
3. These techniques go beyond what we can discuss here, but they are discussed in detail in Prudence Rice, *Pottery Analysis: A Sourcebook* (Chicago: University of Chicago Press, 1987), pp. 371–405. More detailed applications of these methods are described in Jacqueline Olin and Alan Franklin, eds., *Archaeological Ceramics* (Washington, DC: Smithsonian Institution, 1982).
4. See Carla Sinopoli, *Approaches to Archaeological Ceramics* (New York: Plenum, 1991), pp. 53–67.
5. Timothy Pauketat and Thomas Emerson, "The Ideology of Authority and the Power of the Pot," *American Anthropologist* 93 (1991):919–941.
6. J. A. Riley, "Pottery Analysis and the Reconstruction of Ancient Exchange Systems," in *The Many Dimensions of Pottery,* ed. Sander van der Leeuw and Alison Pritchard (Amsterdam: University of Amsterdam, 1984), pp. 55–74.
7. Carla Sinopoli, "The Organization of Craft Production at Vijayanagara, India," *American Anthropologist* 90 (1988):580–597; also "Learning about the Past through Archaeological Ceramics: An Example from Vijayanagara, India," in *Research Frontiers in Anthropology, Volume I: Archaeology,* ed. Carol R. Ember, Melvin Ember, and Peter N. Peregrine (Upper Saddle River, NJ: Prentice Hall, 1998), pp. 365–388.
8. Gregory Johnson, *Local Exchange and Early State Development in Southwestern Iran* (Museum of Anthropology, University of Michigan, Anthropological Papers, No. 51).
9. Ibid., p. 139.

9

Lithic Analysis

OVERVIEW

9.1   What Are Lithics Made From?

9.2   How Are Chipped Stone Tools Made?

9.3   What Types of Chipped Stone Tools Are There?

9.4   What Types of Ground Stone Tools Are There?

9.5   How Do Archaeologists Analyze Lithics?

9.6   What Can Archaeologists Learn from Lithic Analyses?

9.7   Summary

H umans made the first stone tools some two million years ago. The first ceramics were made only ten thousand years ago. That means that lithics have been in use by humans more than two hundred times as long as ceramics! Lithics are, in fact, the primary archaeological remains for more than 99 percent of human history, and that's really a very good thing because the analysis of stone tools can tell us an enormous amount about the past. Before learning something about how archaeologists analyze stone tools, let's learn a bit more about stone tools themselves.

9.1 WHAT ARE LITHICS MADE FROM?

Lithics is a general term applied to all types of stone artifacts, but in this chapter we are only going to consider stone tools, not personal ornaments, statues, or other forms of artwork made of stone. There are two major groups of stone tools: (1) ground stone tools and (2) chipped stone tools.

Ground stone tools are manufactured in a variety of ways, but, as the name suggests, they all typically involve grinding the stone into a desired shape. Creating ground stone tools often begins with **pecking** the surface of the stone, that is, hitting the stone with a harder one to physically crush the surface into powder where the two stones meet. Slowly, by pecking away the surface of the stone, it can be shaped into its desired form. Once the form is achieved, the stone is then ground and polished, usually with sand. Making ground stone tools is a laborious and slow process, but the tools themselves are usually very robust. A wide variety of stone can be used to produce ground stone tools. Most frequently some form of igneous rock is employed because of its hardness and ability to be polished. Sometimes specific types of stone might be preferred, for example, basalts for mortars, pestles, and stones to grind seeds and nuts because the surface of the basalt retains a coarseness even after continual grinding.

Chipped stone tools are made by removing small chips (or **flakes**) of stone from a larger piece of stone called a **core**. A stone tool is shaped by carefully chipping away at a core until the desired thickness, form, and edge of the tool are achieved. Only a few kinds of stone allow stoneworkers to control the size and location of chips: specifically, flint, chert, and obsidian. **Flint** is a relatively pure form of quartz (about 99 percent) that is made up of pure quartz crystals held together in a matrix of impurities. It is black, grey, or brown and is often semitranslucent. It fractures conicoidally along the matrix of impurities, rather than linearly along the planes of the quartz itself. **Chert** is a less pure form of quartz (about 90 percent) and is more common than flint. It is usually white or grey, but can be almost any color. **Obsidian** is volcanic glass, usually black and translucent. It has no crystalline structure and fractures at the molecular level, producing some of the sharpest edges known. This property also makes it very easy to work.

Flint, chert, and obsidian are all usually found in localized outcroppings, and it is not unusual to find ancient quarries in locations where particularly pure forms of these stones appear. When not directly quarried from an outcropping, all three types of stone can be found in **nodules**—raw globular chunks of stone often with a weathered, chalky surface called a **cortex**. Because not all people on earth had access to high-quality stone, a method of improving poorer stone, called heat treating, was developed. In **heat treating** stoneworkers bake a flint or chert nodule in a high temperature (350°–500° F) for thirty to fifty hours. This was often accomplished by burying nodules underneath a hearth for several days. Heat treating apparently increases the density of the matrix of impurities that hold the quartz together, allowing fracture to occur both along the matrix of impurities and along the lines of the crystalline structure of the quartz. It may also cause microfractures to form within the nodule. In either case, heat treating significantly increases the workability of the stone.

The manufacture of ground stone tools may seem pretty straightforward, but I'll bet you're at least a little confused about the process of making chipped stone tools. A lot of lithic analysis is actually focused on examining variations in the way stone is chipped, so it's probably a good idea to take a closer look at how chipped stone tools are made before going much farther.

9.2 HOW ARE CHIPPED STONE TOOLS MADE?

Chipped stone tools are made by chipping away at a big piece of flint, chert, or obsidian until a tool of the desired form is achieved. But the way that chipping proceeds takes on some fairly standardized forms and is based on a unique facet of the stone used to make these tools. When struck, flint, chert, and obsidian all fracture in a conical manner, exactly like a car windshield does when it is hit straight on by a rock. The force of the blow moves outward through the rock from the point of percussion, making a conical shape that, if the force meets an edge and is directed back into the rock, will break off a piece of the stone. If you've ever seen a car windshield hit by a rock or a window hit by a BB you'll understand what I mean. A small cone of the glass

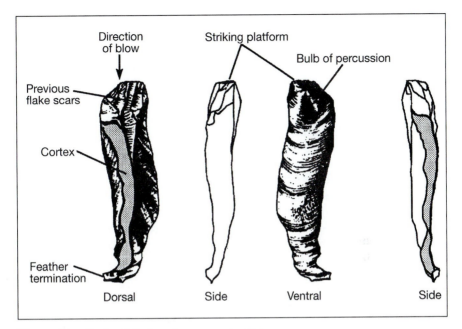

Figure 9.1   Basic attributes of a percussion flake.

Source: Robert Kelly. 1998. "Lithic Analysis: Chipped Stone Tools and Waste Flakes in Archaeology," in *Research Frontiers in Anthropology*, Volume I: Archaeology, edited by Carol R. Ember, Melvin Ember, and Peter N. Peregrine. Prentice Hall, Upper Saddle River, NJ, Fig. 2.

is broken off, with the point at the location where the rock or BB first struck. The key for making stone tools is that if the force of the blow is directed at an edge, it causes a flake of stone, rather than a cone, to be knocked off. The force of the blow, distance from the edge, and its direction all factor into the size and shape of the flake that is chipped off. Stoneworkers learn to regulate how and where they hit rocks and thus learn to control the size and shape of flakes they chip off them. By carefully chipping away at a nodule, stoneworkers essentially carve the stone by removing flakes of particular sizes and shapes until they achieve the desired tool.[1]

Percussion flaking is the most common way stoneworkers remove flakes. In **percussion flaking**, flakes are driven off a piece of stone by striking it with another stone, an antler, or even a piece of hardwood. This type of flaking results in "classic" flakes like those illustrated in Figure 9.1. When these flakes are struck off using a stone, it is called a **hard hammer technique**, and the flakes produced tend to be large and thick. Striking flakes from a piece of stone with an antler or piece of hardwood is called a **soft hammer technique**, and the flakes produced tend to be long and thin. Pressure flaking is the other common way stoneworkers remove flakes. In **pressure flaking**, flakes are pried or pushed off a piece of stone by pressure from an antler tine or other soft tool. This results in very small and extremely thin flakes with no obvious **bulb of percussion**.

The flakes produced during the process of making a chipped stone tool are distinct, and archaeologists have classified them into three basic types. **Primary flakes** (also called *decortication flakes*) are large thick flakes struck off a nodule when removing the cortex and preparing it for working. They are fashioned by a hard hammer technique and can be easily identified because they have a piece of the cortex on them. **Secondary flakes** (also called *reduction flakes*) are large flakes struck off a piece of stone to reduce its size and/or thickness. They are usually produced using a hard hammer technique and can be identified by their size and by the number of flake scars (the marks where earlier flakes were struck off the nodule) they carry. Secondary flakes usually have only a couple of very large scars. **Tertiary flakes** (also called *production flakes*) are smaller flakes struck off a piece of stone to shape it into a tool. These are usually created by a soft hammer technique and so are thinner and finer than either primary or secondary flakes. They usually carry more flake scars as well. Some kinds of tools require additional work, which produces unique types of flakes. Pressure flakes (sometimes called *retouching flakes*) are tiny extremely thin flakes pinched or pushed off a tool to finish shaping it or to resharpen or reshape it. They are produced by a pressure flaking technique and are usually so thin that light can be seen through them. **Notching flakes** result from putting hafting notches in stone tools by pressure flaking and thus are small thin flakes. They also have a unique, half-cone shape that clearly identifies them.

9.3 WHAT TYPES OF CHIPPED STONE TOOLS ARE THERE?

Now that we have a better idea of how chipped stone tools are made, let's take a look at some of them. The one that probably comes to mind when you think of a chipped stone tool is a projectile point. **Projectile points** come in all shapes and sizes, from tiny triangular arrow heads only a centimeter or so in length to large spearpoints 15 or more centimeters long. Projectile points also show a variety of hafting styles. **Hafting** is the term given to the manner in which a projectile point (or other stone tool) is attached to a handle or shaft. Projectile points are usually hafted by placing notches so that sinew or fiber chord can be wrapped around the point to hold it in place on a spear or arrow shaft. These notches are often distinctive and are frequently used (as we will see) to classify projectile point types.

Projectile points may be the most obvious chipped stone tool, but they are not the most common. The most common chipped stone tool is the flake. **Flake tools** can be either created on purpose or simply struck off in the process

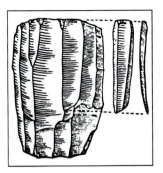

Figure 9.2 A prepared core and blade.

Source: From *The Old Stone Age* by François Bordes, World University Library, McGraw Hill Book Company. Copyright © 1968 by François Bordes.

Figure 9.3 Some chipped stone tools of the Upper Paleolithic Period: (a) Chatelperronian knife point; (b) Gravettian knife point; (c) Trapezoid blade; (d) Perigordian (Gravettian) graver or burin; (e) Aurignacian nosed graver; (f) Aurignacian burin; (g) Magdalenian graver; (h) strangulated blade; (i) nosed scraper; (j) end-scraper; (k) Solutrean piercer or "hand drill;" (l) double-ended grattoir; (m) Magdalenian blade core; (n) saw blade fragment; (o) Magdalenian concave end-scraper or "spokeshave."

Source: From K. P. Oakley. Courtesy of The Natural History Museum, London.

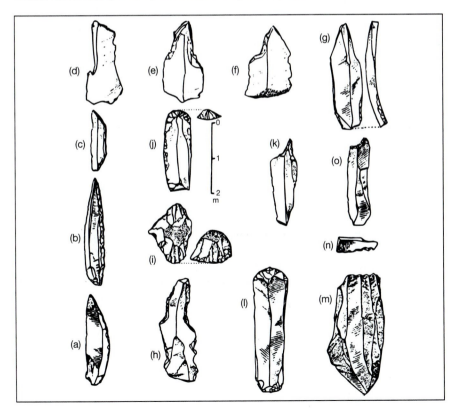

of making some other tool. In either case, they are sharp, plentiful, and can be used for a wide variety of tasks. Purposely created flake tools include **backed flakes**, which are usually decortication flakes that retain a piece of the cortex on one side and a sharp edge on the other, so that users can hold the flake with the cortex toward their hands, providing a safe and easy grip. **Blades** , the other type of purposely created flake tool, are usually made from a **prepared core**, which has been shaped to easily produce blades. A prepared core looks somewhat like a faceted jewel, and from each facet a blade can be struck. In a sense, stoneworkers "unwrap" a prepared core, striking blades from around its exterior continuously until the core becomes so small that useful blades cannot be removed. Blades can be used as is, they can be modified into other tools, or they can be combined into what are called composite tools. For example, a series of small blades can be placed into a goat jaw in place of the teeth to make an effective sickle for harvesting grasses.

There are a lot of other tools made from chipped stone, too. Knives are one common type sometimes confused with projectile points because of the similar shape and because both can be notched for attaching to a handle. Drills are other chipped stone tools that are commonly found, and they tend to be obvious in their distinctive "T" shape. **Scrapers**, another common tool, are used to scrape the meat from a hide and are distinctive in having one edge chipped on an extreme oblique angle. **Burins** are less common chipped stone tools but are still regularly found. They have a single, sharp point used for engraving wood or bone. Finally, in some places hoes are made from chipped stone. These are often obvious due to their size and shape.

9.4 WHAT TYPES OF GROUND STONE TOOLS ARE THERE?

Now that we have taken a good look at how chipped stone tools are made and at the variety of chipped stone tools found in the archaeological record, let's take a look at ground stone tools. As I explained earlier, ground stone tools are usually made from granite or basalt and are shaped by grinding them against other stones or with a sand and water mix, rather than by striking flakes from them. Thus, ground stone tools take a lot of effort to produce, and because of that their use falls into a much narrower range than that of chipped stone tools. They are used for tasks that cause the tool to take a repeated beating during use, which would either continually knock flakes from a chipped stone tool or outright break it. Ground tools are also used when a highly polished finish is desired.

Perhaps the most common use of ground stone tools is to work wood, and the most common form of woodworking tool is the axe. Ground stone axes come in three basic forms: full-grooved (an axe with a hafting groove

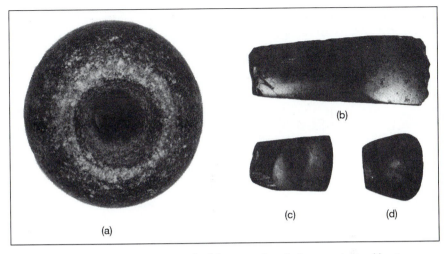

Figure 9.4   Some ground stone tools: (a) a mace head of green stone with an hourglass perforation photographed from above; (b) a polished axe head of a greenish-grey stone; (c) an adze of a greenish-grey stone; (d) a fragmented diorite (?).

Source: Reprinted with the permission of Simon & Schuster from *A Complete Manual of Field Archaeology* by Martha Joukowsky. Copyright © 1980 by Martha Joukowsky.

running all the way around it), three-quarter-grooved (an axe with a hafting groove running three-quarters of the way around it, usually flat on the ungrooved side), and ungrooved, which is usually called a **celt**. Adzes are celts with a channeled blade used for carving. Stone axes do not get nearly as sharp as metal ones, but they are effective when used correctly. They are hafted on a flexible shaft (rather than the very stiff shaft that metal axes are hafted onto), and they are used in short, rapid swings, which take advantage of the flexible shaft to accelerate the axe head. Wood is not really cut with a stone axe but is rather pulped or mashed by the axe blade.

A second common use of ground stone tools is in processing seeds and nuts. One of two combinations of tools is used for these tasks: the mortar and pestle or the mano and metate. A mortar is basically a large stone bowl, while a pestle is a hand-held stone rod used to grind or pound items in the mortar. Similarly, a metate is a large rectangular stone, often with a depressed area in the center, and a mano is a smaller, flat stone used in combination with the metate to grind seeds or nuts.

A third common use of ground stone tools is where highly polished items are needed or desired. Some of these items are often called birdstones, bannerstones, or boatstones, but they are all known to be atl-atl weights. An **atl-atl** is a wooden or bone shaft with a hook on the end to help throw a spear. Weights are often attached to atl-atls to add force to the throw, and these

Figure 9.5   An atl-atl in use. Note the weight attached to the shaft.

Source: Courtesy the William S. Webb Museum of Anthropology. University of Kentucky.

weights are typically highly polished dense stone because of its beauty and weight. Similarly, stones used to weight a bolas (a three-ended chord that is thrown at the legs of animals to ensnare them) are often of ground stone because of its durability and beauty. Finally, many decorative items that may or may not be used as utensils, such as pipes, gorgets, figurines, and the like, are made of ground stone for similar reasons: durability and beauty.

9.5 HOW DO ARCHAEOLOGISTS ANALYZE LITHICS?

Now that we know something about stone tools and how they are made, we can take a look at some of the ways archaeologists analyze them. Techniques of lithic analysis can be divided into four major groups: form, use, manufacture, and dimension.

Formal analysis, the description of a stone item's physical form, is by far the most common and most fundamental aspect of lithic analysis. Formal analysis has deep roots in archaeology and is still one of the basic sets of knowledge all archaeologists (in the United States anyway) have to learn. For this discussion let's consider only projectile points, as they are the most widely studied lithics. Three basic aspects are considered in the formal analysis of projectile points: shape, edge, and notching. Material and manufacturing technique also play a part, but not as large a one as these others. In examining a projectile point's shape, archaeologists consider whether the point is triangular or lancolate (that is, much longer than wide), and whether the edges are excurvate or incurvate. In considering the projectile point's edge, archaeologists determine whether it shows evidence of beveling, of serration, or of grinding. Finally, they examine the **notching** style, if any is present (see Figure 9.6). Typical styles of notching include corner notching, side notching, basal notching, stemming (not really a style of notch but more a style of forming the end of the projectile point), and fluting (also not really a notch but a long flake of stone removed from each side of the projectile point to thin it).

Once archaeologists have identified the shape, edge, and notching of a projectile point, they can go to reports from the area where the point was found, or to more general catalogues of projectile point types, and determine the point's typology. Knowledge of typology provides information on dating the deposit in which the point was found, on cultural affiliations, and perhaps on trade and exchange. In addition to simple typology, formal analysis can also provide some information about the point's use. Small, triangular points suggest the hunting of birds or small game, while larger points suggest the hunting of larger animals. Serrated edges are often used to hunt animals with thick hides, while points with large barbs (as are created in corner notching) are used to hunt animals that are likely to run or otherwise try to remove the point from their bodies.[2]

The use to which a particular stone tool was put can often be more adequately discovered through a technique called *use-wear analysis*. **Use-wear analysis** is based on examining, usually under a high-powered microscope, the patterns of wear, which have been found to be directly correlated with how the tool was used. In one classic study, Dorothy Garrod and Dorothea Bate were able to demonstrate that microlithic blade tools had been used to cut grasses (wheat and barley) because of the patina that built up on them from the silica in the grass stems.[3] In another interesting study, Lawrence Keeley examined Acheulean artifacts (associated with *Homo erectus*) from three sites in England and found that hand axes were multipurpose tools for cutting meat and wood and even for digging (see Figure 9.7).[4] He also found that, at one site, what archaeologists had defined as chopping tools were actually rarely used, but that flakes apparently struck from them were often used. So, what archaeologists thought were tools (choppers) were actually debris from making flakes, and what archaeologists thought were debris (flakes) were actually tools! Oddly, there are some who still believe use-wear analysis is inherently subjective, even though empirical and experimental tests have demonstrated great reliability.

Recently, archaeologists have also realized that information about stone tool manufacture can often provide much of the information about style, cultural affiliation, and use that formal analysis can, in addition to an

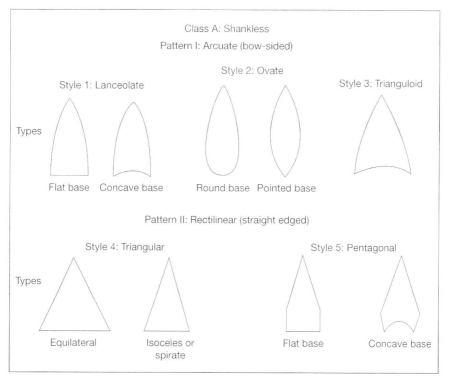

Pattern II: Rectilinear (straight edged)

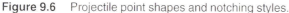

Figure 9.6   Projectile point shapes and notching styles.

Source: "Projectile point shapes and notching styles" from *Artifacts of Prehistoric America* by Louis A. Brennan, copyright © 1980 Stackpole Books. Reprinted by permission of Stackpole Books.

understanding of the organization of stone tool production. The reason for this is simple, though perhaps not obvious. Stone tools are made by striking flakes from a core or nodule of stone. Particular types of flakes (for example, notching flakes) appear only when particular types of tools are being made. Similarly, different groups worked stone in slightly different ways, and those subtle differences can be apparent in the flakes left from their stoneworking. More significantly, if all or most of those flakes can be recovered, then the process of how the tool was made can be reconstructed and, in turn, the tool can be readily inferred. The act of rebuilding a nodule from the flakes struck from it is called **refitting** (see Figure 9.8). Although time consuming and tedious, refitting studies allow archaeologists to physically go through the process (albeit in reverse) of tool-making. They can see precisely how stoneworkers chose to work the stone and, in reality, come close to entering stoneworkers' minds, seeing how decisions were made.

Finally, **metrical analyses** are finding that subtle variations in the sizes and shapes of chipped stone artifacts can yield a wealth of information about

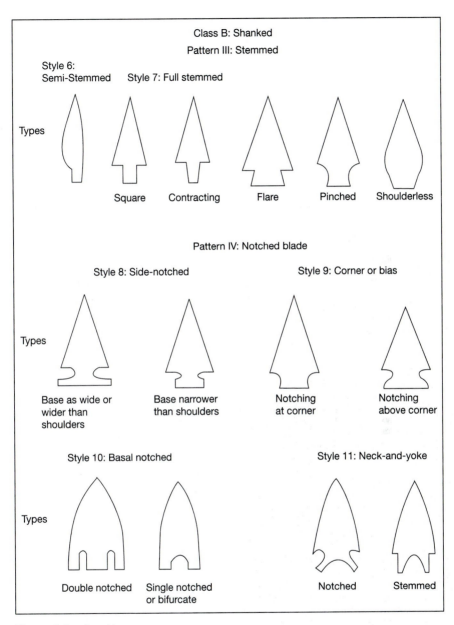

Figure 9.6 *(cont.)*

manufacture, use, and even social organization. Traits commonly measured for metrical analyses include thickness, maximum length, maximum width, and the like. As with metrical analysis of ceramics, archaeologists are finding

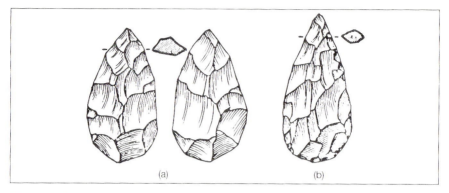

Figure 9.7   Acheulean hand axes.

Source: From *The Old Stone Age* by François Bordes, World University Library, McGraw Hill Book Company. Copyright © 1968 by François Bordes.

Figure 9.8   A refit stone tool.

Source: From Fig. 7, p. 363 by Toby Morrow, in *Stone Tools: Theoretical Insights into Human Prehistory*, G. Odell (ed). Copyright © 1996 Plenum Publishing Corporation. Reprinted by permission of Plenum Publishing Corp. and the author.

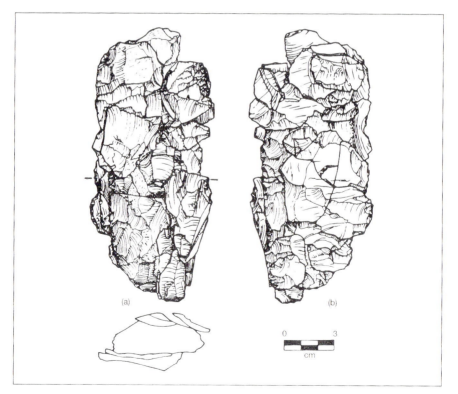

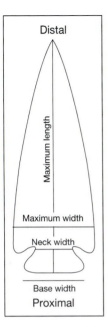

Figure 9.9 Standard metrical measurements made of chipped stone tools.

Figure 9.10 African (a–e) and western Eurasian (f–i) Middle Paleolithic projectile points, illustrating differences.

Source: From Fig. 1, p. 82 by John Shea, in *Projectile Technology,* by Heidi Knecht (ed.). Copyright © 1997 by Plenum Publishing Corporation. Reprinted by permission of Plenum Publishing Corporation.

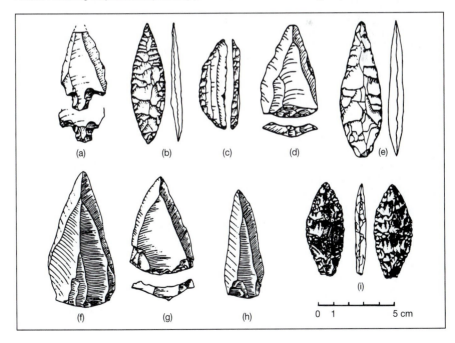

that by combining typological information gained through formal analysis with metric data, very fine typologies can be created, some of which can yield valuable insights. For example, John Shea recently used metrical analysis to aid in understanding how projectile points might have been used by Middle Paleolithic hunters in Europe and Africa.[5] Shea's research is rooted in an ongoing debate among archaeologists about whether Middle Paleolithic peoples used stone points for projectiles, or whether they were simply knives or other cutting utensils. Shea employed a variety of analytic techniques, including formal and use-wear analysis, to examine this question, but one of the most telling was his use of metrical analysis. He found that both European and African Middle Paleolithic points shared metrical patterns related to known projectile point types. However, only African and Near Eastern Middle Paleolithic points showed use-wear related to known projectile points. Shea suggests this may point to behavioral differences between European Neandertal populations and archaic *Homo sapiens* populations living at the same time in Africa and the Near East.

9.6 WHAT CAN ARCHAEOLOGISTS LEARN FROM LITHIC ANALYSES?

Some of what can be learned from lithic analysis has already been hinted at in the examples just given, but let's take a closer look at categories of information about which lithics can help archaeologists learn. Specifically, let's consider the information lithic analysis can provide archaeologists about dating, technology, and social organization.

Dating archaeological deposits is the single most common goal to which lithic analysis is directed. From the very beginning of archaeological research, archaeologists realized that stone tool technology and stone tool forms changed regularly over time, and that those changes could be used to establish local and regional chronologies. Indeed, some of the earliest publications in lithic analysis focus on establishing chronologies, and, in credit to those pioneering archaeologists, many are still in use today.

The exploration of technology can lead to valuable insights about both ancient societies and ancient peoples themselves. One common area of investigation focuses on evidence for craft specialization and whether specialists worked for political leaders.[6] But even more interesting are studies of lithics that consider how and why individuals may have chosen to make or use particular styles of stone tools. For example, Steven Rosen considers the long transition of stone tools to metal tools in terms of individual preferences and choices.[7] He demonstrates that stone tools survived in many contexts well after the introduction of metal. Why? Rosen argues that people made distinct

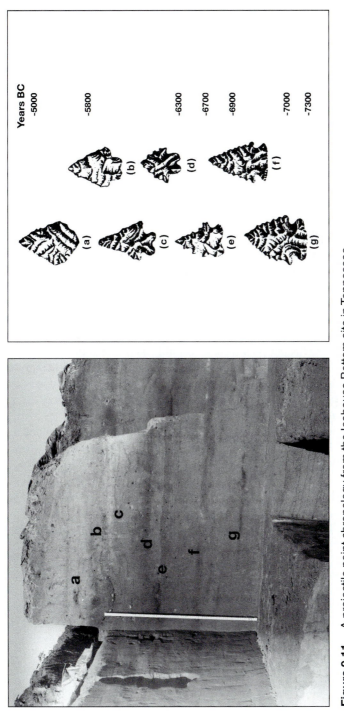

Figure 9.11 A projectile point chronology from the Icehouse Bottom site in Tennessee.

Source: Jefferson Chapman. 1985. *Tellico Archaeology.* Knoxville: Tennessee Valley Authority, Fig. 1.15.

choices about stone versus metal tools, some based on the functional benefits of one or the other for performing a specific task, but some also based on cultural or economic grounds. For example, metal tools might not have been adopted until they became readily accessible, because of either the opening of trade or the development of craft specialists to produce them. In either case, what we see by examining the use of stone is individuals making active choices about the tools they use.

Archaeologists have also attempted to understand how stoneworkers thought by examining how stone tools were made, that is, how stoneworkers conceived the tool they wanted and how they shaped that tool out of the stone. Perhaps the most fascinating aspect of this work is that being done on the stone tools of our ancient, protohuman ancestors. The technological transitions in early stone tool production—from knocking simple flakes from a core, to making specifically shaped tools (such as hand axes) from a core, to making large flakes of a particular size and shape (such as blades) and reshaping *those* flakes into the desired tools—mark dramatic advances in forethought and planning abilities. In one study, Thomas Wynn evaluated the intelligence necessary to produce Acheulean hand axes dating to roughly 300,000 years ago in terms of classic (Piagetian) theories of child development.[8] He found that the *Homo erectus* peoples producing these hand axes were capable of several types of adult human thought and concluded that, in terms of organizational ability, *Homo erectus* peoples were as capable as modern humans.

While it is fascinating that stone tools are able to provide some insight into the thought processes of stoneworkers, we might reasonably wonder how studying stone tools illuminates features of social organization. As was the case with ceramics, there are many ways in which tools reflect the way people live. Two good examples related to stone tools focus on settlement mobility and social differentiation. In terms of settlement mobility, clear differences are present in the lithic manufacturing techniques employed by nomadic and by sedentary peoples. These differences often relate to access to quality stone and the ability to carry or store it. In a comparative study of archaeological sites from North America, William Parry and Robert Kelly found that prepared core technology and "curation" (reworking tools so they can be used for a long period of time) was more common on sites associated with nomadic peoples.[9] In terms of social differentiation, "elites" tend to have access to both a greater quantity and greater diversity of all types of material items. So, by identifying households or (through the analysis of grave goods) individuals themselves who have greater access to stone tools—particularly exotic ones or ones requiring intense or specialized labor to produce—archaeologists can examine some aspects of social differentiation. Richard Yerkes examined use-wear patterns on stone tools from a long-term habitation in the American Bottom region called the Labras Lake site and found that Mississippian patterns of stone tool use at the site differed significantly from earlier patterns.[10] Specif-

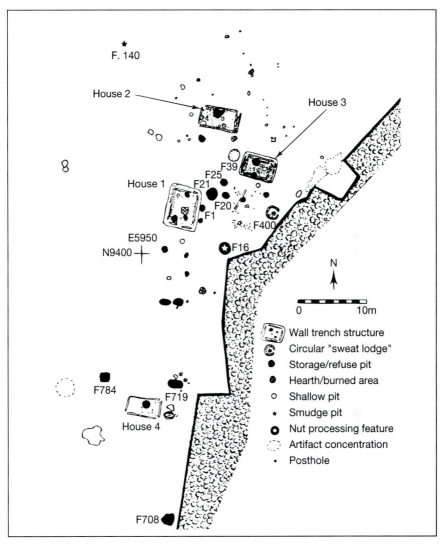

Figure 9.12 Map of the Labras Lake central cluster of houses.

Source: From *Prehistoric Life on the Mississippi Floodplain* by Richard Yerkes, copyright © 1987, University of Chicago Press, p. 86. Reprinted by permission of The University of Chicago Press.

ically, he found that a central cluster of three houses in the community had tools for producing craft items such as shell beads. He suggests, based on this and other evidence, that these houses were the residential unit of a community leader who exercised some control over craft production and exchange.

9.7 SUMMARY

Stone tools are made either by striking flakes from a core of stone, in essence "carving" the stone into shape, or by grinding the surface of the stone into a desired shape. In either case, archaeologists have developed analytical techniques to examine tool manufacture and use. These techniques include formal analysis, use-wear analysis, refitting, and metrical analysis. By examining stone tools with these techniques, archaeologists can both place them into a typology to aid in chronological dating and gain valuable evidence about social organization and even past ways of thinking. Thus, like ceramic analysis, lithic analysis provides many unique inroads into the past.

SUGGESTED READINGS

Keeley, Lawrence. 1980. *Experimental Determination of Stone Tool Uses*. Chicago: University of Chicago Press. The "bible" on use-wear analysis and mandatory reading for anyone interested in the subject.

Knecht, Heidi, ed. 1997. *Projectile Technology*. New York: Plenum. A recent collection of articles combining both archaeological and ethnographic data into an interesting and informative analysis of projectiles.

Odell, George, ed. 1996. *Stone Tools: Theoretical Insights into Human Prehistory*. New York: Plenum. An excellent collection of articles on lithic analysis, demonstrating some of the range of both techniques used and questions addressed.

Whittaker, John. 1994. *Flintknapping: Making and Understanding Stone Tools*. Austin: University of Texas Press. An outstanding introduction to lithics, their production, and their analysis. Well written and comprehensive, this is mandatory reading for anyone interested in lithic analysis.

NOTES

1. An outstanding introduction to stoneworking is given by John Whittaker, *Flintknapping: Making and Understanding Stone Tools* (Austin: University of Texas Press, 1994).

2. The relationship of form to use is critically analysed by Margaret Nelson, "Projectile Points: Form, Function, and Design," in *Projectile Technology*, ed. Heidi Knecht (New York: Plenum, 1997), pp. 371–384.

3. Dorothy Garrod and Dorothea Bate, *The Stone Age of Mount Carmel* (Oxford, UK: Oxford University Press, 1937).

4. Lawrence Keeley, "The Functions of Paleolithic Flint Tools," *Scientific American* 237 (1977):108–126.

5. John J. Shea, "Middle Paleolithic Spear Point Technology," in *Projectile Technology,* ed. Heidi Knecht (New York: Plenum, 1997), pp. 79–106.

6. An ongoing debate about craft specialization at Cahokia is illuminating in this regard, as all sides are able to present good evidence for their particular points of view. See, for example, Timothy Pauketat, "Specialization, Political Symbols, and the Crafty Elite of Cahokia," *Southeastern Archaeology* 16 (1997):1–15; and Richard Yerkes, "Specialization in Shell Artifact Production at Cahokia," in *New Perspectives on Cahokia,* ed. James Stoltman (Madison, WI: Prehistory Press, 1991), pp. 49–65.

7. Steven Rosen, "The Decline and Fall of Flint," in *Stone Tools: Theoretical Insights into Human Prehistory,* ed. George Odell (New York: Plenum, 1996), pp. 129–158.

8. Thomas Wynn, "The Intelligence of Later Acheulean Hominids," *Man* 14 (1979):371–391.

9. William Parry and Robert Kelly, "Expedient Core Technology and Sedentism," in *The Organization of Core Technology,* ed. J. K. Johnson and C. A. Morrow (Boulder, CO: Westview Press, 1987), pp. 285–304.

10. Richard Yerkes, "Lithic Analysis and Activity Patterns at Labras Lake," in *Alternative Approaches to Lithic Analysis,* ed. Donald Henry and George Odell (Archaeological Papers of the American Anthropological Association, No. 1, 1989), pp. 183–212.

Floral and Faunal Analysis

OVERVIEW

10.1   How Do Archaeologists Find Remains of Ancient Plants and
       Animals?

10.2   What Kinds of Plant Remains Are Found in the Archaeological
       Record?

    10.2.1   Microbotanical Remains

    10.2.2   Macrobotanical Remains

10.3   What Kinds of Animal Remains Are Found in the Archaeological
       Record?

    10.3.1   Microfaunal Remains

    10.3.2   Macrofaunal Remains

10.4   What Information Do Archaeologists Obtain from Plant and Animal
       Remains?

10.5   Summary

In a review of Northrop Frye's book *The Stubborn Structure*, novelist Stephen Vizinczey asked, "Is it possible that I am not alone in believing that in the dispute between Galileo and the Church, the Church was right and the centre of man's universe is the earth?"[1] Archaeologists would accept this as an excellent question, for the earth—and particularly the plants and animals that inhabit it—shapes human cultures. Without knowledge of the environment a group of people lived in, archaeologists can never hope to fully understand those people and their world. For that reason, among others, identifying the flora and fauna that surrounded and were used by the people inhabiting an archaeological site is an important facet of any archaeological research project. It is also perhaps the most complicated, and archaeologists have to rely on specialists—**archaeobotanists,** who study plant remains, and **zooarchaeologists,** who study animal remains—for most analyses. Because floral and faunal analyses are such specialties, we will only scratch the surface of them here. We will briefly consider the variety of floral and faunal materials archaeologists collect and the kinds of analyses done by archaeobotanists and zooarchaeologists. Before we get to that, however, let's first consider how archaeologists collect plant and animal remains.

10.1 HOW DO ARCHAEOLOGISTS FIND REMAINS OF ANCIENT PLANTS AND ANIMALS?

The simplest way to collect plant and animal remains is to screen excavated soil. **Screening** simply means passing excavated soil through a mesh screen in order to recover small pieces of material. Screens come in a variety of forms. The simplest is just a box with the screen in the bottom. More complex systems have screens suspended from a tripod or set atop a frame so that the person doing the screening doesn't have to support the weight of the screen and soil. Some mechanical systems, where a motor shakes the screen as material is thrown into it, have also been developed. Typically archaeologists use about a ¼-inch mesh screen, but if soil conditions permit, and if they want to recover very small materials, a screen as small as ⅛ of an inch might be used. Soil will have to be very dry and fine-grained for this small a screen. One way to help soil go through a small screen (or even a larger one if the soil is composed of

Figure 10.1   Screening excavated soil.

clay) is to use water to break up the soil and make it flow through the screen: This is typically called water-screening.

Related to water-screening is the most important method for recovering plant and animal remains: **flotation**. Flotation is based on the idea that because most plant and animal remains are lighter than the soil they are embedded in, they tend to float in water more readily than soil (which dissolves or sinks). The simplest way to do flotation is to pour a small amount of soil into a large container of water and quickly skim off the material that floats, using a kitchen strainer. More sophisticated systems use either a shower head or a compressed-air bubbler located at the bottom of a large container of water (often a 55-gallon drum) to create an upward current in the water that forces material to the surface. The most sophisticated systems include a sluiceway that feeds floated materials through a series of increasingly smaller sieves, often ending in a carburetor screen or muslin bag trapping even the tiniest material. In any of these systems, the addition of chemicals to increase water's density can make it possible to float increasingly heavier materials.[2]

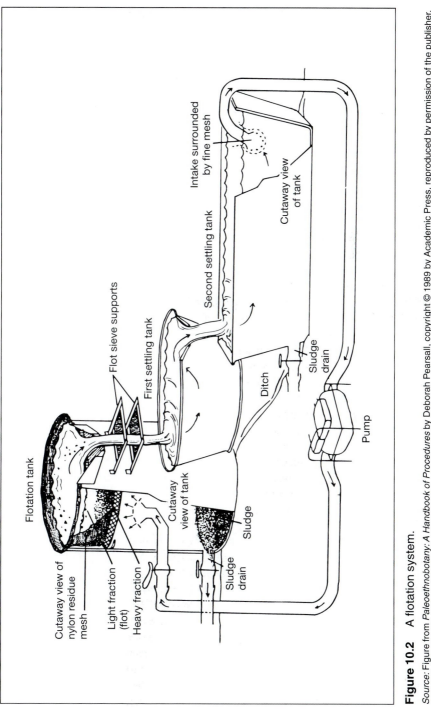

Figure 10.2 A flotation system.

Source: Figure from *Paleoethnobotany: A Handbook of Procedures* by Deborah Pearsall, copyright © 1989 by Academic Press, reproduced by permission of the publisher.

Chemicals can also be used directly on soil samples to isolate desired materials. For example, to recover pollens from a soil sample they must be separated from the soil. This is usually done by removing all the nonpollen materials through a series of chemical processes: Carbonates are removed with hydrochloric acid, silicates with hydrofluoric acid, organics with a series of acetic acid rinses, and so on. All that remains of the sample at the end of this processing are the pollen grains themselves.[3] Such chemical processing is obviously much more complicated than screening and flotation and is usually only performed by trained soil scientists or botanists, not by archaeologists.

10.2   WHAT KINDS OF PLANT REMAINS ARE FOUND IN THE ARCHAEOLOGICAL RECORD?

Now we know how archaeologists recover material, but we still don't know what those materials are. What kinds of plants survive in the archaeological record? The answer is: a surprising variety. Different conditions allow different kinds of plant remains to survive, but almost every site will contain some, and some sites will contain quite a lot of plant remains. Archaeobotanists divide this diversity of plant remains into two broad categories: microbotanical remains and macrobotanical remains.

10.2.1   Microbotanical Remains

Microbotanical remains are the smallest of the plant remains found in the archaeological record—remains so small that we need a microscope to see them. Two kinds of microbotanical remains are commonly analyzed: pollens and phytoliths. **Pollens** are essentially plant sperm. Pollen is composed of three separate layers, and only the outermost layer, called the exine, survives in archaeological context. The exine is made of an organic material called sporopollenin that decays extremely slowly in low-oxygen environments. Since the exine is the outermost of three layers, it always has at least one aperture allowing access to the interior layers. The locations and shapes of these apertures, as well as the overall shape and surface structure of the exine itself, differ between species of plants. Hence the number, location, and shape of apertures, as well as the shape and surface of the exine, can be used to identify the plant species it came from.[4]

Phytoliths differ from pollens in that they are part of the physical structure of plants. Phytoliths are really small rocks formed in the spaces between the living cells of a plant by silica brought into the cells with water. Once the plant dies and decays, these small silica rocks remain and retain the shape of

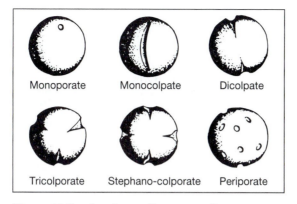

Figure 10.3 Aperture patterns on pollens.

Source: Adapted from Kapp 1969: 22–25, 27, in *Paleoethnobotany: A Handbook of Procedures* by Deborah Pearsall, copyright © 1989 by Academic Press.

the cells they surrounded. Not all plants produce phytoliths, and not all that do have shapes that distinguish them from other plants. However, many do, and there appear to be gross differences in the phytoliths of some plant families, such as grasses—differences that can be used to identify the family, if not the genera, of the phytolith's origin. The use of phytoliths in archaeology is also relatively new, and not as many species of plants have uniquely identified phytoliths. However, because they are made of silica, they are almost indestructible and can be recovered from almost any kind of archaeological deposit. For this reason their analysis is likely to become increasingly common in archaeology.[5]

10.2.2 Macrobotanical Remains

Macrobotanical remains are those plant materials that can be seen with the naked eye. They tend to be seeds and wood fragments, but nuts and other fruits sometimes survive in the archaeological record and are recovered. Archaeologists recover macrobotanical remains by either screening or flotation. Because macrobotanical remains can be heavy, flotation is sometimes done in water made denser than normal through the addition of chemicals (often zinc chloride). Once macrobotanical remains have been collected, they are sorted into gross categories of similar materials (nuts, seeds, and so on) and then analyzed by archaeobotanists.

In analyzing macrobotanical remains, archaeobotanists attempt to use features of the remains, such as size, shape, and surface characteristics, to define the genus or species of plant the remains are from. For seeds, the features most commonly examined are, in addition to size and shape of the seed,

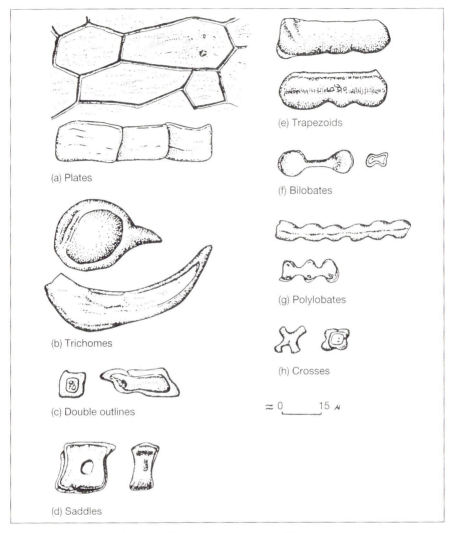

(a) Plates

(b) Trichomes

(c) Double outlines

(d) Saddles

(e) Trapezoids

(f) Bilobates

(g) Polylobates

(h) Crosses

Figure 10.4   The eight basic divisions of grass phytoliths.

Source: Adapted from Brown 1984: 362–364, in *Paleoethnobotany: A Handbook of Procedures* by Deborah Pearsall, copyright © 1989 by Academic Press.

the characteristics of the seed coat, including its color, and the location of the embryo. For nuts, common features used for identification include the shape and color of the shell, the shape of the meat or meat cavity, and, if it has been preserved, the shape, color, and surface of the husk. Finally, wood can be identified by examining thin sections under magnification for the wood's porosity, the location of vessels, and the type and arrangement of tissue in the wood itself. Such features allow archaeobotanists to identify plants with great accuracy.

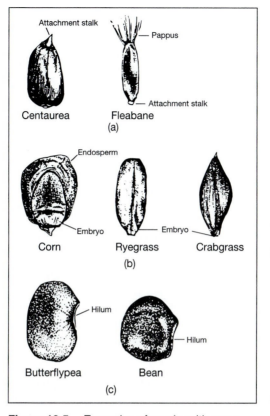

Figure 10.5 Examples of seeds, with some diagnostic features noted. Group (a) are from the daisy family; group (b) are from the grass family; and group (c) are from the bean family.

Source: Figure from *Paleoethnobotany: A Handbook of Procedures* by Deborah Pearsall, copyright © 1989 by Academic Press, reproduced by permission of the publisher. Camera art by permission of Deborah M. Pearsall.

Archaeobotanists are aided in identification by having type collections of known plant species. In fact, many archaeobotanists begin their research on a particular archaeological site by collecting specimens of plants growing in the surrounding area. The reason for this is twofold: first, to identify plants common in the present environment, plants whose pollen or seeds might accidentally "pollute" an archaeological sample; and second, to create a collection to help identify plants in the archaeological record. While there are texts and handbooks for plant identification, none are complete, and none provide a good sense of the range of variation within a given species of plant. Collecting plants in a given area provides archaeobotanists with a sense of the

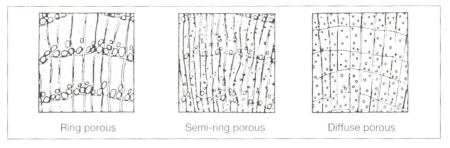

| Ring porous | Semi-ring porous | Diffuse porous |

Figure 10.6   Diagnostic patterns in wood thin sections.

Source: Figure from *Paleoethnobotany: A Handbook of Procedures* by Deborah Pearsall, copyright © 1989 by Academic Press, reproduced by permission of the publisher. Camera art by permission of Deborah M. Pearsall.

variation present and with examples of uncommon species that may well not be illustrated in standard reference works.

10.3   WHAT KINDS OF ANIMAL REMAINS ARE FOUND IN THE ARCHAEOLOGICAL RECORD?

Like plant remains, we have learned how animal remains are recovered, but are there really that many animal remains in the archaeological record? Don't animals all decay? The answer is no. Just as was the case of plant remains, different environmental conditions allow different types of animal remains to survive. Zooarchaeologists have divided the range of animal materials that might be found into two broad categories: microfaunal remains and macrofaunal remains.

10.3.1   Microfaunal Remains

Microfauna are the remains of small animals such as mice, birds, and fish; of insects; and of snails or other mollusks. They usually consist of bones or shells, but may also include scales (from fish), whole body segments (from insects), and even hair, blood, or soft tissue where conditions are right for preservation. Microfauna are typically recovered through screening and flotation, and in either case they are often mixed up with macrobotanical remains collected from the same soil. Thus, the first step in the analysis of macrobotanical remains and microfauna is the same—separating the screened or floated materials into gross categories. A first division of these materials, then, is into flora and fauna. Once the fauna have been identified, they are further divided into fish, bird, mammal, mollusk, and insect remains. Once that is finished the work of zooarchaeologists begins.

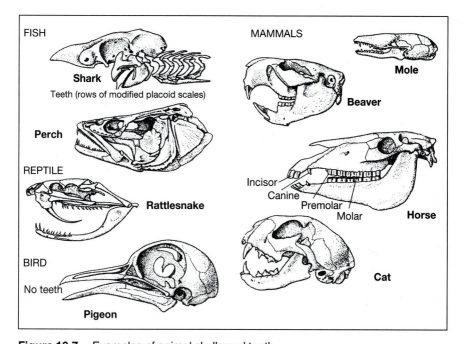

Figure 10.7 Examples of animal skulls and teeth.

Source: Illustration from *Collier's Encyclopedia, Vol. 2.* Copyright © 1997 by Atlas Editions, Inc. All rights reserved. Used by Permission.

Zooarchaeologists can usually identify the genus or species of an animal based on its skull. Skull forms and sizes differ markedly among animals. Also important for identification are teeth, which vary in size and shape and usually preserve well in the archaeological record. Less useful for identification are the pelvis and spine; the least useful are long bones and ribs. Fish can be identified by their skulls and teeth as well, and often by the shape and surface characteristics of their scales. The form, thickness, and surface characteristics of mollusk shells can yield very precise identifications, as can the exoskeletons of insects and crustaceans.[6]

10.3.2 Macrofaunal Remains

Macrofauna are the remains of large animals. They are often recovered in the process of excavation, but may also be recovered through screening. Zooarchaeologists identify macrofauna, like microfauna, on the basis of skull size and shape. Extensive comparative studies of macrofauna allow zooarchaeologists to use long bone and tooth measurements to make fine-scale identification of animal species and the sex and age of particular animals within a species.[7]

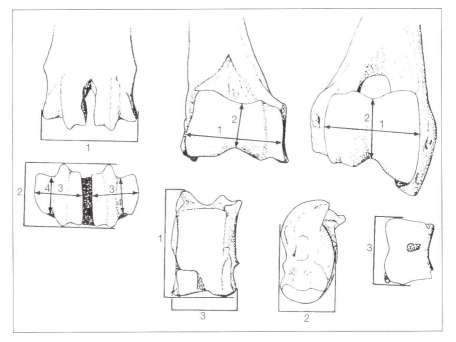

Figure 10.8   Some of the metric measurements used in analyzing long bones.

Source: From *The Archaeology of Animals* by Simon Davies, copyright © 1987 Yale University Press. Reprinted by permission of Yale University Press and Routledge, UK.

For both microfauna and macrofauna, a good comparative collection is a great aid in identification. The reasons for this are similar to those given earlier for plants. Comparative collections often contain animals not illustrated in standard reference works and they allow zooarchaeologists to gain a sense of the variation present within animal species. Unlike their method with plants, zooarchaeologists do not usually make a new collection of animals representing each site on which they are working, but instead rely on extant museum collections or on collections they have acquired during their careers.

10.4   WHAT INFORMATION DO ARCHAEOLOGISTS OBTAIN FROM PLANT AND ANIMAL REMAINS?

Thus far we have learned how archaeologists collect plant and animal remains, what those remains typically are, and how they are analyzed by archaeobotanists and zooarchaeologists. But what does it all mean? Why go to the trouble of collecting this information and having specialists analyze it? What do plant and animal remains tell us about the past? The simple answer is: a lot. Let's consider just a few of the things we can learn from plant and animal remains.

One of the most important things floral and faunal analysis can do is reconstruct past environments, commonly called **paleoenvironments**. The recreation of a paleoenvironment for a particular site is one of the keys to understanding why and how people lived there. For example, Tell es-Sweyhat is located in a place that would not, on the surface, seem a likely location for a large city. The region is very arid, vegetation is sparse, and there are almost no game animals. But floral and faunal remains from the site tell us that the environment in 2150 B.C. was very different from what it is today. Macrobotanical remains suggest the climate was wetter then and that vegetation was more plentiful.[8] Microfauna support that conclusion, and macrofauna demonstrate that deer were common in the region.[9] The presence of deer suggests that there must have been large stands of trees nearby, too, an idea backed up by the presence of diverse wood remains in the collections of macrobotanical remains. By knowing that the paleoenvironment was wetter, had a greater diversity of plants, and contained a group of game animals including deer, we have a much better sense of why and how people lived at Tell es-Sweyhat.

A second type of information floral and faunal analysis provides is knowledge of ancient diets. By examining the plants and animals used by a group of people, we can create a good picture of what they ate. Of particular interest to many archaeobotanists and zooarchaeologists is the origins of domestication, that is, when food collection changed to food production. Indeed, some might argue that archaeobotany and zooarchaeology were born because of interest in this question. The origins of domestication are thought to be an important watershed in human history, a point where humans came to shape and control their environment, a point where they gained the ability to significantly increase the production of food. Determining where and when this happened was a question that turned on the ability to distinguish domesticated from wild plants and animals, and this, obviously, needed the trained eye of specialists: archaeobotanists and zooarchaeologists. For example, the distinction between domesticated and wild goats hinges on subtle differences in the cross-sectional shape of the horn. This was only learned after a zooarchaeologist spent months examining collections of wild and domesticated goats and then examining collections from the time when domestication was starting. From those examinations he was able to trace the shift in cross-sectional shape through the archaeological record, showing clearly the transition from wild to domestic.[10]

Floral and faunal analysis can also tell us how humans used the environment around them, that is, which species were exploited and which were not. No human group uses all the possible resources in its environment, and choices are often very culturally biased. In the United States, for example, we find it strange to eat dog, yet dog is considered a delicacy in other parts of

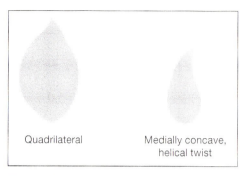

Quadrilateral

Medially concave,
helical twist

Figure 10.9   Cross sections of goat horn
cones, showing the change from wild
(quadrilateral) to domestic (concave and
twisted).

the world. All human groups focus on some resources and ignore others. What people use and what they ignore can lead to important insights about their culture, and archaeobotanists and zooarchaeologists can often discern those focal or ignored resources. For example, the examination of wood remains from the FAI-270 project in the American Bottom demonstrates that by around A.D. 500 people started using upland woods (oak and hickory) for fuel rather than lowland woods (elm, ash, willow, birch, and so on).[11] Why? One answer might be deforestation of the lowlands, although those woods were still used in constructing houses. Another answer might be that upland woods, like oak and hickory, produce more heat than lowland woods and might have become preferred for fuel. These kinds of subtle changes in plant use point to decisions made by ancient peoples and often lead to understandings about past lives that can be acquired in no other way.

10.5   SUMMARY

Floral and faunal remains are an important part of any archaeological assemblage. They provide unique information on the environment at the time an archaeological deposit was created and how humans adapted to and used it. Floral and faunal remains are collected by screening excavated soil or by using a system of water flotation to separate them from surrounding soil. Microbotanical remains include pollen and phytoliths; macrobotanical remains include seeds, nuts, and wood fragments. Microfaunal remains include mollusks, small mammals, birds, reptiles, and insects; macrofaunal remains include all forms of large animals. The analysis of floral and faunal remains is conducted by

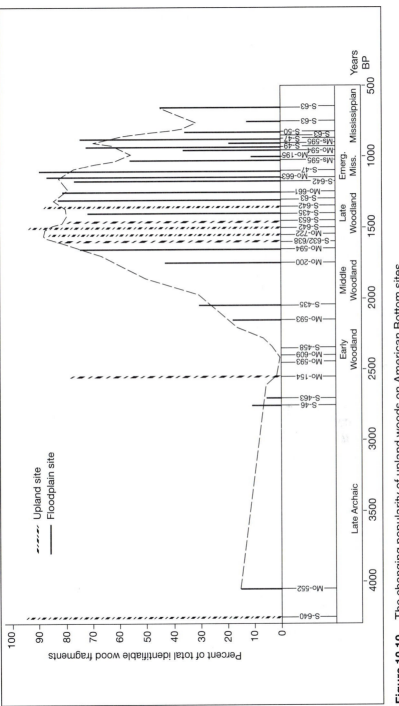

Figure 10.10 The changing popularity of upland woods on American Bottom sites.

Source: From *American Bottom Archaeology* by Charles Bareis and James Porter, copyright © 1984, University of Illinois Press, Fig. 75, p. 211. Courtesy of the Board of Trustees of the University of Illinois.

specialists—archaeobotanists and zooarchaeologists—who bring a highly detailed knowledge of taxonomy and identification to the examination of these remains. Archaeologists are willing go to the trouble and expense of collecting and analyzing plant and animal remains because they provide otherwise unattainable information about human groups and how they used the world around them.

SUGGESTED READINGS

Davies, Simon. 1987. *The Archaeology of Animals*. New Haven, CT: Yale University Press. A good introduction to zooarchaeology. It combines information on data collection and analysis with summaries of major questions in zooarchaeological research.

Grayson, Donald. 1984. *Quantitative Zooarchaeology*. New York: Academic Press. A detailed and thorough introduction to quantitative analyses of faunal remains.

Miller, Naomi. 1998. "The Analysis of Archaeological Plant Remains," in *Research Frontiers in Anthropology*, ed. Carol R. Ember, Melvin Ember, and Peter N. Peregrine. Upper Saddle River, NJ: Prentice Hall. A basic and easy to read introduction to archaeobotany.

Pearsall, Deborah. 1989. *Paleoethnobotany: A Handbook of Procedures*. New York: Academic Press. This is perhaps the best single source on archaeobotany (which Pearsall calls paleoethnobotany). It covers data collection, analysis, and interpretation in clear and concise detail.

Redding, Richard. 1998. "The Study of Human Subsistence Behavior Using Faunal Evidence from Archaeological Sites," in *Research Frontiers in Anthropology*, ed. Carol R. Ember, Melvin Ember, and Peter N. Peregrine. Upper Saddle River, NJ: Prentice Hall. A good basic introduction to zooarchaeology focusing on subsistence studies and highlighting some of the ongoing controversies in the field.

NOTES

1. Stephen Vizinczey, "Rules of the Game," *Times of London* (November 12, 1970).
2. An excellent overview of flotation systems is given in Deborah Pearsall, *Paleoethnobotany: A Handbook of Procedures* (New York: Academic Press, 1989), pp. 15–75.
3. Ibid., pp. 269–277.
4. Ibid., pp. 246–251.
5. Ibid., pp. 311–328.
6. For an overview of the work of zooarchaeologists, see Simon Davies, *The Archaeology of Animals* (New Haven, CT: Yale University Press, 1987), pp. 23–46.
7. See Donald Grayson, *Quantitative Zooarchaeology* (New York: Academic Press, 1984).

8. Naomi Miller, "Sweyhat and Hajji Ibrahim: Some Archaeobotanical Samples from the 1991 and 1993 Seasons," in *Subsistence and Settlement in a Marginal Environment*, ed. Richard Zettler (Philadelphia: Museum Applied Science Center for Archaeology, University of Pennsylvania, Research Papers in Science and Archaeology, Volume 14, 1997), pp. 95–122.

9. Jill Weber, "Faunal Remains from Tell es-Sweyhat and Tell Hajji Ibrahim," in *Subsistence and Settlement in a Marginal Environment*, ed. Richard Zettler (Philadelphia: Museum Applied Science Center for Archaeology, University of Pennsylvania, Research Papers in Science and Archaeology, Volume 14, 1997), pp. 133–167.

10. Charles A. Reed, "A Review of the Archaeological Evidence on Animal Domestication in the Prehistoric Near East," in *Prehistoric Investigations in Iraqi Kurdistan*, ed. Robert Braidwood and Bruce Howe (Chicago: University of Chicago Press, 1960).

11. Sissel Johannsen, "Paleoethnobotany," in *American Bottom Archaeology*, ed. Charles Bareis and James Porter (Urbana: University of Illinois Press, 1984), pp. 197–214.

Dating Archaeological Materials

OVERVIEW

11.1   Relative Dating

   11.1.1   Association

   11.1.2   Seriation

11.2   Absolute Dating

   11.2.1   Radiocarbon

   11.2.2   Thermoremnant Magnetism

   11.2.3   Thermoluminescence

   11.2.4   Dendrochronology

   11.2.5   Some Less Common Dating Techniques

11.3   Summary

O n the first day of my introduction to my archaeology class several years ago I handed out the syllabus and asked if there were any questions. A student raised his hand and said, "It says here we're gonna do dating techniques. Does that mean we're gonna learn how ta pick up chicks?" No, sorry. Hope you weren't thinking that yourself. Dating here means assigning an age to an archaeological deposit or artifact, not . . . well, not "picking up chicks" anyway. Archaeologists typically define two primary forms of archaeological dating: relative and absolute. Let's take a close look at both.

11.1 RELATIVE DATING

Relative dating refers to methods used to assign a date to an archaeological deposit or artifact through its context with other materials. The two primary forms of relative dating are **association** and **seriation**. Association is used all the time and, indeed, some might argue that all archaeological dating relies in some way on association. Seriation was once a very popular method of relative dating, but it fell into disfavor when radiocarbon dating became common. It is making a comeback today because of its ability to assign relative dates to materials either that are too close in time to distinguish using an absolute dating technique or that cannot be dated using another technique. In addition, seriation is free (archaeologists do it themselves) and so can be performed on any suitable assemblage without having to worry about the costs.

11.1.1 Association

The basic idea behind dating by association is that if you know the date of a given item and it is found within a deposit of interest or in association with an object of interest, it is reasonable (under most circumstances) to assign the same date to the associated deposit or object. It is best if the associated material is directly dated by some absolute method, but in most cases dates are assigned on the basis of **artifact typology** or the use of **reference fossils**. Using artifact typology archaeologists assign a date to an archaeological deposit based on the types of artifacts found in it. For example, I have dated the Bjorklunden site based on the types of projectile points we've found there. We know they

Figure 11.1   Clear stratigraphy visible in an eroded section of Tell Othmann, Syria.

were made during specific time periods, and we know those time periods from other dated contexts. So when they are found elsewhere (as at Bjork-lunden), we assume that site must date to the same general time period. Similarly, using reference fossils archaeologists assign a date to a deposit based on known dates of those fossils. Many preliminary dates (usually confirmed later using some absolute method) from ancient human sites in east Africa, for example, are based on fauna associated with the site, particularly porcine.

Another general way of doing associative dating is based on natural processes that create a regular **stratigraphy** at a site. In some parts of the world (northern Europe in particular) annual accumulations of sediments called *rythmites* or *varves* can be used to determine how many years in the past a deposit was created. Similarly, less regular but still discrete accumulations of wind-blown (loess) or water-borne (alluvium) soils can sometimes correlate a site in a specific deposit with a known date elsewhere. This kind of associative dating is used all the time with volcanic deposits (known as *tuffs*), where materials buried in or near a tuff will be dated based on the date of the tuff, sometimes taken hundreds of miles away. Using strata in this way is a very common method of dating and at some level underlies all archaeological dating, since only a tiny proportion of materials is physically dated.

11.1.2 Seriation

The other primary method of relative dating, **seriation,** uses artifact typologies to create a time series that is purely relative, although it can be tied into an absolute chronology if one or more of the artifacts can be associated with dated materials. The basic premise of seriation is that artifact types come into use and go out of use slowly. Thus, if we were to look at the whole range of, say, ceramic types on a site, at any given point some types will be more popular than others. The less popular ones will be either coming into use or going out

Figure 11.2 Method of constructing a seriation graph. Frequencies of the types in each collection are drawn as bars along the top of graph-paper strips. These are arranged to discover the type-frequency pattern and are fastened to a paper backing with paper clips. When the final arrangement has been determined, a finished drawing may be prepared.

Source: James A. Ford, A Quantitative Method for Deriving Cultural Chronology (1962). Courtesy of the General Secretariat of the Organization of American States.

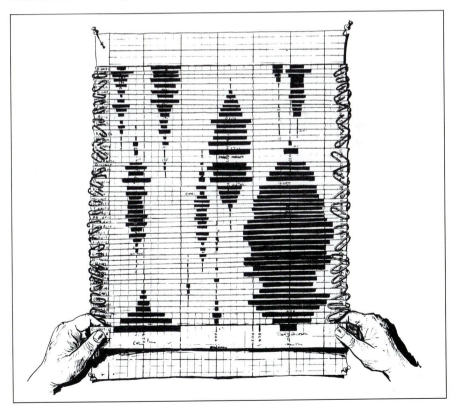

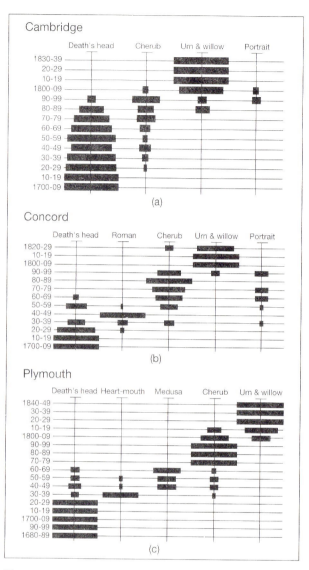

Figure 11.3   Seriation graphs showing sequences of headstone decorative styles in three Massachusetts cemeteries.

Source: From "Death's Heads, Cherubs, and Willow Trees: Experimental Archaeology in Colonial Cemeteries" by Edwin Dethlefsen and James Deetz. Reproduced by permission of the Society for American Archaeology from *American Antiquity* 31 (4) 1966.

of use. By charting the percentages of each type, we should be able to create a logical series showing the comings and goings. The traditional way of doing this is to create "battleship" diagrams, although more sophisticated statistical and graphical methods have also been developed.[1]

Perhaps the most well-known example of seriation comes from a study of the design motifs used on headstones in Massachusetts cemeteries. The study, by Edwin Dethlefsen and James Deetz, was designed to examine the extent to which headstones reflected social changes in colonial society.[2] While they found fascinating relationships between the primary design motifs—death's head, cherub, and urn and willow—and Massachusetts's transition from a Puritan colony to one of the United States, their study has been more influential as an illustration of the validity of seriation. As Figure 11.3 illustrates, the changes in design motifs are obvious in the seriation diagrams and clearly demarcate temporal periods in colonial Massachusetts; that is, the typological series provides a way to define temporal periods that could be used for dating the context of the headstones.

11.2   ABSOLUTE DATING

Absolute dating refers to methods used to assign a date to an archaeological deposit or artifact that provides a true chronometric date of when the deposit or artifact itself was made or discarded. Of course, the simplest form of absolute dating is when an artifact has the date written on it, as coins do. Indeed, in many parts of the Old World coins are extensively used for dating. Where writing is present in archaeological contexts, for example in the Near East, dates are sometimes even written on artifacts. Most artifacts are not so easily dated, though, and archaeologists (with the help of chemists, physicists, and others) have developed a large number of ways to date artifacts, ecofacts, and features. Of these, only a handful are regularly used in archaeology, among them radiocarbon, thermoremnant magnetism, thermoluminescence, and dendrochronology. These common techniques are the ones I will focus on here, although I'll also mention some less common and newer techniques.

11.2.1   Radiocarbon

Radiocarbon dating was the first feasible absolute dating method developed and is still the most widely used. It can be used to date virtually any organic material from roughly 100 years ago to nearly 100,000 years ago (although its accuracy drops dramatically after about 50,000 years ago). It is based on the fact that two common forms of carbon exist in the atmosphere, a stable form

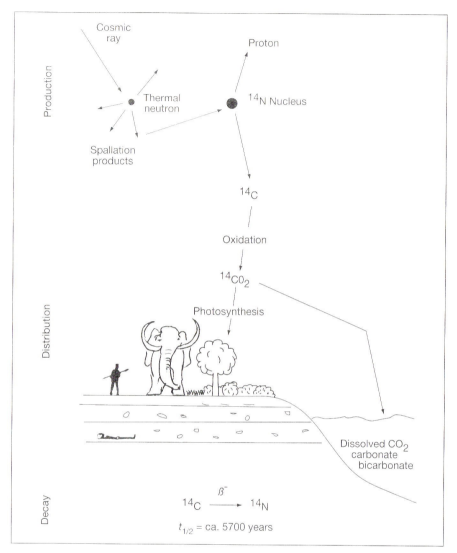

Figure 11.4   The carbon-14 cycle.

Source: "The carbon-14 cycle" from "Radiocarbon Dating" by R. E. Taylor, copyright © 1997, from *Chronometric Dating in Archaeology* by R. E. Taylor and M. J. Aitken, eds., Plenum Publishing, Fig. 3.1, p. 67.

(carbon-12) and an unstable form (carbon-14). These two forms exist in a fairly constant ratio, even though the unstable form is always breaking down into nitrogen. The ratio is constant because at the same time existing carbon-14 is breaking down into nitrogen, new carbon-14 is being created in the upper atmosphere where carbon atoms are bombarded with solar radiation. Once created, carbon-14 quickly attaches with oxygen to become carbon dioxide and then moves into the earth's carbon cycle. It is breathed in by animals, taken up by plants in photosynthesis, ingested by animals eating the plants, and so on. Thus carbon-14 is always circulating around the planet and is constantly being absorbed by all living organisms. When an organism dies, the carbon-14 in its body begins to break down into nitrogen, and since it is no longer eating or breathing, it is no longer adding new carbon-14 to its body. Hence the ratio of carbon-14 to carbon-12 slowly decreases as the carbon-14 decays. Because carbon-14 decays into nitrogen at a constant rate, we can use the ratio to determine how long ago the organism died.[3]

Several methods have been devised to measure the ratio of carbon-14 to carbon-12 in a piece of organic material. The first, and simplest, is simply to extract all the carbon from the sample and then place it in a shielded container and measure the number of particles being released from it. The source of the particles is the breakdown of carbon-14 into nitrogen, and, since the breakdown of carbon-14 takes place at a constant rate, the number of particles released over a given time is directly proportional to the amount of carbon-14 present in the sample. More recently a technique called *accelerator mass spectroscopy* (or AMS) has been developed that physically measures the number of carbon-14 and carbon-12 atoms in a sample. The technique is complicated, but basically pure carbon is extracted from a sample, then several atoms of that

Figure 11.5 A calibration curve for converting radiocarbon dates into calendar dates.

Source: Figure "A calibration curve for converting radiocarbon dates into calendar dates" by Stuiver and Pearson, from *Radiocarbon Dating* by Sheridan Bowman, copyright © 1990, University of California Press, Fig. 18, p. 46. Reprinted by permission of Dr. Minze Stuiver.

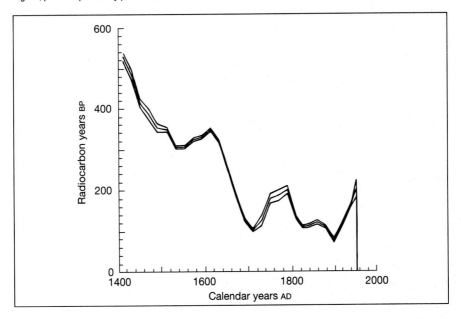

carbon are ionized and accelerated toward a magnet that separates the carbon atoms by weight. Carbon-14, with two extra neutrons, is heavier than carbon-12 and thus separates from it and can be measured, as can the carbon-12, giving a precise ratio of the two.

When radiocarbon dates are reported they are given in years before present (B.P.). These are typically called *radiocarbon years* and have to be corrected for changes in the overall ratio of carbon-14 to carbon-12 in the atmosphere in order to be converted into calendar years A.D. and B.C. Because the ratio of carbon-14 to carbon-12 has changed over time, a strictly linear relationship between the ratio in a sample and the age of the sample doesn't exist. However, excellent "calibration curves" for correcting the date based on changes in the ambient ratio are available and are being improved all the time. Today, it is not at all unusual to be able to determine within twenty-five to fifty years the age of a sample several thousand years old.

Almost any organic remains can be dated using radiocarbon dating, but charcoal is among the best. Wood, bone, seeds, cloth, and the like are all datable with radiocarbon. The amount of sample needed depends on the technique being used, the anticipated age of the material, and the type of material itself. AMS dating requires a much smaller sample than traditional methods, and more recent materials require a smaller sample than older materials (since there is more carbon-14 available to measure in newer materials). A typical sample of burned wood from a hearth anticipated to be from roughly 2,000 years ago would require at least 10 grams of material using one of the traditional methods of counting, but only about 10 milligrams using AMS methods.

11.2.2 Thermoremnant Magnetism

While radiocarbon dating is by far the most common dating technique used in archaeology, thermoremnant magnetic techniques are also frequently used. **Thermoremnant magnetism** refers to a magnetic moment induced into an item by heat. Thermoremnant magnetic techniques are based on two basic principles. First, when soil is heated to a high temperature, its atoms are freed from the soil matrix and all tend to line up with the earth's magnetic field. This creates a subtle magnetic moment in the soil, which is directed at the earth's magnetic pole. Second, the earth's magnetic pole has both moved and reversed its polarity over time. Thus the polarity and direction of the magnetic moment in the sample soil points to the location of the magnetic pole at the time the soil was heated. The location of the magnetic pole has been mapped for much of human prehistory, and by knowing where the pole was when the sample was heated, we can estimate when the soil was heated.[4]

One of the reasons thermoremnant magnetic techniques are popular is that suitable samples can often be found, even on sites with poor preservation of organic materials (needed for radiocarbon dating). All people make fires, and many of them heat the soil to the point where the soil molecules are freed

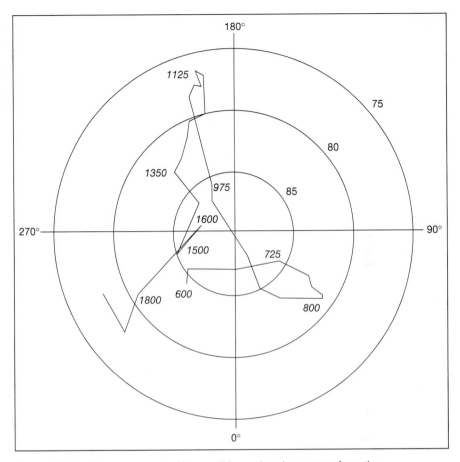

Figure 11.6 The movement of the earth's north pole as seen from the southwestern United States.

Source: Robert Sternbert, 1997, "Archaeomagnetic Dating," in R. E. Taylor and M. J. Aitken, eds., *Chronometric Dating in Archaeology,* Copyright © 1997 Plenum Publishing, Fig. 11.1, p. 330.

from the soil matrix. Thus most archaeological sites have hearths, and in many cases multiple hearths, from which samples can be collected. To collect a sample, archaeologists simply take a block of soil out of a hearth or other burned soil feature after carefully measuring and noting on the sample the direction of present-day magnetic north. In the lab, the magnetic moment of the sample can be measured, and the location of magnetic north when it was heated can then be determined. The accuracy of the technique is therefore limited mostly by the accuracy of measuring the current direction of magnetic north when the sample is collected.

11.2.3   Thermoluminescence

Another technique based on the heating of materials is dating by **thermoluminescence.** Thermoluminescent dating can be used on any item that has been subjected to high heat and is particularly useful for dating ceramics. When an item like a ceramic piece is heated to a high temperature, electrons normally "trapped" in the item are freed. Once the item is cooled, it is bombarded by radiation in the environment, and electrons once again start being trapped in it. By heating the item again and measuring the number of electrons that are freed (by measuring the amount of light given off), we can estimate the date of the initial heating. Before heating, however, we must determine the ability of the item to trap electrons, as well as the average amount of radiation the item was subject to before being collected. Both of these are unique to each item dated, which is one of the drawbacks to this technique—dates for each item have to be individually calibrated. But the real benefit of thermoluminescent dating is its ability to date materials, particularly ceramics, for which no other technique is available.[5]

11.2.4   Dendrochronology

The last of the more common absolute dating techniques is quite different from the three we've already looked at. **Dendrochronology** is based on the fact that a tree grows a ring of new tissue during each year of its life. The thickness of the tissue is directly related to the amount of moisture and sunlight the tree obtained during that year. In any given area, all the trees of a particular species will have a similar pattern of thin and thick rings. By comparing the growth rings from trees in archaeological contexts with a regional "master sequence," we can make a good estimate of when the tree was cut down.[6] Where do archaeologists find samples of wood with growth rings? There are a surprisingly large number of places. One of the best has been structural beams and pilings which are usually thick enough to provide a good sequence of growth rings. In the dry conditions of the southwestern United States and the waterlogged conditions of northern Europe, large wooden beams and pilings have been preserved and have provided samples allowing dendrochronological dates of remarkable accuracy—in some cases down to a single year! In fact, entire construction sequences of ancient pueblos have been worked out based on dendrochronological dating of their structural beams.[7]

11.2.5   Some Less Common Dating Techniques

In addition to the four techniques just described, there are a large number of less frequently used dating techniques. Some are specific to only a certain type of material. Others have only recently been developed and are therefore

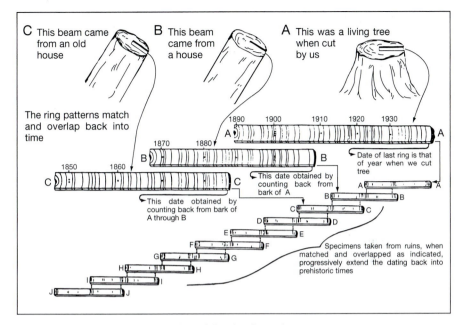

Figure 11.7   The basic principles of dendrochronology.

Source: Bannister, Bryant and Smiley, Terah L. 1955. "Dendrochronology." In *Geochronology, Physical Science Bulletin No. 2:* ed. T. L. Smiley. Tucson: University of Arizona.

not widely used. Still others require very specific environmental conditions to prove accurate.

Obsidian hydration can be used only on obsidian and hence is limited in its application. It is based on the fact that, when fractured, obsidian begins to absorb water from the surrounding environment, called hydration.[8] A thin layer of hydrated rock builds up on the obsidian over time, and how long ago a piece of obsidian was fractured can be estimated by measuring the thickness of this hydrated layer. A problem with the technique is that the speed with which this layer builds up is dependent on both the amount of water in the environment and the temperature, so dates based on it are specific to particular locations. Similar to obsidian hydration dating is a technique called **cation ratio**. When exposed to weathering, some elements (cations) leach out of rocks faster than others. By measuring the ratio of fast-leaching elements to slow-leaching elements, we can estimate when the rock was exposed to weathering. If the ratio is high (more fast-leaching elements), the rock was exposed recently; if the ratio is low (about equal fast- and slow-leaching elements), the rock was exposed long ago. This technique is particularly useful for dating petroglyphs but could potentially be used to date any rock broken by humans.[9]

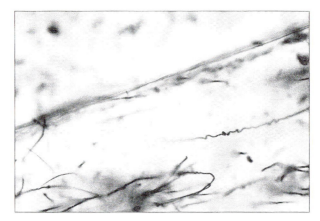

Figure 11.8   Photomicrograph of a thin section of obsidian. The hydration rim front is visible as a distinct boundary extending inward from the outer surface of the artifact.

Amino acid racemization is a dating technique that can only be used on bone. Amino acids in living tissue polarize light to the left. After death, they begin to change into a form that polarizes light to the right. By measuring the ratio of left-polarizing to right-polarizing amino acids in bone, we can estimate how long ago an organism died. This process is highly temperature-sensitive, and (like obsidian hydration) can only be used in situations where temperature history is well known. Bone can also be dated by measuring the amount of specific chemicals—in particular fluorine and uranium—it has absorbed from the surrounding environment. Like amino acid racemization, this is highly temperature-dependent and is also dependent on the chemicals in the environment itself. The real utility of these methods is that they can be used to determine if a given bone is from the same time as another (potentially radiocarbon dated) from the same location.[10]

11.3   SUMMARY

Archaeologists have a wide variety of techniques available to them to assign dates to archaeological artifacts or deposits. There are two primary types of archaeological dating techniques: relative and absolute. Relative dating techniques assign a date to an item based on its association with another item with a known date. Techniques of relative dating include direct association, stratigraphic association, and seriation. Absolute dating techniques assign a true calendar date to an item. Among the most frequently used absolute dating techniques are radiocarbon, thermoremnant magnetism, thermoluminescence, and dendrochronology. Less frequently used techniques include obsidian hydration, cation ratio, amino acid racemization, and bone chemical absorption. Each technique has its own benefits and drawbacks. Most can only be used on a specific type of material. Many are dependent on local environmental conditions. All have common problems and errors associated with them. Because of these potential problems, most archaeologists use a variety of techniques on any given site in order to cross-check assigned dates.

SUGGESTED READINGS

Aitken, Martin J. 1990. *Science-Based Dating in Archaeology*. New York: Longman. A sometimes difficult but thorough overview of absolute dating techniques used in archaeology written by one of the main figures in the field.

Bowman, Sheridan. 1990. *Radiocarbon Dating*. Berkeley: University of California Press. A brief, easy to read, and very informative introduction to radiocarbon dating.

Fleming, Stuart. 1976. *Dating in Archaeology: A Guide to Scientific Techniques*. New York: St. Martin's Press. An older introduction to absolute dating techniques, but I still think it is one of the best. Fleming's introductions to the techniques are clear and are general enough to still be current.

Taylor, R. E., and M. J. Aitken, eds. 1997. *Chronometric Dating in Archaeology*. New York: Plenum. A collection of articles on various methods of absolute dating. Most of the articles are difficult, but they convey state-of-the-art information about these techniques.

NOTES

1. See R. Lee Lyman, Steve Wolverton, and Michael J. O'Brien, "Seriation, Superposition, and Interdigitation: A History of Americanist Graphic Depictions of Culture Change," *American Antiquity* 63 (1998):239–261.
2. Edwin Dethlefsen and James Deetz, "Death's Heads, Cherubs, and Willow Trees: Experimental Archaeology in Colonial Cemeteries," *American Antiquity* 31 (1966):502–510.
3. Good recent overviews are Sheridan Bowman, *Radiocarbon Dating* (Berkeley: University of California Press, 1990); and R. E. Taylor, *Radiocarbon Dating: An Archaeological Perspective* (Orlando, FL: Academic Press, 1987).
4. For more detailed information about thermoremnant magnetic dating and its application in archaeology see the papers in Jeffrey Eighmy and Robert Sternberg, eds., *Archaeomagnetic Dating* (Tucson: University of Arizona Press, 1990).
5. See Martin Aitken, *Thermoluminescence Dating* (Orlando, FL: Academic Press, 1985).

6. M. G. L. Baillie, *A Slice through Time: Dendrochronology and Precision Dating* (London: Batsford, 1995).

7. Jeffrey Dean, "Aspects of Tsegi Phase Social Organization: A Trial Reconstruction," in *Reconstructing Prehistoric Pueblo Societies,* ed. William Longacre (Albuquerque: University of New Mexico Press, 1970), pp. 140–174.

8. See Stuart Fleming, *Dating in Archaeology* (New York: St. Martin's Press, 1976), pp. 148–163.

9. A good introduction is given in David Whitley and Ronald Dorn, "Rock Art Chronology in Eastern California," *World Archaeology* 19 (1987):150–164.

10. A good overview of these techniques and their problems is given by Stuart Fleming, *Dating in Archaeology* (New York: St. Martin's Press, 1976), pp. 181–201.

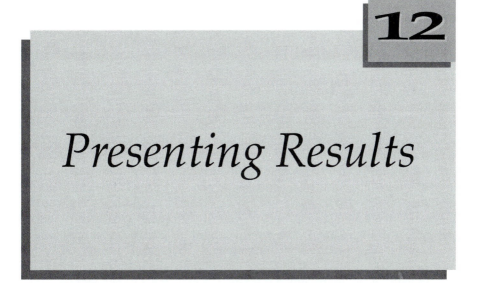

Presenting Results

OVERVIEW

12.1   Why Publish?

12.2   What Types of Publication Are There?

12.3   What Are the Standard Forms of Publication?

12.4   Are There Nonprint Forms of Publication?

12.5   Summary

$\mathbf{E}$arlier I said that archaeologists who don't publish their results are no better than looters. As we'll see in the next chapter, failure to publish is also considered unethical. Why is publication of results such a big deal? Because, as I hope you'll remember from Chapter 5 on excavation, archaeologists destroy their data (the context between and among artifacts, ecofacts, and features) as they collect them, and it is incumbent upon all archaeologists to record and disseminate what they have destroyed. Without a clear and accessible documentary record, an excavated site no longer exists. With a clear published record, any interested scholars can go back to the site any time they choose and, indeed, re-create the site in their own living rooms if they want to.

12.1 WHY PUBLISH?

Well, then, isn't archiving the records and storing the collected material enough? Why is there a need to publish? There are several reasons. One is that publication provides broad accessibility to the information gained through an archaeological project. Publications are purchased by individuals and libraries around the world; the recovered archaeological record thus becomes accessible literally anywhere on earth. The accessibility publication offers should be obvious enough. Archival records and materials stored in one place allow scholars located there to access the materials but no one else. Publication provides any interested parties with access through their library, a bookstore, or even the Internet. Publication also ensures that material will remain accessible through time. Archival records and materials may be accidentally lost or destroyed, but publications are spread widely enough that if one copy is lost, many others are available for researchers to examine.

A second reason for publication is that through a process called **peer review** publishing provides a chance for the rest of the field to examine and critique archaeological work *before* it becomes a part of the permanent record. Peer review helps to ensure the quality of the information presented. The process of peer review begins when a manuscript is submitted to a journal or publisher. The manuscript is usually evaluated first in the journal's or the publisher's editorial office. If it seems worthy of publication, it is then sent out to several (usually two to four) established scholars. Based on those scholars' evaluations, the editor or editorial board of the journal or publisher decides whether to publish the manuscript. Often a manuscript is judged worthy of publication if particular revisions are made to address concerns of the reviewers, a process commonly termed "revise and resubmit." Among the major archaeological journals, the typical acceptance rate for manuscripts submitted for evaluation is 20 to 30 percent.

A third and perhaps less obvious reason for publishing results is that the conventions of publication allow archaeologists, through **citation**, to situate their work in the context of previous work and permit future archaeologists to bring work into the web of accepted archaeological knowledge. Indeed, citation is the way knowledge is established and transmitted through the archaeological community. It is not enough for information to be published; it must be utilized for it to constitute knowledge. Think about it. If no one had picked up on the theories of gravity Newton put forward in *Principa Mathematica*, it wouldn't have been a very big deal, would it? But because other scholars recognized that Newton's theories worked well and used them

Figure 12.1   How citation helps an author build an argument.

Source: Based on Bruno Latour. 1987. *Science in Action*. Cambridge, MA: Harvard University Press, Fig. 1.3, p. 38.

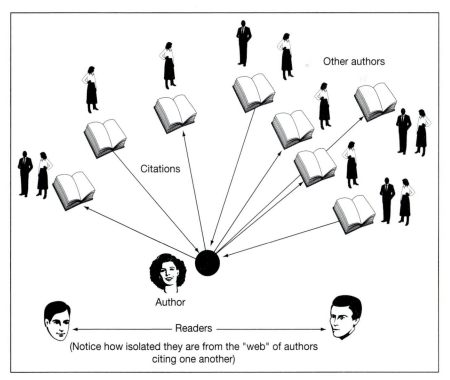

in their own research, we can send spacecraft to Jupiter today. For authors, citation means that their ideas have become real. They have been accepted into the realm of knowledge and are being used by others. They may, of course, be subject to debate or even attack, but they are still being used. Death, in terms of publication, means being ignored. So for authors, citation allows their ideas to live on in future research.[1]

What about the people making the citation? Why cite others when writing a professional publication? There are three basic reasons. First, citation allows authors to create a framework quickly and easily so that readers can understand what is new or different or important about the new work. Second, citation provides a kind of shorthand for conveying ideas, at least for other scholars in the discipline. Citing specific works can tell the reader a lot about what authors are doing, their methodological or theoretical orientation, and the focus or purpose of their research. Not citing important works can sometimes say even more (that authors don't want to accept the knowledge or ideas conveyed in them). For example, I cited Bruno Latour as the source for my ideas about citation. That places me in a fairly "radical" camp that views science as a social and historical phenomenon, rather than a purely objective and rational one. If I were to cite, for example, Karl Popper instead of Latour, I would place myself in a different camp.

Third, citation is one of the central elements in the rhetoric of scientific discussion. It is a primary way in which arguments are built and supported (and I am using the term rhetoric in its traditional sense, as the skill of argumentation). How? First of all, personal observations, reactions, feelings, or the like are not acceptable in scientific papers. If you want to express an idea you have to support it either with empirical data or with reference to someone else's data. Citation allows you to do the latter. Second, if you make any statement of truth or knowledge in a scientific paper you need to back it up, to show that it is a legitimate claim. Citation allows you to do that also. Third, and most important, if you make a claim to truth or knowledge that you know will be controversial, the best (and perhaps only) way to head off controversy is to show that you are not alone in making that claim, that others have made it, too. Again, this is something citation allows you to do.[2]

I like to think of publication as a big discussion among a group of scholars, similar to one that might be going on at a party. Imagine you're watching a group of people standing around having a lively discussion. You wouldn't just jump in and speak your mind without knowing what the arguments are, would you? No. You'd more likely listen for a while. Reading the published literature is like listening to the ongoing discussion. When you understand what's being discussed, you might find yourself wanting to add something, but you wouldn't just sound off. You'd weigh in slowly, perhaps adding to an idea someone else already put forward. That would be like publishing an article and citing another scholar's ideas. What you would like is for your idea to become the focus of continued discussion, right? The worst thing that could happen would be for everyone to look briefly askance at you and go on with their own discussion, ignoring what you said. This is again like citation— your ideas need to be heard and accepted in order to become part of the discussion.

12.2   WHAT TYPES OF PUBLICATION ARE THERE?

What contributions do archaeologists make to the ongoing discussions? Well, there are several types of standard publications, each with its own focus and purposes.

Site reports and **research reports** are the most basic types of archaeological publication. They relate new findings to the archaeological community. Site reports describe the results of survey and excavation projects. They often contain much of the raw data that were collected: descriptions of artifacts, ecofacts, and features, where and how much of each were found, maps, drawings, photographs, and the like. Research reports are more focused and more detailed. They usually describe the results of artifact or ecofact analyses and explain the impact or importance of those analyses. Site and research reports, then, are the source of basic information about the archaeological record.

Literature reviews and **syntheses** attempt to pull together a large volume of literature into a coherent picture. A regional synthesis might attempt to summarize all the site reports for a given area and create from them a broad perspective on the archaeological record for that area as well as the area's culture-history. A review of research reports might take a large number of lithic analyses and attempt to condense from them some fundamental insight into how lithic tools are manufactured or used. Within the archaeological community, literature reviews and syntheses are considered secondary sources. They take the original research and digest it for more general use. Literature reviews and syntheses, then, are not substitutes for the original site and research reports (the primary sources) but rather are useful for gaining general insights into the archaeological record and for helping to locate and evaluate important primary sources on a given subject.

Among the rarest of archaeological publications are **theoretical statements**. Where other sciences have subdisciplines devoted to theory, archaeology has always been data-oriented, and that shouldn't be all that surprising. After all, archaeology is really a set of methods and techniques, and that is what the field has traditionally focused on. In the 1970s, however, there came a realization that what constitutes data is theoretically informed. When we are doing archaeological research we start with a question, develop a model answer, and then collect data to evaluate that answer. Since the answer is based on some set of theory, the data we want to go after is theory-dependent, too. Beyond this notion of theory-dependent data collection, one school of thought suggests that archaeology should be developing theory to understand and explain the relationships between material culture and behavior.[3] Today such theoretical discussions are more common than in the past, but even papers that address theoretical issues usually do it within the guise of a research report or literature review. The purely theoretical statement is still a rarity in archaeology.

Finally, archaeology has always held the public's interest, and archaeologists have regularly published popular accounts of their work aimed at the general public. *Archaeology* magazine is a good example of this type of literature. Articles are generally written by scholars directly involved in the research being presented, and what is presented is usually up to date and informative. How do these reports differ from those previously described? Well, they usually contain only a minimum of actual data. Data are summarized and interpreted rather than directly presented. Second, citations are kept to a minimum and are not used as shorthand allusions to other literature or to bolster an argument as they are in scholarly literature. Finally, review is of a different kind. Editors seek well-written, interesting, and exciting material, and editors will turn down even the most important of discoveries if they think it won't interest a popular audience. Thus entertainment value is weighed more heavily than scientific value in popular reports and reviews.

12.3   WHAT ARE THE STANDARD FORMS OF PUBLICATION?

Although there are only four common types of publication, archaeologists obviously publish on a wide variety of topics. Site and research reports, syntheses, theoretical statements, and popular reports provide a framework for conveying ideas—they certainly don't limit them. Nor do they necessarily limit the forms of publication such work can take. By form I mean the organization or structure within which a particular type of archaeological publication is presented.

Dissertations are the reports of major research projects undertaken by graduate students as part of the requirements for earning a Ph.D. The project and the dissertation are done independently by the students but are closely monitored by students' advisors and by committees of three or four other scholars. Before starting the project students undergo preliminary or qualifying examinations by the committee in which the goals and methods of the project are scrutinized. If students pass, then they go out and complete the project. Once complete, the project reports, or dissertations, are read by the committee, which again examines the students. If the students pass this exam then they are awarded the Ph.D. So, dissertations are a rather strange form of publication. They are always the work of students, and almost always carry the mark of being written by naïve scholars. Tangential material and discussions are often included, frequently to please committee members rather than to directly further the arguments being made. Finally, dissertations are often verbose, packed with information that would never be published elsewhere. This last feature of dissertations makes them both excellent sources of data and information and often difficult sources to use.

Dissertations, when accepted by the students' committee, are deposited in the library of the university where they become a part of the library's permanent collection. Copies are usually kept in the department as well. At most institutions copies are also sent to University Microfilms International (UMI), which makes a microfilm copy to keep on file. Abstracts for all dissertations are published within a year or so of their completion in the serial *Dissertation Abstracts International*. Once a dissertation is listed, libraries and scholars can order copies from UMI. This actually makes dissertations one of the more accessible forms of publication because they never go out of print. UMI produces copies on demand and keeps dissertations on file forever. In addition, scholars can always locate a copy of a needed dissertation at the institution where it was completed.

Books and monographs are primary forms of publication in archaeology. They are particularly important forms for site reports because they allow for long, detailed discussions of excavation methods, data recovery and analysis, and interpretation of the archaeological record. Books are also important as edited volumes, that is, collections of shorter articles, each of which forms a chapter of a longer, unified book. Edited volumes allow a group of scholars to discuss a particular site, region, or topic within a common framework and usually provide a good introduction and an informative conclusion on the volume's focal topic. Books are formally distinguished from monographs by having an index, but they are more informally recognized as being produced by a professional publishing company. Monographs are more frequently produced by museums, university departments, and research organizations. Thus monographs are often published in small numbers and can only be found in research libraries. Some monographs are only produced in a few dozen copies (or less) and form one aspect of what is known as the "grey literature" of archaeology.

The term **grey literature** refers to archaeological reports with limited distribution and no peer review. These are often "contract" reports, written to describe the results of archaeological salvage work, but they also include some research reports produced by university or museum departments and even survey and excavation reports produced by amateur societies. While many grey literature publications are of high quality and contain valuable information, they are problematic because (1) their quality is not ensured through peer review and (2) the information they contain has a limited chance to become a part of the knowledge base with which the archaeological community works. Remember that information only becomes useful knowledge when it is cited and used by other scholars. Because of the very nature of this grey literature, it has a limited chance to be read and cited by other scholars and thus has a limited chance of becoming part of the archaeological knowledge base.

There are two schools of thought on the growing body of archaeological grey literature. One school sees it as beneficial to the discipline. Increasing costs of publication and diminishing returns on investments have led many professional publishing companies to shy away from publishing archaeological books and monographs. The grey literature ensures that materials lacking a broad interest base are at least produced in some form that is available to the archaeological community, if only in limited numbers. The other school of thought sees grey literature as a problem, primarily because there is no easy way to distinguish important works from poor ones. Scholars might have to go through a considerable amount of work simply to compile a bibliography of grey literature materials on a subject of interest, more work (and often expense) to acquire those materials, and after all that find little of use.

There is truth in both schools of thought, and the archaeological community as a whole recognizes a need to address the issue of grey literature. In fact, a number of groups are attempting to compile centralized bibliographies, some even annotated, on this grey literature. Perhaps the most successful to date has been the National Park Service, whose National Archaeological Database provides a massive, on-line bibliography of archaeological literature, including not only grey literature but also books, monographs, and a form of publication we have not yet discussed, journal articles.

Journal articles are arguably the most important form of archaeological publication. Literally dozens of professional archaeological journals publish hundreds of articles each year. Virtually all of these articles are peer reviewed, and thus there is some guarantee of quality or importance. Most journals cover a specific area of archaeological interest, such as a particular region (midwestern United States) or a particular type of artifact (lithics or ceramics). Thus finding material on a topic of interest is relatively easy, as we can simply browse those journals that cover that particular topic and be relatively assured that what we read will be of high quality.

It is important to note that the form of publication does not limit the topic or type. Any of the types of publication we discussed previously can be presented in any of these forms. Site and research reports are often presented as dissertations; many edited books are really lengthy theoretical statements; literature reviews and syntheses are often found in journals. Nothing intrinsically prevents any particular topic from being presented in any of these forms. The combination of a wide variety of topics and of publication forms makes archaeological literature diverse and flexible.

12.4 ARE THERE NONPRINT FORMS OF PUBLICATION?

So far I have only described printed forms of publication, but there have always been ways to convey information about the archaeological record outside of print media. In recent years the expansion of cable television, computers and the Internet, and ease of travel have led to a greater emphasis on nonprint forms of "publication" in archaeology. I put "publication" in quotes here because these forms are really not "publications" per se, but rather are additional ways archaeologists have available to get their ideas into circulation.

With the growth of cable television in the late 1980s and 1990s, a wide variety of television programs and documentary films on archaeology have been produced. These offer a new venue for conveying information about the archaeological record to both peers and the general public. Public television's *Nova* series, TBS's *National Geographic Explorer,* and the Discovery Channel group (including the Learning Channel and the History Channel) regularly offer documentary films on archaeology. In fact, the Discovery Channel's daily *Discovery News* regularly covers recent archaeological finds. These television programs provide archaeology with an outlet for public education that is unmatched by any print media. It is important to note, however, that some of these programs do not reflect good, scientific archaeological research of the kind I am presenting in this book (and particularly in this chapter), that is, with a firm grounding in the relevant literature. It is often very hard to know whether a program is founded on good research, but there are two useful guides. First, if the ideas presented contradict what is already known or accepted, those ideas must be carefully scrutinized. Second, if the ideas have been put forward for peer review and have been rejected, then that calls those ideas into question. Neither of these conditions should make you reject the ideas in a documentary outright, but they should make you wary of them.

Unlike television, computer-based forms of publication have not yet reached their apparent potential. Only a handful of computer-based resources are available today, but they offer a tantalizing view of what is possible. For example, the CD-ROM *Excavating Occaneechi Town* brings together a comprehensive set of maps, photographs, and textual descriptions of a thoroughly excavated eighteenth-century Indian village in North Carolina.[4] It allows users to explore areas of interest by an unstructured and self-directed path and to grasp, in a way not possible through print, the process of how archaeologists piece together the archaeological record to create a picture of the past. A more exciting picture of the past is provided through virtual reality. The University of Pennsylvania Museum of Anthropology and Archaeology Web page, for example, provides a three-dimensional "fly-by" of the ancient city of Corinth in addition to a changing set of "virtual exhibits" on a variety of topics.[5] These kinds of virtual reality reconstructions bring the past to life in a way print media simply cannot.

The World Wide Web provides an entirely new way for archaeologists to archive data and present results. Not only are data on the Web available to scholars twenty-four hours a day, seven days a week, but they are also available to anyone, anywhere on earth! Large sets of data, complete with maps, drawings, and photographs, can be readily archived on the Web—indeed, whole sets of excavation records and even entire museum collections are being put on-line. One excellent example is the Perseus Project based at Tufts University. The project was started in 1985 with the idea of creating a digital library of classical Greek literature. It has expanded tremendously since then and contains not only several hundred texts, but also detailed information on ceramics, works of art, buildings, and archaeological sites of the ancient Greek world.[6] The Perseus Project offers a clear picture of how effective the Web can be for conveying information about the archaeological record to a world audience. One word of caution, though: Lots of sites on the World Wide Web are based on truly bad archaeology or offer gross misrepresentations of the archaeological record. The two guides just discussed for evaluating documentaries (examining how the information relates to current knowledge and the extent to which that information has been evaluated and accepted by other archaeologists) should always be applied to Web sites.

While documentary films and computer-based media are two of the newer means archaeologists have available to convey information about the archaeological record, attending and giving lectures and workshops have always been important means of disseminating the results of archaeological research. National and regional meetings of professional organizations offer scholars a chance to describe recent findings in an open forum and provide the opportunity to test ideas before sending them off to journals for review. Public lectures offer archaeologists a chance to describe their work to the general public, and some organizations, such as the Archaeological Institute of America, have hosted such lectures for decades.

Workshops are generally more focused, often hands-on, venues for teaching specific topics or methods in archaeological research. Many national meetings hold concurrent workshops on a variety of topics from lithic analysis to historic preservation law. They offer a small group the chance to intensely investigate the topic in an open forum. Workshops are sometimes also held for the general public. Local amateur groups, for example, might provide workshops on excavation to promote historic preservation in their area and to gain additional training for themselves. In either case, workshops offer a valuable opportunity for learning.

12.5   SUMMARY

In order for archaeological data to become knowledge it must be published. Publication not only makes data accessible but, through the processes of peer review and citation, brings those data into the ongoing archaeological discourse. Archaeologists publish several types of work, from site or research reports to literature reviews to theoretical statements. Archaeologists publish their work in several forms as well. Most professional archaeologists produce a dissertation at least once in their career, and most produce several books or monographs as well. Journal articles are the primary form of archaeological publication. In addition to these print forms of publication, archaeologists also disseminate data through television and computers and orally in lectures, conferences, and workshops. The diversity of types and forms of publication in archaeology is no accident. Archaeological research and archaeological findings are so diverse that no single type or form of publication would ever be satisfactory for it all. In addition, by using a diversity of publication types and forms, archaeology assures that its audience will be broad.

SUGGESTED READINGS

American Psychological Association. 1994. *Publication Manual of the American Psychological Association* (4th ed.). Washington, DC: American Psychological Association. This probably looks like a strange resource for an archaeology book, but most archaeology publications follow APA style. This book also offers a good overview of the publication process and the elements of a good journal article.

Heizer, Robert, Thomas Hester, and Carol Graves. 1980. *Archaeology: A Bibliographical Guide to the Basic Literature.* New York: Garland Publishing. An older but still useful guide to archaeological literature of all types.

Latour, Bruno. 1987. *Science in Action.* Cambridge, MA: Harvard University Press. Latour presents a controversial view of how scientists create knowledge by following established ideas back to the starting points. For this chapter, discussions of scientific literature are key, but the book is useful for anyone wishing to understand how scientists really work.

McCloskey, Donald. 1985. *The Rhetoric of Economics.* Madison: University of Wisconsin Press. McCloskey also presents a controversial view of how scientists develop arguments in writing. His focus is on economics, but his insights are applicable to all scientific disciplines.

Weeks, John M. 1998. *Introduction to Library Research in Anthropology* (2nd ed.). Boulder, CO: Westview Press. A clear introduction to the literature of anthropology, written in an easy manner specifically for students.

NOTES

1. My ideas about citation were largely influenced by Bruno Latour, *Science in Action* (Cambridge, MA: Harvard University Press, 1987).

2. For a more comprehensive discussion of this, see Donald McCloskey, *The Rhetoric of Economics* (Madison: University of Wisconsin Press, 1985).

3. A key work is Michael Schiffer, *Behavioral Archaeology* (New York: Academic Press, 1976).

4. Stephen Davis, Patrick Livingood, Trawick Ward, and Vincas Steponaitis, *Excavating Occaneechi Town* (Chapel Hill: University of North Carolina Press, 1997).

5. The Museum's Web address is www.museum.upenn.edu.

6. The Perseus Project site is www.perseus.tufts.edu.

Legal and Ethical Issues

OVERVIEW

13.1 What Laws Regulate Archaeology in the United States?

13.2 What Principles Regulate the Behavior of Professional Archaeologists?

13.3 Summary

M ore than 150 years ago Alexis de Tocqueville noted: "Scarcely any political question arises in the United States that is not resolved, sooner or later, into a judicial question."[1] That is certainly true with the question of how to deal with the past. The past is a political figure, and, as I noted in the Preface, is regularly used for political purposes. It should be no surprise, then, that legal issues play a major role in archaeology, both in the United States and elsewhere in the world. In this chapter I will outline some of the history of archaeological legislation in the United States and the impact it has on research. At the end of the chapter I will discuss the Society for American Archaeology's code of ethics, which can be taken as a set of laws guiding the individual behavior of archaeologists.

13.1   WHAT LAWS REGULATE ARCHAEOLOGY IN THE UNITED STATES?

Archaeological legislation in the United States began with the **Antiquities Act of 1906**, which made it a felony to damage or remove archaeological or historical sites on government property.[2] This act established all the basic ideas that stand behind current legislation, and it is important to understand those ideas before continuing. A basic idea behind the law is that the archaeological record is part of the public record, just as are marriage licenses, death certificates, real estate titles, and the like. Just as we cannot go around simply throwing away or burning titles to real estate, we cannot destroy the archaeological record—it, too, is a public document. A second basic idea in the law is that the federal government assumes the responsibility for protecting the archaeological record. In essence, they "claim" the archaeological record for all U.S. citizens.

A federal government laying claim to all antiquities found within its borders is not unusual in the world; in fact, many countries today have laws that basically outlaw the personal ownership of antiquities.[3] Obviously, this is not the case in the United States, for while the law establishes the principle that the archaeological record is part of the public record, it formally protects only that part of the archaeological record found on federal land or in the course of an activity where federal funds are involved. This is a third important principle in archaeological legislation that has its roots in the Antiquities Act of 1906.

The **Historic Sites Act of 1935**, a logical extension of the Antiquities Act, declared a national policy to identify and protect important archaeological and historic sites on federal land.[4] If you think about it, this is necessary to enforce the Antiquities Act, but it also goes farther. It makes it part of federal policy to actually go out and find sites in order to preserve and protect them. This policy was further developed and strengthened through the **Historic Preservation Act of 1966**, which established the National Register of Historic Places and the National Trust for Historic Preservation.[5]

The **National Register of Historic Places** is a list of historic properties and archaeological sites that have been nominated, evaluated, and approved as significant parts of U.S. history. Sites on the National Register are protected to the extent that they cannot be wantonly altered or destroyed (although both alteration and demolition can be done with approval from a state or federal historic preservation officer). The establishment of the National Register, however, has had much broader impact than simply creating a list of important sites. Part of the act that created the National Register also created a fund of money, the National Trust for Historic Preservation, to be used in evaluating sites for the National Register. In order to locate and evaluate National Register–eligible sites and to disburse funds from the National Trust, the Historic Preservation Act also required each state to create a liaison officer for historic preservation. It is from this requirement that the current network of state archaeologists emerged.[6]

Together, these laws have been very effective in promoting archaeology and historic preservation. Perhaps the best example is a federal highway project that built the Interstate 270 bypass around St. Louis, Missouri, known in American archaeology as the FAI-270 project. The bypass happened to cut across one of the richest archaeological areas in North America, known as the American Bottom. In the 1100s some 50,000 or more people inhabited the American Bottom region, and the largest settlement north of Mexico—Cahokia—contained at least 10,000 of them. Over a seven-year period, dozens of archaeological sites were excavated as highway construction proceeded.[7]

Archaeological crews followed highway surveyors as they mapped the location of the highway, identifying where the highway ran across archaeological sites. Test excavations were performed, and when significant archaeological deposits were located, complete salvage excavations were undertaken.[8] Archaeological work proceeded year-round. Dozens of supervisors and scores of workers, all supported by federal money, excavated, catalogued, and analyzed the millions of artifacts, ecofacts, and features found.

A generation of midwestern archaeologists was trained by the FAI-270 project, and archaeology as a whole still benefits from the more than twenty detailed monographs that came out of the project, some of them arguably among the finest excavation reports published in midwestern archaeology. This project illustrates how well these laws have worked to foster archaeology and historic preservation.

More recently, Congress passed the **Native American Graves Protection and Repatriation Act of 1990** (NAGPRA), which provides absolute protection to Native American graves on federal land, and which makes it a felony to collect, possess, or transfer human remains of known affinity to an existing Native American culture except by the members of that culture." This extends to all objects found in grave contexts and to sacred or ritual objects and other important "objects of cultural patrimony." The law also mandated that institutions receiving federal money that had such remains or objects notify representatives of the affiliated culture and establish a process to "repatriate" those remains and objects, that is, to transfer them to the affiliated Native American group for curation.

In some ways this is a continuation of the logic of the historic preservation laws. Recall the basic principles: Antiquities are part of the public record claimed for all citizens, and they are the responsibility of the federal government to find and protect. Federally recognized Native American groups, however, are legally sovereign nations. Thus, antiquities relating to those groups are part of *their* public record, not the United States's, and should be held in trust by the sovereign groups themselves for their citizens. NAGPRA, therefore, turns the responsibility of managing the archaeological record of another sovereign nation (a federally recognized Native American group) over to that nation. The sovereign nation can choose whether to accept the responsibility. If it accepts it, then NAGPRA requires that all pieces of its archaeological record held in federal agencies or in agencies receiving federal funds be turned over to that nation.

In other ways NAGPRA seems to contradict the history of U.S. historic preservation, at least in the way it has been implemented. One of the major problems with the law stems from identifying to which Native American group archaeological materials belong. Once we go back into prehistory, it is often impossible to follow ancestry. Yet some Native American groups have claimed that *all* prehistoric materials are part of their public record and should be repatriated. Indeed, opposing claims have led to conflicts between Native American groups over the deposition of archaeological materials. A second problem with NAGPRA is that some Native American groups who have rather strong claims to particular aspects of the archaeological record are not federally recognized and thus don't fall under the law. Provisions for nonrecognized groups have been developed, but in practice these provisions have opened the contention about who gets what materials to all kinds of political and religious interest groups rather than to sovereign nations.[10]

Finally, one of the more common results of the repatriation process has been reburial of excavated materials. This has led to the bizarre situation of federal funds, under the Antiquities Act and other federal laws, being used to excavate archaeological deposits, which are then, as mandated under NAGPRA, repatriated to Native American groups, who rebury those materials! Some see this as the best of both worlds: Archaeologists can excavate materials, record context, and get the data they want; the sovereign Native American nations get control of the record of their past. Others see it as an extraordinary contradiction that needs to be fixed.[11]

Perhaps the most famous NAGPRA case to date concerns "Kennewick Man," a possibly 9,200-year-old skeleton found in July of 1996 along the Columbia River in Washington state. The find is remarkable in several ways. First, it is one of only a half-dozen or so skeletons from this early a date in the New World. Second, it is very well preserved for its early date. Third, it shows clear evidence of death from violence (a projectile point is embedded in the skeleton). Finally, there is some tantalizing evidence that this individual, as well as others from similarly ancient contexts, do not show some of the typical skeletal features found among contemporary Native Americans, suggesting that they may be from a population of early North American inhabitants that died out. Unfortunately, before any of these interesting facets of the skeleton could be examined, the U.S. Army Corps of Engineers decided to repatriate the remains to the Confederated Tribes of the Umatilla Indian Reservation, as the remains were found on Corps land within the reservation. An injunction filed by a group of archaeologists stopped the repatriation and has led to a long and bitter legal battle among the archaeologists, the Corps of Engineers, the Umatilla and other Native American groups, and even several non-Native American groups who want to claim the remains.[12]

At the core of the battle is the question: To whose public record does this skeleton belong? If this is an individual who is related to contemporary Native Americans, then can the Umatilla speak for all Native American groups, even though 9,000 years may separate them? Or should other Native American groups, who may also be descended from this individual or his group, also have a say in what happens? If this is an individual who appears not to be related to contemporary Native Americans, then should the U.S. government decide what happens to his remains? Underlying these questions is a deeper struggle between archaeologists and Native Americans over whose wishes and ideas carry the most weight. This is a worst case scenario for both sides. In recent years archaeologists and Native Americans have tried to work together, forming a mutually beneficial relationship that is now breaking down over conflicts of interest and mistrust stemming from NAGPRA. There is no easy answer to this issue, even after the court decides on the Kennewick Man case. The legal issues faced by archaeologists in the United States are likely to become more, not less, complex in the future, regardless of how this case is decided.

13.2   WHAT PRINCIPLES REGULATE THE BEHAVIOR OF PROFESSIONAL ARCHAEOLOGISTS?

The legislation I've just described defines how the public as a whole, and archaeologists in particular, are legally expected to treat the archaeological resources we encounter. But what about the behavior of individual archaeologists? Is any behavior that does not violate one of these laws acceptable behavior for professional archaeologists? Are there standards in addition to these legal ones to which professional archaeologists should be expected to adhere? In 1996, the Society for American Archaeology formally announced that there were additional guidelines archaeologists must follow by adopting the following Principles of Archaeological Ethics.[13]

Principle 1: Stewardship

"The archaeological record, that is, in situ archaeological material and sites, archaeological collections, records, and reports, is irreplaceable. It is the responsibility of all archaeologists to work for the long-term conservation and protection of the archaeological record by practicing and promoting stewardship of the archaeological record. Stewards are both caretakers of and advocates for the archaeological record. In the interests of stewardship, archaeologists should use and advocate use of the archaeological record for the benefit of all people; as they investigate and interpret the record, they should use the specialized knowledge they gain to promote public understanding and support for its long-term preservation."[14]

Archaeologists, according to this principle, are expected to not only uphold historic preservation laws but also go beyond them to actively promote stewardship and protection of archaeological resources through education, outreach, and even lobbying for the care and protection of archaeological sites.

Principle 2: Accountability

"Responsible archaeological research, including all levels of professional activity, requires an acknowledgment of public accountability and a commitment to make every reasonable effort, in good faith, to consult actively with affected group(s), with the goal of establishing a working relationship that can be beneficial to all parties involved."[15]

The archaeology laws make it clear that archaeology focuses on caring for a unique segment of the public record. This principle stems directly from that idea. Since archaeology is done for the benefit of the public, archaeologists must be accountable to the public; that is, they have to make their findings known and accessible. In addition to this, however, archaeology is an inherently political activity, and any archaeological research will have political implications for some group. When such an impacted group is known, archaeologists are expected to consult with the group on a regular basis and to be receptive to and understanding of the political implications of their activities.

Principle 3: Commercialization

"The Society for American Archaeology has long recognized that the buying and selling of objects out of archaeological context is contributing to the destruction of the archaeological record on the American continents and around the world. The commercialization of archaeological objects—their use as commodities to be exploited for personal enjoyment or profit—results in the destruction of archaeological sites and of contextual information that is essential to understanding the archaeological record. Archaeologists should therefore carefully weigh the benefits to scholarship of a project against the costs of potentially enhancing the commercial value of archaeological objects. Wherever possible, they should discourage, and should themselves avoid, activities that enhance the commercial value of archaeological objects, especially objects that are not curated in public institutions, or readily available for scientific study, public interpretation, and display."[16]

This principle stems directly from the principle of stewardship and is in line with the historic preservation laws previously discussed. In terms of stewardship, archaeologists are expected to preserve the archaeological record. To the extent that the buying and selling of artifacts foster the destruction of the archaeological record, archaeologists are expected to dissuade commercialization. In terms of historic preservation law, the archaeological record is part of the public record. Any activity that takes the archaeological record out of public access, such as the private collecting of artifacts, must also be actively discouraged by professional archaeologists.

Obviously, this is one of the more ticklish of the Principles of Archaeological Ethics. Throughout this book I have made it clear that amateur archaeologists are welcomed as informants and assistants. But most amateur archaeologists are also collectors. What are archaeologists to do? In my case I have encouraged amateurs to allow their collections to be documented (photographed and recorded) and asked that they seriously consider donating their collection to public institutions, perhaps through their wills.

Principle 4: Public Education and Outreach

"Archaeologists should reach out to, and participate in, cooperative efforts with others interested in the archaeological record with the aim of improving the preservation, protection, and interpretation of the record. In particular, archaeologists should undertake to: (1) enlist public support for the steward-ship of the archaeological record; (2) explain and promote the use of archaeological methods and techniques in understanding human behavior and culture; and (3) communicate archaeological interpretations of the past. Many publics exist for archaeology including students and teachers; Native Americans and other ethnic, religious, and cultural groups who find in the archaeological record important aspects of their cultural heritage; lawmakers and government officials; reporters, journalists, and others involved in the media; and the general public. Archaeologists who are unable to undertake public education and outreach directly should encourage and support the efforts of others in these activities."[17]

This principle stems directly from the first on stewardship and is, in essence, simply an extension of it. The logic is this: If archaeologists are to promote the stewardship of the archaeological record, they need to make it clear why such stewardship is important. That is where public education and outreach come in. Helping the public to understand what archaeology is, what archaeologists do, and why archaeology is important also helps the public to understand why it is important to protect the archaeological record.

Principle 5: Intellectual Property

"Intellectual property, as contained in the knowledge and documents created through the study of archaeological resources, is part of the archaeological record. As such it should be treated in accord with the principles of steward-ship rather than as a matter of personal possession. If there is a compelling reason, and no legal restrictions or strong countervailing interests, a researcher may have primary access to original materials and documents for a limited and reasonable time, after which these materials and documents must be made available to others."[18]

This principle might seem fairly innocuous, but it was perhaps the most controversial of all of them. Why? Well, there is a long-standing tradition in archaeology that the excavators of a site have exclusive right to the material they have excavated. In many ways this makes sense. The excavators not only know the most about the site, and thus are most able to accurately report on it, but also have put in a lot of hard work excavating the site and should be given the opportunity to gain the rewards of publishing the collected data. Unfortunately, some archaeologists (and even some institutions) have treated their collections not as parts of the public record held in their trust but as their own private collections. These archaeologists and institutions have actively prevented other archaeologists and the public from using the collections. This principle makes it clear that such practices are not appropriate.

Principle 6: Public Reporting and Publication

"Within a reasonable time, the knowledge archaeologists gain from investigation of the archaeological record must be presented in accessible form (through publication or other means) to as wide a range of interested publics as possible. The documents and materials on which publication and other forms of public reporting are based should be deposited in a suitable place for permanent safekeeping. An interest in preserving and protecting in situ archaeological sites must be taken into account when publishing and distributing information about their nature and location."[19]

This principle really follows from the previous one, for in many cases the reason given for preventing access to collections was that excavators had not finished examining and publishing them. As I have noted a few times, archaeologists have not been very good about publishing materials in a timely manner. This principle says, in essence, that archaeologists can control material they have excavated for a reasonable time, but if they haven't worked on or published it in a timely manner, they must allow other archaeologists the opportunity to work on and publish that material. In addition, this principle implies that publication must be in a form that preserves the information and that provides access to other researchers. The reason should be clear enough from our discussion of archaeological literature. Archaeologists' reports are, quite literally, the only real knowledge we have about excavated sites, and thus it is vital to make that information both secure and available.

Principle 7: Records and Preservation

"Archaeologists should work actively for the preservation of, and long-term access to, archaeological collections, records, and reports. To this end, they should encourage colleagues, students, and others to make responsible use of collections, records, and reports in their research as one means of preserving the in situ archaeological record, and of increasing the care and attention given to that portion of the archaeological record which has been removed and incorporated into archaeological collections, records, and reports."[20]

This principle is an extension of principles 5 and 6, making it more clear that collections are not the property of the individual or institution who excavated them but rather are held in trust for the public. Thus archaeologists have the responsibility to ensure that collections and their associated records are well cared for. This principle, however, contains an important additional point. It states that archaeologists should not only maintain collections but also actively encourage their use by others. Research done on existing collections has been something of a rarity in archaeology, but if we take the principle of stewardship seriously, then we really must try to use existing materials before excavating—and hence destroying—additional sites.

Principle 8: Training and Resources

"Given the destructive nature of most archaeological investigations, archaeologists must ensure that they have adequate training, experience, facilities, and other support necessary to conduct any program of research they initiate in a manner consistent with the foregoing principles and contemporary standards of professional practice. . . ."[21]

This final principle is a fairly obvious one. It tells archaeologists not to undertake a project unless they have the training and support to complete it with excellence. Once a site is excavated, it can never be excavated again. Ensuring that all excavations are done with the highest levels of excellence in mind is vital, and this principle reminds us of that.

13.3   SUMMARY

A number of key laws regulate archaeology in the United States. The Antiquities Act of 1906 established the basic principles underlying all of them: (1) The archaeological record is a part of the public record; (2) the federal government takes responsibility for protecting the archaeological record; but (3) this is only on federal lands or in the course of federally funded projects. These basic principles were developed and expanded in the Historic Sites Act of 1935 and the National Historic Preservation Act of 1966. They were extended to sovereign Native American governments through the Native American Graves Protection and Repatriation Act of 1990.

The individual behavior of archaeologists is also regulated by a set of ethical principles established, in the United States, by the Society for American Archaeology in 1996. They are based on the fundamental premise that stewardship of the archaeological record and regular dissemination of information about the archaeological record are key to the behavior of professional archaeologists.

SUGGESTED READINGS

Lynott, Mark. 1997. "Ethical Principles and Archaeological Practice: Development of an Ethics Policy," *American Antiquity* 62(4):589–599. A formal presentation of the Society for American Archaeology's code of ethics and how it was developed.

Lynott, Mark J., and Alison Wylie, eds. 1995. *Ethics in American Archaeology: Challenges for the 1990s*. Washington, DC: Society for American Archaeology. A good collection of articles about the Society for American Archaeology's code of ethics, how it was developed, and the desired impact on American archaeology.

McGimsey, Charles. 1972. *Public Archaeology*. New York: Seminar Press. An older but still useful overview of historic preservation laws and practice in the United States.

Smith, George, and John Ehrenard, eds. 1991. *Protecting the Past*. Boca Raton, FL: CRC Press. By far the best single source on historic preservation in the United States. The essays in this book cover the entire range of topics from laws and their implementation to the practice of cultural resource management.

Vitelli, Karen, ed. 1996. *Archaeological Ethics*. Walnut Creek, CA: Alta Mira. A collection of articles from *Archaeology* magazine which are both readable and informative.

NOTES

1. Alexis de Tocqueville, *Democracy in America,* the Henry Reeve text, rev. Francis Bowen, further corrected and ed. Phillips Bradley (New York: Knopf, 1945/1840).
2. Public Law 59–209 (16 U.S.C. 431–433).
3. Many of these are discussed in H. F. Cleere, ed., *Archaeological Heritage Management in the Modern World* (London: Unwin Hyman, 1989).
4. Public Law 74–292 (16 U.S.C. 461–467).
5. Public Law 89–665 (16 U.S.C. 470).
6. For a brief overview see John Fowler, "The Legal Structure for the Protection of Archaeological Resources," in *Protecting the Past,* ed. George Smith and John Ehrenhard (Boca Raton, FL: CRC Press, 1991), pp. 21–25.
7. Charles Bareis and James Porter, *American Bottom Archaeology* (Urbana: University of Illinois Press, 1984).
8. Ibid., pp. 1–14.
9. Public Law 101–601 (25 U.S.C. 3001–3013)
10. See, for example, Clement Meighan's discussion of the reburial of materials from a West Virginia burial mound in "Burying American Archaeology," *Archaeology* 47 (1994):64.
11. Ibid.
12. A good summary of this extraordinary case was put together by Andrew Slayman, "A Battle over Old Bones," *Archaeology* 50 (1997):16–23.
13. Mark J. Lynott and Alison Wylie, eds., *Ethics in American Archaeology: Challenges for the 1990s* (Washington, DC: Society for American Archaeology, 1995); also Mark Lynott, "Ethical Principles and Archaeological Practice: Development of an Ethics Policy," *American Antiquity* 62 (1997):589–599.

14. Society for American Archaeology, "Principles of Archaeological Ethics," *American Antiquity* 61 (1996):451.

15. Ibid.

16. Ibid., pp. 451–452.

17. Ibid., p. 452.

18. Ibid.

19. Ibid.

20. Ibid.

21. Ibid.

14

Research Opportunities

OVERVIEW

14.1   How Can I Gain Field Experience in Archaeology?

14.2   Summary

I n Oscar Wilde's only novel, *The Picture of Dorian Gray*, the character of Lord Henry (often thought to be Wilde's own self-portrait) lamented that the value of experience was misunderstood, that it was "merely the name men gave to their mistakes."[1] Most archaeologists would probably agree, but they would not be bothered in the way Lord Henry is. Archaeologists know that they learn by making mistakes. There is no substitute for experience in archaeology—archaeologists learn archaeology by doing archaeology. Indeed, the Register of Professional Archaeologists requires a total of fifty-two weeks—a full year!—of archaeological experience before awarding certification as professional archaeologists. Because mistakes on an archaeological site can be extremely destructive, it is important that archaeological experience be gained, and mistakes made, under the supervision of experienced archaeologists who can recognize those mistakes and fix them before they become grave problems. So, if you want to become an archaeologist, you'll need to gain lots of experience by doing research with trained, professional archaeologists. In this chapter I'll describe some of the ways you can gain experience in archaeological research and offer some ideas about whom to contact for more detailed and up-to-date information.

14.1 HOW CAN I GAIN FIELD EXPERIENCE IN ARCHAEOLOGY?

The typical—and probably easiest—way to gain experience is through a **field school**. The term *field school* is what archaeologists call a formal field archaeology experience under the supervision of trained professionals. Many universities and colleges offer field schools, as do a few state historical societies and local amateur archaeological societies. All involve trained professionals whose job it is to oversee the work performed by student archaeologists. In a way, a field school is like an apprenticeship. If you want to learn how to do archaeology, a field school is the best possible place.

Most field schools last six to eight weeks, and most are held during the summer months when colleges and universities are on break. One of the odd things about field schools is that you almost always have to pay for them. I recall that in the first field school I attended we were so excited about archaeology that we put in extra hours in the evenings and on weekends—extra hours for which our supervisor threatened to make us pay extra! If you are a college or university student you can usually recover some of the costs of attending a field school by applying for academic credit. Many field schools are designed as summer courses offering credit, and, even if they are not, students can often arrange to make a field school count as an independent study or internship.

Finding field schools is not difficult. Probably the easiest place to start looking is on the bulletin boards in the anthropology department of your college or university. Most fields schools advertise by sending out fliers to anthropology departments, and most departments post them in an obvious location. There are, however, a number of more formal places to look. Each year the Archaeological Institute of America publishes a comprehensive, international list of field schools as the *Archaeological Fieldwork Opportunities Bulletin*. This resource is available in many libraries or can be purchased through the Kendall/Hunt publishing company (4050 Westmark Drive, Dubuque, Iowa 52002. Tel: 800-228-0810). The National Park service also publishes a more general list of historic preservation training opportunities in the United States as the *Cultural Resources Training Directory*. This directory is available on-line at www.cr.nps.gov/crm/dir or can be obtained through the National Park Service, Archaeology and Ethnography Program (1849 C Street, N.W., Washington, DC 20240. Tel. 202-343-4101). There is also an on-line list of field schools that can be reached through either the National Park Service (www.cr.nps.gov) or the Archaeology Virtual Subject Library (www.lib.uconn.edu/ArchNet).

You can attend a number of more focused, often noncredit field schools. Two of the best in the United States are run by the Crow Canyon Archaeological Center and the Center for American Archaeology. Both nonprofit educational and research organizations offer a variety of short archaeological training programs for adults, special programs for high school and middle school students, and special interest programs on subjects such as flintknapping, ceramics, and the like. The focus of research for the Crow Canyon Archaeological Center is the region surrounding Mesa Verde National Park in Colorado. The focus of research for the Center for American Archaeology is the lower Illinois River valley. You can contact the Crow Canyon Archaeological Center on the World Wide Web at www.crowcanyon.org or by telephone at 800-422-8975. You can contact the Center for American Archaeology at www.caa-archaeology.org or by telephone at 618-653-4316.

If you have already completed a field school or aren't all that interested in paying for a research opportunity, there are still opportunities for volunteer work. Many college and university departments—and most museums—have volunteer positions. Volunteers do many things, from cataloguing artifacts to leading museum tours.

Opportunities to volunteer can be found through many of the same resources where field schools are listed, as many field schools also accept volunteers. In addition, however, several federal agencies have special volunteer programs. The National Park Service is one, and their programs are listed in the *Cultural Resources Training Directory*. The U.S. Forest Service has volunteer opportunities listed on its Web page (www.fs.fed.us/recreation/opp_to_vol.html) and in a publication called *Passport in Time*, available from the Passport in Time Clearinghouse (P.O. Box 31315, Tucson, AZ 85751-1315. Tel. 800-281-9176). The Bureau of Land Management also lists volunteer opportunities on its Web page (www.blm.gov/education/volunteer) and through its Environmental Education and Volunteers Group (1849 C Street, Suite LS-406, Washington, DC 20240. Tel. 202-452-5078).

Many local amateur archaeological societies also have research opportunities available. As I have said before, amateur archaeologists are often the most knowledgeable people around, and professional archaeologists are usually very interested in keeping on their good side. For that reason, many professional archaeologists provide research opportunities for local amateurs, from weekend excavation or survey at a nearby site to lab work processing or analyzing artifacts collected previously. Joining an amateur society often provides openings to do archaeological research in a variety of venues.

You can find information about local amateur societies on the World Wide Web through the Archaeology Virtual Subject Library (www.lib.uconn.edu/ArchNet) and the Society for American Archaeology (www.saa.org/Publications/AOA/alliorg.html). Contact information for amateur societies in the United States is listed in print annually in the fourth issue of the journal *North American Archaeologist*.

Very rarely, paid research opportunities arise, but usually some experience is necessary. Frankly, there are more archaeologists than paid positions out there. However, the pundits keep saying that archaeology is a growing field, and I have to admit that I have never had a problem placing students with professional archaeology firms. To find a paid archaeology position, it is probably best to go through the archaeologists at your college or university. They can make the contacts for you and serve as references. However, jobs are often listed in the *SAA Bulletin*; professional archaeology firms (which you can contact for job opportunities) are also listed on the Society for American Archaeology Web page (www.saa.org).

14.2   SUMMARY

Field experience is an essential part of learning to be archaeologists. Field schools are the best possible places to gain field experience. You can gain additional field experience by volunteering, by taking additional field courses, or even by obtaining paid positions doing archaeology. Don't try to gain experience yourself—it's unethical and destructive. If you do "dig" by yourself and are found out, you may well find yourself in prison, and you will probably be ostracized by the archaeological community. As intriguing as archaeology is, try to remember that it is also extraordinarily destructive. So I repeat: Don't think that you have the skills of a professional archaeologist and go and dig a site yourself. Trust the profession, and value yourself enough to learn the skills and knowledge necessary to do archaeology. That is a challenge you will never regret.

SUGGESTED READINGS

Archaeological Institute of America (annual). *Archaeological Fieldwork Opportunities Bulletin*. Dubuque, IA: Kendall/Hunt. A key resource for finding field schools and volunteer field positions.

National Park Service (annual). *Cultural Resources Training Directory*, U.S. Government Printing Office, Washington, DC. A resource with information on a wide variety of seminars, workshops, and field schools for archaeology, most aimed at people with some background in archaeology.

NOTE

1. Oscar Wilde, *The Picture of Dorian Gray* (New York: Harper and Row, 1965/1891), p. 52.

Glossary

Absolute dating refers to methods used to assign a date to an archaeological deposit or artifact that provides a true chronometric date for when the deposit or artifact itself was made or discarded.

Accession catalogues are used in the lab after artifacts and ecofacts are initially processed (washed and conserved) and provide the numbers (called *accession numbers*) with which artifacts and ecofacts are marked for storage. The accession catalogue is the primary record for all materials after excavation.

Accession records describe and record what was found during an archaeological investigation.

Activity areas are locations on a site where a group of artifacts associated with a particular activity (for example, stoneworking, pottery making, food processing) are found together. Often the artifacts found are the refuse from the activity.

Aerial photographs, taken from airplanes or satellites, provide unique, large-scale views for archaeological reconnaissance.

Amino acid racemization is an absolute dating technique that can only be used on bone. It is based on the fact that amino acids in living tissue polarize light to the left. After death, the amino acids begin to change into a form that polarizes light to the right. By measuring the ratio of left-polarizing to right-polarizing amino acids in bone, archaeologists can estimate how long ago an organism died.

Antiquities Act of 1906 made it a felony to damage or remove archaeological or historical sites on government property.

Applique is the technique used by potters to add paste or other material to the surface of a ceramic object.

Arbitrary levels are used to give vertical control to an excavation where stratigraphy is poor or nonexistent.

Archaeobotanists are specialists who study plant remains from archaeological contexts.

Archaeological survey refers to methods used to examine an area to determine if archaeological deposits are present.

Artifacts are items of human manufacture or modification that can be collected or otherwise removed from a site.

Artifact typologies place materials in a geographic or temporal context with other, similar artifacts. Archaeologists can use typologies to assign dates to an archaeological deposit based on the types of artifacts found in it.

Association refers to a method of relative dating based on the idea that if you know the date of a given item and it is found within a deposit of interest or in association with an object of interest, it is reasonable (under most circumstances) to assign the same date to the associated deposit or object.

Atl-atls are wooden or bone shafts with hooks on the end used to help throw spears.

Balks are thin (usually 10-to 25-centimeter) walls of unexcavated soil left between test pits in cases where stratigraphy is very complicated or where sites are very deep.

Behaviorist theories suggest that the archaeological record is really a snapshot of ancient behavior.

Blades are long, thin, purposely created flake tools, usually made from a **prepared core**. Blades can be used as is, they can be modified into other tools, or they can be combined into what are called **composite tools**.

Block approach refers to an excavation strategy in which archaeologists open a large area of soil at one time, excavating down across the whole block at once either by arbitrary levels or by cultural strata defined by a **sounding**.

Body shape refers to the overall form of a ceramic object.

Bottom-up strategy refers to a strategy of archaeological survey in which archaeologists begin the survey at an established site and work outward from it, attempting to find related sites.

Bulb of percussion is left on a stone when a flake is knocked from it. It has a round shape radiating out from the **striking platform**.

Burins are chipped stone tools that have a single, sharp point used for engraving wood or bone.

Burnishing refers to a surface finish made on ceramics by polishing it to a high gloss with a smooth rock.

Cation ratio is an absolute dating technique based on measuring the ratio of particular elements (or cations) that leach out of rocks at differential rates during weathering.

Celts are ungrooved stone axes.

Central place theory was developed by Walter Christaller in the 1930s as a way to model a "perfect" settlement system given interactions between settlements based on a known set of principles.

Ceramics are objects made from clay (or, more accurately, from a **paste**) that have been heated to high temperature (called **firing**) to drive out moisture and make them hard.

Chert is a relatively impure form of quartz (about 90 percent) used to make chipped stone tools.

Chipped stone tools are made by removing small chips (or **flakes**) of stone from a larger piece of stone, called a **core**.

Citation is the act of referring to another scholar's work within the text of one's own work. It allows scholars to situate their work in the context of previous work. Through citation future archaeologists can bring work into the web of accepted archaeological knowledge.

Cluster sampling occurs when researchers select a case by **random sampling** and then include contiguous cases as part of the sample.

Coating refers to adding a slip, wash, or glaze to the surface of a ceramic item.

Coiling is a method of making ceramics in which potters begin with long and often thick strands of clay which they coil to form the basic shape of the desired item.

Context is the relationship between and among artifacts, ecofacts, and features.

Cores are raw pieces of flint, chert, or obsidian from which tools are made.

Cortex is the weathered, chalky surface often found on a nodule of chert, flint, or obsidian.

Culture-historical theory suggests that archaeologists can reconstruct the cultural history of a location from the superpositioning of archaeological materials.

Culture-history is simply a history of the cultures that inhabited a particular location or region.

Daily logs are journals written by members of an excavation crew explaining exactly what work they performed, the conditions of work, what they found, and any other observations or insights the crew members want to add.

Data analysis refers to the processes through which archaeologists obtain information from artifacts, ecofacts, and features that have been recovered through archaeological survey or excavation.

Dendrochronology is a method of absolute dating based on the fact that a tree grows a ring of new tissue during each year of its life. By comparing the growth rings from trees in archaeological contexts with a regional "master sequence," archaeologists can make a good estimate of when the tree was cut down.

Descriptive questions ask about the nature of the archaeological record and can be thought of as questions that start with who, what, when, or where. They ask what material is present, what the state of preservation is, when the material was deposited, and, ultimately, who the material was made by.

Design refers to the shapes, motifs, and symbols added as decoration to the surface of a ceramic object.

Digital imagery refers to aerial images obtained from satellites that provide information on reflected light outside of the visible spectrum.

Dispersal methods of point-pattern analysis attempt to determine whether the patterning of items of interest can be explained by random dispersal from a given point or whether they have been clustered during dispersal.

Dissertations are reports of major research projects undertaken by graduate students as part of the requirements for earning a Ph.D.

Distance methods of point-pattern analysis measure distances from items of interest to all other items of interest. Statistical tests determine whether the items are distributed randomly.

Ecofacts are natural materials that have been used by humans. Typical ecofacts include the remains of plants and animals that were eaten by a group of people.

Eco-functional theories posit that human culture is an adaptation to the environment, and thus culture functions to maintain humans and the environment in a sustainable balance.

Electromagnetic survey is a remote sensing technique utilizing an electromagnetic field to locate buried archaeological deposits.

Ethnoarchaeological studies use ethnographic data to inform the examination of the archaeological record.

Excavation is the careful recovery of buried archaeological data in context.

Excavation records record the process of excavation itself.

Excavation strategies are developed by archaeologists by combining a method of horizontal control and a method of vertical control into an overall plan for uncovering an archaeological deposit.

Excavation units are large units of horizontal control. They are generally made up of test pits joined or expanded to follow archaeological deposits of interest.

Experimental studies attempt to replicate particular ceramic or lithic forms by experimenting with various production methods in order to understand how those items were made.

Feature records are comprehensive and detailed summaries of how a given feature was excavated, what was found in or associated with it, and an interpretation of what the feature represents.

Features are artifacts or ecofacts that cannot be removed from their context. The remains of houses, buildings, or monuments; storage and garbage pits; hearths and ovens; and the like are classified as features.

Field school is formal field archaeology experience under the supervision of trained professionals.

Firing is the process of heating raw ceramics to a high temperature, driving all the water out of the paste, and—depending on the composition of the paste and tempering—causing new chemical bonds to form within the paste.

Flake is the term given to the thin, sharp pieces of stone produced in the process of making stone tools. **Primary flakes** (also called *decortication flakes*) are large, thick flakes struck off a nodule when removing the cortex and preparing it for working. **Secondary flakes** (also called *reduction flakes*) are large flakes struck off a piece of stone to reduce its size and/or thickness. **Tertiary flakes** (also called *production flakes*) are smaller flakes struck off a piece of stone to shape it into a tool. **Pressure flakes** (sometimes called *retouching flakes*) are tiny, extremely thin flakes pinched or pushed off a tool to finish shaping it or to resharpen or reshape it. **Notching flakes** are produced when putting hafting notches in stone tools.

Flake scars are depressions left on flakes or tools where another flake was driven off.

Flake tools can be either created on purpose or simply struck off in the process of making some other tool. In either case, they are sharp, plentiful, and can be used for a wide variety of tasks. Purposely created flake tools include **backed flakes**, which are usually decortication flakes that retain a piece of the cortex on one side and a sharp edge on the other, so that users can hold the flake with the cortex toward their hands to provide a safe and easy grip.

Flint is a relatively pure form of quartz (about 99 percent) used to make chipped stone tools.

Flotation is a method of recovering small floral and faunal remains from soils using water to separate those remains (which tend to float) from the soil.

Formal analysis refers to the process of describing the overall shape of an item as objectively and with as much detail as possible.

Geomagnetic surveying is a method of remote sensing that uses variations in the earth's magnetic field to locate archaeological deposits.

Graph theory refers to a set of powerful mathematical procedures that can be applied to graphs in order to discern unique properties of individual points or of the graph as a whole.

Gravity analysis is a method of regional spatial analysis that explores variations from a predicted level of interaction between settlements.

Gravity surveying is a method of remote sensing that uses deviations in the earth's gravitational field to locate archaeological deposits.

Grey literature refers to archaeological reports with limited distribution and no peer review.

Ground stone tools are manufactured by grinding a stone into a desired shape.

Hafting is the term given to the manner in which a projectile point (or other stone tool) is attached to a handle or shaft.

Hard hammer technique refers to a method of stoneworking in which flakes are struck from a core using a stone.

Heat treating is the process of baking a flint or chert nodule at a high temperature (350°–500° F) for thirty to fifty hours in order to increase the workability of the stone.

Historic Preservation Act of 1966 established the National Register of Historic Places and the National Trust for Historic Preservation.

Historic Sites Act of 1935 declared it a national policy to identify and protect important archaeological and historical sites on federal land.

Horizontal controls refer to techniques used to locate and record artifacts, ecofacts, and features in horizontal (north-south, east-west) space.

Hypotheses are a set of ideas or predictions for how the archaeological record should look if a particular theory holds true.

Incising and engraving are techniques for decorating ceramics that involve cutting linear designs into the surface of an object.

Incrusting refers to the impressing of material into the surface of a ceramic object.

Interpretive theories suggest that we can sometimes recover ancient thoughts, beliefs, motivations, and even feelings from the archaeological record.

Interval data have categories that both are ordered in a meaningful way and have a constant interval between each category.

Isolated pit approach is an excavation strategy that involves excavating many small test pits over a large area in locations defined by random sampling.

Kiln firing is a method of firing ceramics in which the ceramics are exposed to the heat from a fire within an oven-like structure called a kiln rather than to a direct flame.

Level records are completed for each level (arbitrary or stratigraphic) in each unit. They are meant to provide detailed information on how a given level was excavated and what was found in it.

Literature reviews pull together a large volume of literature into a coherent picture.

Lithics is a general term applied to all types of stone artifacts.

Living floors are locations on a site where artifacts associated with a household are found.

Loci, plural of **locus**, is the name archaeologists give to specific locations on a site, such as rooms in a house or major features in an excavation unit.

Lot books are used in the field to record the lots or point-plotted artifacts collected each day.

Lot-locus system refers to a method of archaeological recordkeeping that adds a secondary horizontally and vertically defined unit (the locus) to the lot system, such that the artifacts and ecofacts found in each locus are collected in separate lots.

Lot system refers to a method of archaeological recordkeeping in which all artifacts and ecofacts found together in a single horizontally and vertically defined unit are combined into one group (or lot) for the purposes of collection and analysis.

Macrobotanical remains are those plant materials that can be seen with the naked eye. They tend to be seeds and wood fragments, but nuts and other fruits sometimes survive in the archaeological record and are recovered.

Macrofauna are the remains of large animals.

Mano and **metate** are stone tools. A **mano** is a smaller, flat stone used in combination with the larger **metate** to grind seeds or nuts.

Materialist theories posit that the way humans organize labor and technology to get resources out of the material world is the primary force shaping culture.

Metrical analysis refers to the practice of taking a set of designated measurements from an item of interest and using those measurements to aid in classification and analysis.

Microbotanical remains are the smallest of the plant remains found in the archaeological record; they can only be seen under a microscope.

Microfauna are the remains of small animals such as mice, birds, and fish; of insects; and of snails or other mollusks.

Middens are substantial and well-defined accumulations of artifacts and ecofacts.

National Register of Historic Places is a list of historic properties and archaeological sites that have been nominated, evaluated, and approved as a significant part of U.S. history.

Native American Graves Protection and Repatriation Act of 1990 (NAGPRA) provides absolute protection to Native American graves on federal land and makes it a felony to collect, possess, or transfer human remains of known affinity to an existing Native American culture except by the members of that culture.

Network methods refer to methods of regional analysis based on hypothesized relationships of communication or interaction between settlements in a settlement system.

Nodules are raw globular chunks of chert, flint, or obsidian, often with a weathered, chalky surface called a **cortex**.

Nominal data are also called *categorical data*, since the data are segregated into distinct categories.

Nonrandom sampling refers to methods of choosing cases from a target population in which **random sampling** is not used. Some common forms of nonrandom sampling include snowball sampling, in which cases are selected based on previous cases, and opportunistic sampling, in which cases are selected because they are readily available.

Notching is the practice of chipping small, semicircular notches out of the base or side of a **projectile point** in order to aid in **hafting**.

Obsidian is volcanic glass used to make chipped stone tools. It fractures at the molecular level, producing some of the sharpest edges known.

Obsidian hydration is a method to date when an obsidian tool was made. It is based on the fact that when obsidian is chipped a thin layer of hydrated rock slowly builds up on the fresh surface. The thickness of this hydrated layer can be measured to estimate how long ago the piece of obsidian was chipped.

Operationalization is the process of turning variables into valid and reliable measures.

Ordinal data provide information in categories that are ordered in a meaningful way.

Paddle and anvil method of producing pottery requires potters to use a paddle on the outside of the ceramic object and an anvil on the inside of the ceramic object to "hammer" the surface into shape.

Paleoenvironment is the term given to a past environment.

Paste is the physical material from which a ceramic is made. It consists of the soil itself and both the natural and human inclusions and additions to the soil.

Pecking is a method of making stone tools by hitting one stone with a harder one to physically crush the surface into powder where the two stones meet.

Pedestalling is an excavation technique in which excavated items are left in place (or in situ) on columns of soil until the entire unit is excavated.

Pedestrian survey is a method of archaeological survey in which archaeologists simply walk along scanning the surface of the ground for artifacts.

Peer review is the term given to the process of a publisher providing a chance for other scholars to examine and critique an archaeological work *before* it is published.

Percussion flaking is a technique of chipped stone tool production in which flakes are driven off a piece of stone by striking it with another stone, an antler, or even a piece of hardwood.

Phytoliths are small rocks formed in the spaces between the living cells of a plant by silica brought into the cells with water.

Picking is an excavation technique in which archaeologists use a small metal pickaxe, usually with a 5- to 7-inch pick, to loosen soil, which is then shoveled out of the excavation unit, usually to be screened.

Pinch method is a method of making ceramics in which potters take a lump of clay and shape it by pinching it between their fingers.

Pit firing is a method of firing ceramics using an open or exposed flame as opposed to a kiln.

Point-pattern analysis is a basic form of spatial analysis. It allows archaeologists to identify concentrations of material, trends in artifactual deposition, and the like by examining deviations from random patterns.

Point-plot system is the most basic method of recording context. Every artifact or ecofact is individually recorded (or point-plotted) in terms of its horizontal and vertical location.

Pollens are essentially plant sperm. Pollen is composed of three separate layers, and only the outermost layer, called the exine, survives in archaeological context.

Polychrome is the term given to ceramics decorated with more than two colors.

Predictive surveying uses existing literature and background knowledge about prehistoric settlement in a given region to predict where sites will be located.

Prepared core is a nodule of chert, flint, or obsidian which has been shaped to easily produce blades.

Pressure flaking is a technique of chipping stone in which flakes are pried or pushed off a piece of stone using pressure from an antler tine or other soft tool. This results in very small and extremely thin flakes with no obvious **bulb of percussion**.

Probing involves the use of one of several instruments to explore beneath the ground surface for archaeological deposits.

Processual questions assume that a location's culture-history is known and move beyond it to ask how and why the culture-history takes the form it does. In other words, processual questions ask about the processes of cultural stability and change over time.

Projectile points are stone, bone, or even metal tips used to "arm" spears or arrows.

Punctating is the term given to ceramic decorations made using a pointed implement to press designs into an object, which in some cases even creates holes in it.

Quadrat refers to a rectangular area used for data collection or analysis.

Radiocarbon dating is an absolute dating technique that is based on measuring the ratio of carbon-14 to carbon-12 in a piece of organic material.

Random sampling means one thing: that every case in the target population has the same likelihood of being chosen.

Random walks are a mathematical procedure used to predict a random pattern of dispersal from a point source.

Rank-size analysis is a method of regional analysis that attempts to determine whether any settlements vary from a predicted linear pattern of rank versus size.

Reactionary theories tend to promote two interconnected positions: (1) We can never describe or understand a real past because (2) our knowledge of the past is filtered through our own, uniquely individual interpretations of the archaeological record. In a sense, reactionary theories suggest that sites and artifacts are nothing more than mirrors of ourselves.

Reference fossils are used by archaeologists to assign dates to deposits based on known dates of those fossils.

Refitting is the process of rebuilding a nodule from the flakes struck from it. Refitting studies allow archaeologists to physically go through the process (albeit in reverse) of how a stone tool was made.

Regional analysis refers to a wide range of spatial analysis techniques in which archaeologists attempt to examine how behaviors structure a settlement system.

Relational methods of spatial analysis examine the relationships between various settlements based on a particular characteristic, often size.

Relative dating refers to methods used to assign a date to an archaeological deposit or artifact through its context with other materials.

Reliability means that measurements taken of the same thing will provide the same data time and again, whether those measurements are taken by different people, taken under different conditions, or taken in different locations each time.

Remote sensing covers a variety of techniques that share the ability to locate archaeological deposits below the ground without having to dig.

Replication is the act of repeating an experiment to determine if the same results occur.

Research reports describe the results of artifact or ecofact analyses and explain the impact or importance of those analyses.

Rim and lip stance refers to the shape of the rim and lip of a ceramic vessel relative to the rest of the object.

Sampling refers to the selection of cases for analysis. Most sampling techniques are designed to allow archaeologists to choose a small set of cases that are representative of a larger target population of interest.

Scrapers are distinctive chipped stone tools with one edge having an extreme oblique angle. They are used to scrape the meat from a hide.

Screening simply means passing excavated soil through a mesh screen in order to recover small pieces of material. Water screening uses water to help drive soil through the screen.

Seismic surveying is a method of remote sensing that uses vibrations sent into the earth and reflected back by buried materials to locate archaeological deposits.

Seriation is a method of relative dating using artifact typologies to create a time series that is purely relative, although it can be tied into an absolute chronology if one or more of the artifacts can be associated with dated materials.

Shotgun survey uses archaeologists' intuitive knowledge of prehistoric settlement and landscape to focus survey on places likely to have sites.

Shovel scraping is an excavation technique in which archaeologists use a shovel with a sharpened edge to carve thin slices from the floor of an excavation unit.

Shovel tests are used in archaeological survey and involve taking a shovel full of dirt out of the ground and sifting it through a screen to separate the dirt from artifacts.

Simple random sampling refers to a method of random sampling in which each case in the target population is assigned a unique number, and cases are selected for analysis through the use of a list of random numbers.

Site files usually consist of a set of forms filled out by archaeologists describing the location, cultural affiliations (if known), physical features, state of preservation, and other basic information about a site.

Site reports describe the results of survey and excavation projects.

Sites are locations where archaeological material (artifacts, ecofacts, and features) exist in context.

Slab method refers to a method of producing ceramics in which potters first make large flat slabs of clay which they then join and shape into the desired item.

Smoothing is a technique used to finish the surface of a ceramic piece in which potters use a spatula of wood or ceramic or some other flat tool (indeed, even the bare hand can be used) to smooth the surface of the object.

Soft hammer technique is a method of chipping stone in which an antler or piece of hardwood is used to strike flakes from a core.

Soil chemistry refers to methods used to analyze the chemical composition of soils in order to determine if they reflect human settlement.

Soil interface radar is a remote sensing technique that uses an electromagnetic pulse sent into the ground to search for subsurface archaeological deposits.

Soil resistivity surveying is a remote sensing technique that uses an electric current passed through the ground to search for subsurface archaeological deposits.

Sounding is the term given to a very deep test pit, often dug to find sterile soil.

Stamping refers to using an implement or paddle of some kind to impress designs into the surface of a ceramic object.

Step trenching is an excavation strategy in which individual strata are exposed in a step-like fashion (with each step of a designated size, such as 5 meters by 5 meters) before being excavated across the entire length of the trench.

Sterile soil is soil that lacks archaeological deposits.

Strata are cultural levels that provide vertical control for excavation.

Stratified random sampling is a method of random sampling in which the target population is divided into several distinct categories or **strata**, with random samples taken from each.

Stratigraphic records depict, describe, and provide an initial interpretation of the cultural levels at a given location on a site.

Stratigraphy is the term given to the process of working out the relationships between and among cultural levels.

Striking platform is a flat spot left on a flake at the point where the core was struck to knock the flake from it.

Syntheses are a type of archaeological publication that attempts to pull together a broad range of knowledge about a particular topic or geographical area into a single comprehensive statement.

Systematic random sampling is a method of random sampling in which only two random numbers are used: a random starting number and a random interval number.

Taphonomic theories argue that while the archaeological record may manifest human behavior and even thought when it is deposited, the natural world steps in after deposition and mixes those materials to the point where we often can't be certain what they tell us.

Target population is the entire group of items (sites, artifacts, features, and so on) that archaeologists are interested in analyzing. Since it is rare that archaeologists can actually gain access to an entire target population of interest, the target population is most commonly employed for sampling.

Tempering is material added to the paste of a ceramic to give it properties it does not naturally have and often simply to make it hold together better.

Test excavations refer to excavations made during the initial examination of an archaeological site. Their purpose is to locate archaeological deposits and help archaeologists develop an excavation strategy for the site.

Test pits are small, square excavation units.

Texture is a term used to describe the uniformity of the paste in a ceramic item.

Theoretical statements are a type of archaeological publication that propose or develop a particular explanation or way of understanding human behavior and the effects of humans on the material world.

Thermoluminescence refers to the light energy given off from an item by the "escape" of trapped electrons when the item is heated to high temperature.

Thermoremnant magnetism refers to a magnetic moment induced into an item by heat.

Thiessen polygons are used in regional analysis. They are imaginary polygons that surround a site and demarcate that site's sphere of influence.

Top-down strategy refers to a strategy of archaeological survey that employs random sampling to select areas to survey and usually attempts to cover a large area, generally ignoring previous knowledge or intuitive knowledge about the area.

Trenches are basically long **test pits**.

Trend surface analysis is a method of spatial analysis used to fit equations for relationships among three continuous variables to contour maps.

Troweling is a method of excavation in which archaeologists use a standard mason's pointing trowel (usually a 5-inch or shorter one) with sharpened edges to carve thin slices of dirt from the floor or face of an excavation unit.

Unit of analysis is the unit from which archaeologists take measurements.

Unit records are comprehensive descriptions of the work done in a given unit and the archaeological deposits found there.

Use-wear analysis is a method of stone tool analysis in which the patterns of wear on a stone tool are examined under high-power magnification.

Validity basically means that what is actually being measured is what we *think* is being measured.

Vertical controls refer to techniques used to locate and record artifacts, ecofacts, and features in vertical (up-down) space.

Vertical face trenching is an excavation strategy in which archaeologists expose a vertical face from the ground surface to sterile soil before excavating individual strata across the entire length of the trench.

Wheeler-Kenyon method is an excavation strategy in which archaeologists open large areas of a site at a single time but leave balk walls between excavation units to preserve stratigraphy.

Zooarchaeologists are specialists who study animal remains from archaeological contexts.

Photo Credits

All photographs, except as specified below, are the property of Peter N. Peregrine.

Page xxiii: Image Studios.

Chapter 1.   Page 6: Kal Mullar/Woodfin Camp & Associates;   page 10: Image Studios; page 14: Image Studios.

Chapter 4.   Page 55: Division of Remote Sensing/National Park Service/U.S. Department of the Interior;   page 57: English Heritage Photo Library;   page 59: NASA Headquarters.

Chapter 5.   Page 75: Frank H. McClung Museum;   page 78: Courtesy of the Illinois Transportation Archaeological Research Program, University of Illinois;   page 80: Frank H. McClung Museum;   page 82: Image Studios;   page 83: Image Studios.

Chapter 8.   Page 128: William J. Parry/Plenum Publishing Corporation. From Carla Sinopoli, 1991, *Approaches to Archaeological Ceramics*, p. 24;   page 132 (left): Werner Forman Archive Collection: Edward H. Merrin Gallery, New York;   page 132 (right): Martinez, Maria. Bowl, no date. Blackware, 6¾ × 9½ (17.2 × 24.2 cm). Gift of the IBM Corporation. National Museum of American Art, Washington DC/Art Resource, NY;   page 142: University of Michigan; page 143: Courtesy of Museum of Anthropology, University of Michigan.

Chapter 9.   Page 154: University of Kentucky;   page 161: Frank H. McClung Museum.

Chapter 10.   Page 168: Image Studios.

Chapter 11.   Page 194: Craig E. Skinner.

Index

A

Abri Pataud site, France, 109
Absolute dating
 dendrochronology, 192, 193
 radiocarbon, 187–190
 thermoluminescence, 192
 thermoremnant magnetism, 190–191
Accelerator mass spectroscopy (AMS), 189,
 190
Accession catalogues, 95
Accession numbers, 95
Accession records, 91, 95, 97–103
Accountability, 214–215
Acheulean artifacts, 155, 158, 162
Activity areas, 22
Adovasio, James, 54
Adzes, 153
Aerial photography and surveying, 57–58
Amateur archaeologists, 47, 215, 224
American Bottom region, 138, 162, 178, 179,
 211
Amino acid racemization, 194
Anasazi peoples, 136
Animals. *See* Floral and faunal analysis
Anthropology, 44
Antiquities Act of 1906, 210, 213
Apatite, 127

Aperture patterns on pollens, 170, 171
Applique, 130
Arbitrary levels, 73
Archaeobotanists, 167, 171–173, 177, 178
Archaeological Institute of America, 206, 223
Archaeological record, 20–32
Archaeological site, defined, 23
Archaeological survey. *See* Survey methods
 and strategies
Archaeology magazine, 202
Archaic period, 69
Arnold, Jeanne, 55–56
Arrays, 53–54
Artifacts, defined, 21–22
Artifact typology, 183
Asking questions, 2–5
Association, 183–184
Atl-atls, 153–154
Avebury, 57
Axes, 152–153
Aztalan site, Wisconsin, 58, 60, 62

B

Backed blades, 109
Backed flakes, 152
Balks, 70, 78

Bannerstones, 153
Basal notching, 155
Bate, Dorothea, 155
Behaviorist theories, 24, 25–26
Beryl, 127
Bevel-rim bowls, 143–144
Binford, Lewis, 26, 44
Birdstones, 153
Bjorkland Archaeological Survey, 2, 9
    dating, 183–184
    excavation units at, 3
    projectile points from, 14
    shovel testing at, 10, 50
    site files, 44, 45
    unit of analysis at, 37
Blades, 152
Blanton, Richard, 3
Bloch, Marc, 30
Block approach, 76–78, 80
Boatstones, 153
Body shape, 133, 134
Bone chemical absorption, 194
Books, 203
Boserup, Esther, 6
Bottom-up surveys, 58–59, 62
Braidwood, Robert, 76
Bulb of percussion, 150
Bureau of Land Management, 224
Burial excavations, 79–80
Burial records, 95
Burins, 152
Burnishing, 132

C

Cable television, 205
Cagny-l'Epinette site, France, 87, 88
Cahokia site, Illinois, 56, 211
Calcite, 127
Cation ratio, 193
Celts, 153
Center for American Archaeology, 223
Central place theory, 112–114
Ceramic analysis, 124–145
    body shape, 133, 134
    construction techniques, 127–132
    dating and, 139
    design, 136, 138
    formal, 133
    metrical, 135–137
    paste, 125, 126
        political organization and, 139, 143
        rim and lip stance, 133–135
        social organization and, 139–143
        tempering, 125–126
        texture, 126
        trade and, 139
Ceramics. *See also* Ceramic analysis
    defined, 12
    Neolithic period, 27, 28
    as primary forms of data, 12–13
    from Valley of Oaxaca project, 13
Chaco Canyon, New Mexico, 55
Chert, 147, 148
Chipped stone stools
    manufacture of, 147–150
    types of, 150–152
Christaller, Walter, 112–113
Chumash sites, Santa Barbara Channel
        Islands, 55–56
Citation, 199–200
Cluster sampling, 39–40, 112
Coating, 130
Coiling method of pottery construction, 127,
        128
Colombia river, 120, 121
Commercialization, 215
Comparative collections, 176
Computer-based media, 205–206
Context, 18, 68
    defined, 23
    destruction of, 24
    recording, 87–89
Cores, 147
Corner notching, 155
Cortex, 147
Corundum, 127
Crop marks, 57
Crow Canyon Archaeological Center, 223
Culture-historical theory, 24–25
Culture-history, 5
Custer, Jay, 63

D

Dacey, Michael, 107–108
Daily field record form, 96–97
Daily logs, 92
Dalan, Rinita, 56
Data analysis, 12–15, 17
Data collection, 9–12, 37
Data evaluation, 15–17
Data types, 35–36

Dating archaeological materials, 182–196
  absolute dating
    dendrochronology, 192, 193
    radiocarbon, 187–190
    thermoluminescence, 192
    thermoremnant magnetism, 190–191
  amino acid racemization, 194
  bone chemical absorption, 194
  cation ratio, 193
  ceramic analysis and, 139
  lithic analysis and, 160
  obsidian hydration, 193–194
  relative dating
    association, 183–184
    seriation, 183, 185–187
Deetz, James, 187
Dendrochronology, 192, 193
Descriptive questions, 4–5, 7, 8
Design, ceramic analysis and, 136, 138
Dethlefsen, Edwin, 187
Diamond, 127
Dibble, Harold, 87
Digging techniques, 81–83
Digital imagery, 57–58
Discriminant analysis, 110
Dispersal methods, 110–112
Dissertation Abstracts International,
    203
Dissertations, 202–203
Distance methods, 108–110
Diyala plains, Mesopotamia, 113–114
Documentary films, 205, 206
Domestication, origins of, 177
Domestication of Europe, The (Hodder), 27
Drills, 152

E

Early Bronze Age, 70
Early Dynastic settlement, 113–114
Ecofacts, defined, 22
Eco-functional theories, 5
Electromagnetic survey, 55, 56
Emerson, Thomas, 138
Engraving, 130
Ethical issues, 214–218
Ethnoarchaeological studies, 133
Excavation methods and strategies, 11–12,
    66–85. *See also* Recordkeeping
  digging techniques, 81–83
  horizontal controls, 68–70
  reasons for, 67–68

  remote sensing and, 53, 56
  special-case, 79–81
  standard, 74–79
  vertical controls, 68, 70–73
Excavation records, 89, 92–95
Excavation units, 69
Exine, 170
Experimental studies, 133

F

FAI-270 project, 178, 211–212
Feature records, 93–95, 98–99, 101
Features, 14, 73, 80
  defined, 22
Fiber tempering, 125–126
Field numbers, 101
Field schools, 222–223
Firing, 131
Flakes, 147, 149–150, 156
Flake scars, 150
Flake tools, 150, 152
Flannery, Kent, 69–73, 77
Flint, 147–148
Floodplains, 50
Floral and faunal analysis, 166–181
  collection, 167–170
  information obtained from, 176–178
  macrobotanical remains, 171–174
  macrofaunal remains, 175–176
  microbotanical remains, 170–171
  microfaunal remains, 174–175
Flotation, 168–171, 174
Fluorite, 127
Formal analysis
  ceramics, 133
  lithics, 154–155, 160
Formative period, 69
Formative Processes of the Archaeological Record
    (Schiffer), 27–29
Frye, Northrop, 167

G

Garrod, Dorothy, 155
Geomagnetic surveying, 11, 52–53, 56
Giza, pyramids at, 14
Goldstein, Lynn, 58, 60, 62
Graph theory, 115
Gravity analysis, 118–119
Gravity surveying, 56
Gregg, Susan, 112

Grey literature, 45, 203–204
Grit tempering, 126
Grog tempering, 126
Ground stone stools
    manufacture of, 147
    types of, 152–154
Growth rings, 192
Guilá Naquitz, Mexico, 69–73,
        77
Gypsum, 127

H

Hafting, 150
Hammond, Norman, 120–121
Hard hammer technique, 149, 150
Heat treating, 148
Hermeneutic process, 27
Historic Preservation Act of 1966, 211
Historic Sites Act of 1935, 211
Hiwassee Island site, 75–76
Hodder, Ian, 27, 119
Homo erectus, 155, 162
Horizontal controls, 68–70
Howarth/Nelson site, Pennsylvania, 54–55
Howe, Bruce, 76
Hypotheses, 7

I

Ice Bottom site, Tennessee, 161
Incising, 130
Incrusting, 130
Intellectual property, 216–217
Interpretive theories, 27
Interval (ratio) data, 35
Iron Age, 136, 137, 140–143
Isolated pit approach, 76

J

Jarmo, 76, 77
Johnson, Gregory, 113–114, 143–144
Journal articles, 204

K

Kalahari region, Africa, 112
Kaminaljuya site, Guatemala, 96–103
Keeley, Lawrence, 155
Kelly, Robert, 162
Kennewick Man, 213
Kenyon, Kathleen, 78

Kiln firing, 131–132
Knives, 152
Kowalewski, Stephen, 118
!Kung, 111, 112

L

Labras Lake site, 162, 163
Landowner and collector interviews,
        47
Latour, Bruno, 200
Lectures, 206
Legal issues, 210–213
Level records, 90–92
Lévi-Strauss, Claude, 41
Literature reviews, 201
Literature search, 44–47
Lithic analysis, 146–165
    chipped stone stools
        manufacture of, 147–150
        types of, 150–152
    dating and, 160
    formal, 154–155, 160
    ground stone stools
        manufacture of, 147
        types of, 152–154
    metrical analysis, 156–157, 159–160
    social organization and, 162
    technology and, 160, 162–163
    use-wear analysis, 155–156, 160
Lithics. *See also* Lithic analysis
    from Bjorklunden, 14
    defined, 12
    as primary forms of data, 12–13
Living floors, 22
Loci, 70
Long bones, 175, 176
Lot books, 95
Lot-locus system, 89
Lot system, 87
Lower Paleolithic, 87
Lubaantun, 120–121

M

Macrobotanical remains, 171–174
Macrofaunal remains, 175–176
Magnetometer, 51, 52
Mano, 153
Massachusetts cemeteries, headstones in, 186,
        187
Materialist theories, 5, 24
Matthiae, Paolo, 70

Mayans, 62, 120–121
Measurement, 34–37. *See also* Sampling
   types of data, 35–36
   units of analysis, 37
   validity and reliability, 36–37
Metate, 153
"Method and Theory in American Archaeol-
   ogy" (Phillips and Willey), 24, 25
Metrical analysis
   ceramics, 135–137
   lithics, 156–157, 159–160
Microbotanical remains, 170–171
Microfaunal remains, 174–175
Middens, 22
Middle Bronze Age, 70
Middle Paleolithic period, 160
Middle Uruk period, 143
Mississippian people, 58, 115–116,
   162–163
Model building, 5–8
Mogollon peoples, 136
Moh's scale, 126, 127
Mold method of pottery construction, 127,
   129
Monographs, 203, 212
Monte Albán, Oaxaca, Mexico. *See* Valley
   of Oaxaca Settlement Pattern
   Project
Mortar and pestle, 153
Munsell color chart, 126

N

Naram-Sin of Akkad, 70
National Park Service, 204, 223, 224
National Register of Historic Places,
   211
Native American Graves Protection and
   Repatriation Act of 1990 (NAGPRA),
   212–213
Neandertal populations, 160
Neolithic period, 27, 28, 119–120
Network methods, 114–116
Neutron activation analysis, 133
Nodules, 148
Nominal (categorical) data, 35
Nonprint forms of publication, 205–206
Nonrandom sampling, 40
Notching flakes, 150, 156
Notching style, 155
Nunamuit Ethnoarchaeology (Binford),
   26
Nuts, 172

O

Obsidian, 147, 148
Obsidian hydration, 193–194
Oneota people, 58, 133
Operationalization, 17, 37
Opportunistic sampling, 40
Ordinal data, 35
Orthoclase feldspar, 127

P

Paddle and anvil method of pottery construc-
   tion, 127, 128
Paleoenvironments, 177
Parry, William, 162
Paste, 125, 126
Pauketat, Timothy, 136
Pecking, 147
Pedestalling, 79–80
Pedestrian surveys, 9–10, 48–50
Peer review, 198
Percussion flaking, 149
Perseus Project, 206
Phillips, Philip, 24, 25
Phosphates, 56
Photographic records, 100, 101
Phytoliths, 170–172
Picking, 83
Pinch method of pottery construction,
   127
Pit features, 14–15
Pit firing, 131
Plants. *See* Floral and faunal analysis
Point-pattern analysis, 106–112
   dispersal methods, 110–112
   distance methods, 108–110
   quadrat methods, 107–108
Point-plot system, 87
Political organization, ceramic analysis and,
   139, 143
Pollens, 170, 171
Polychrome, 132
Polyvinyl acetate, 80
Popper, Karl, 200
Predictive surveys, 62–63
Prepared core, 152
Preservation, 217–218
Pressure (retouching) flakes, 150
Pressure (retouching) flaking, 149–150
Primary (decortication) flakes, 150
Primate distribution, 117
Principles of Archaeological Ethics, 214–218

Probing, 50–51
Processual questions, 4–8
Projectile points, 150, 154–157, 159–161
Publication, 17, 45, 197–208, 217
    nonprint forms of, 205–206
    reasons for, 198–201
    standard forms of, 202–204
    types of, 201–202
Public education and outreach, 216
Puleston, Dennis, 61, 62
Punctating, 130

Q

Quadrat methods, 107–108
Quartz, 127, 147–148

R

Radiocarbon dating, 187–190
Radiocarbon years, 190
Ramey Incised pottery, 138
Random sampling, 38–39, 76
Random walks, 110–112
Range site, 78
Rank-size analysis, 117–118
Raw and the Cooked, The (Lévi-Strauss),
    41
Reactionary theories, 29, 30
Reconstructing Archaeology (Shanks and
    Tilley), 29
Recordkeeping, 86–104, 217–218
    accession records, 91, 95, 97–103
    of context, 87–89
    excavation records, 89, 92–95
Redman, Charles, 125
Reference fossils, 183, 184
Refitting, 156
Regional analysis, 106
    central place theory, 112–114
    network methods, 114–116
    relational methods, 116–121
Regression analysis, 111
Relational methods, 116–121
Relative dating
    association, 183–184
    seriation, 185–187
Reliability, 36
Remote sensing, 11, 51–56
Research opportunities, 221–225
Research process, 1–19
    asking questions, 2–5
    data analysis, 12–15, 17

data collection, 9–12, 37
    model building, 5–8
    publication (*see* Publication)
    result evaluation, 15–17
Research reports, 201, 204
Retouched blades, 109
Riley, A. J., 139
Rim and lip stance, 133–135
Roman ceramics, 139, 140
Rosario phase, 13
Rosen, Steven, 160
Rythmites, 184

S

St. Louis, Missouri, 78
Sampling, 17–18, 38–40
    cluster, 39–40, 112
    nonrandom, 40
    random, 38–39, 76
    stratified, 39, 58
Sanders, William, 6
Satellite imagery, 57–58, 59, 63
Schiffer, Michael, 27–29
Scrapers, 152
Screening, 83, 167–168, 171, 174
Sde Divshon site, Negev desert, 107–108
Secondary (reduction) flakes, 150
Sectioning, 80
Seeds, 171–173
Seismic surveying, 56
Seriation, 183, 185–187
Shanks, Michael, 29, 30
Shea, John, 160
Shell tempering, 126
Shotgun surveys, 62, 63
Shovel scraping, 82–83
Shovel testing, 10, 50
Side notching, 155
Silica, 170–171
Simple random sampling, 38, 39
Sinopoli, Carla, 136, 137, 139–143
Site files, 44–47
Site reports, 201, 204
Sites, locating, 44–47
Skinner, G. William, 113
Skull forms and sizes, 175
Slab method of pottery construction, 127
Smoothing, 127
Snowball sampling, 40
Social organization
    ceramic analysis and, 139–143
    lithic analysis and, 162

Society for American Archaeology, 215, 224
Society of Archaeological Ethics, 214
Soft hammer technique, 149
Soil chemistry, measuring, 56
Soil interface radar, 55–56
Soil probe, 50–51
Soil resistivity surveying, 53–54
Sounding, 68
Spatial pattern analysis, 105–123
    context and, 106, 121–122
    point-pattern analysis, 106–112
        dispersal methods, 110–112
        distance methods, 108–110
        quadrat methods, 107–108
    regional analysis, 106
        central place theory, 112–114
        network methods, 114–116
        relational methods, 116–121
Special-case excavation methods and strategies, 79–81
Sporopollenin, 170
Stamping, 130
Standard excavation strategies, 74–79
State number-county abbreviation-site number, 45
Stemming, 155
Step trenching, 74–76
Stewardship, 214
Stonehenge, 57
Stone tools. *See* Lithics
Strata, 70–71
Stratified sampling, 39, 58
Stratigraphic records, 92–93, 101–103
Stratigraphy, 70–75, 78, 79, 184
Stubborn Structure, The (Frye), 167
Superimposed architecture, 80–81
Survey methods and strategies, 43–65
    aerial photography and surveying, 57–58
    bottom-up surveys, 58–59, 62
    landowner and collector interviews, 47
    literature search, 44–47
    pedestrian surveys, 9–10, 48–50
    predictive surveys, 62–63
    probing and testing, 50–51
    remote sensing, 11, 51–56
    shotgun surveys, 62, 63
    top-down surveys, 58
Susiana plains, Iran, 143
Syntheses, 201
Systematic random sampling, 38–39

T

Talc, 127
Taphonomic theories, 27
Technology, lithic analysis and, 160, 162–163
Teeth, 175
Television, 205
Tell es-Sweyhat, Mesopotamia, 7–9, 14, 29, 30, 37
    excavation strategies at, 11, 12, 74, 75, 81
    excavation units and survey areas at, 8
    floral and faunal remains from, 177
    geomagnetic surveying at, 52–53
    gravity surveying at, 56
    recordkeeping at, 89
    tombs at, 15–16
Tell Mardikh (ancient Ebla), Syria, 70–71
    excavation of, 78–79
Tempering, 125–126
Tertiary (production) flakes, 150
Test excavations, 10
Test pits, 68–70
Texture, 126
Theoretical statements, 201
Theory-dependent data collection, 202
Thermoluminescence, 192
Thermoremnant magnetism, 52, 190–191
Thiessen polygons, 120, 121
Thin section analysis, 133
Tikal, Mexico, 61, 62
Tilley, Christopher, 29, 30
Tippecanoe River, Indiana, 39, 48–49
Tocqueville, Alexis de, 210
Topaz, 127
Top-down surveys, 58
Trade, ceramic analysis and, 139
Trenches, 68–70
Trend surface analysis, 111
Troweling, 82
Tuffs, 184

U

Umatilla people, 213
Underhill, Anne, 133
U.S. Forest Service, 224
Unit records, 95
Units of analysis, 37
University Microfilms International (UMI), 203
Upper Paleolithic period, 109, 151
Use-wear analysis, 155–156, 160
Utensils. *See* Ceramics

V

Validity, 36
Valley of Oaxaca Settlement Pattern Project, 3–4, 12, 16, 69
  ceramic analysis at, 13
  pedestrian survey of, 9–10
  population growth model, 6–7, 15, 34–36
  rank-size distributions for, 118
  survey boundaries of, 4
Varves, 184
Vertical controls, 68, 70–73
Vertical face trenching, 75
Vijayanagara site, India, 136, 137, 140–143
Vizinczey, Stephen, 167
Volunteer programs, 223–224

W

Water-screening, 168
Wentworth Size Classification Scale, 126

Whallon, Robert, 109–110
Wheeler, Mortimer, 78
Wheeler-Kenyon method, 78, 79
Wheel method of pottery construction, 127, 129–130
Willey, Gordon, 24, 25
Wood, 172, 174, 178, 179, 190, 192
Woodworking tools, 152–153
Workshops, 206
Works Progress Administration (WPA), 75
World Wide Web, 205–206, 223, 224
Wynn, Thomas, 162

Y

Yerkes, Richard, 162–163

Z

Zagros mountains, 76
Zooarchaeologists, 167, 174–175, 177, 178